AF556153

Dark Tourism

Dark Tourism

Satendra Tripathi

RANDOM PUBLICATIONS
NEW DELHI (INDIA)

Dark Tourism

ISBN 978-93-5111-543-4

Published in 2015 in India by

RANDOM PUBLICATIONS

4376-A/4B, Gali Murari Lal, Ansari Road
New Delhi-110 002
Phone : +9111-43580356, 011-23289044, 011-43142548
e-mail: sales@randompublications.com,
info@randompublications.com, randomexports@gmail.com

Type Setting by : Friends Media, Delhi-110089
Printed at : Thomson Press (India) Ltd

Preface

Dark tourism has been defined as tourism involving travel to sites historically associated with death and tragedy. More recently it was suggested that the concept should also include reasons tourists visit that site, since the site's attributes alone may not make a visitor a 'dark tourist'. Thanatourism, derived from the ancient Greek word thanatos for the personification of death, refers more specifically to violent death; it is used in fewer contexts than the terms 'dark tourism' and 'grief tourism'.

The main draw to dark locations is their historical value rather than their associations with death and suffering. While there is a long tradition of people visiting recent and ancient settings of death like travel to gladiator games in the Roman colosseum, attending public executions by decapitation for example, and visiting the catacombs, this has been studied academically only relatively recently. Travel writers were the first to describe their tourism to deadly places like P.J. O'Rourke who called his travel to Warsaw, Managua, and Belfast in 1988 'holidays in hell', or Chris Rojek talking about 'black-spot' tourism in 1993 or the 'milking the macabre' Academic attention to the subject originated in Scotland: The term 'dark tourism' was coined in 1996 by Lennon and Foley, two faculty members of the Department of Hospitality, Tourism & Leisure Management at Glasgow Caledonian University.

The term 'thanatourism' was first mentioned by A.V. Seaton in 1996, then Professor of tourism marketing at University of Strathclyde Glasgow. As of 2014, innumerable studies on definitions, sub-categorizations, like Holocaust tourism, slavery-heritage tourism etc, and labels exist, and the term continues to be molded outside academia by authors of travel literature. There is very little empirical research on the perspective of the dark tourist.

I would like to thank my team for standing beside me throughout my career and writing this book. My special thanks go to "Random Publications" who have published the book.

– Satendra Tripathi

Contents

1

Dark Tourism: Understanding Visitor Motivation at Sites of Death and Disaster

DARK TOURISM

To understand the purpose and findings of this study, it is necessary to first understand the concept of dark tourism and its related terms. The term dark tourism was first coined by two researchers, Malcolm Foley and J. John Lennon, as a means of describing, "...the phenomenon which encompasses the presentation and consumption of real and commodified death and disaster sites". In their book Dark Tourism: The Attraction of Death and Disaster, Lennon and Foley refine this definition even further by noting what actions do and do not constitute dark tourism. For instance, friends and family visiting sites of dark tourism is not categorized as dark tourism. Conversely, "It is those who visit due to serendipity, the itinerary of tourism companies or the merely curious who happen to be in the vicinity who are, for us, the basis of dark tourism". For the authors, it appears tourist motivations play an almost inconsequential role in dark tourism. However, in the aforementioned article, they do concede that motivations may play some role in the dark tourism experience. They quote, "These visitors may have been motivated to undertake a visit by a desire to experience the reality behind the media images and/or personal association with inhumanity".

THANATOURISM

Tony Seaton coined a similar label in his definitive article, *From Thanatopsis to Thanatourism: Guided by the Dark*. In it, he describes thanatourism as being, "...travel to a location wholly, or partially, motivated by the desire for actual or symbolic encounters with death, particularly, but not exclusively, violent death, which may, to a varying degree be activated by the person-specific features of those whose deaths are its focal objects". Seaton furthers this definition by adding two factors. First, thanatourism is behavioural; the concept is defined by the traveler's motives rather than attempting to specify the features of the destination. Unlike Lennon and Foley's concept, Seaton recognizes that individual motivations do play a role in death and disaster tourism. Secondly, thanatourism is not an absolute; rather it works on a continuum of intensity based on two elements. First, whether it is the single motivation or one of many and secondly, the extent to which the interest in death is person–centered or scale–of– death centered:

1. Travel to watch death, *i.e.* public hangings or executions;
2. Travel to sites after death has occurred, *i.e.* Auschwitz;
3. Travel to internment sites and memorials, *i.e.* graves and monuments;
4. Travel to re–enactments, *i.e.* Civil War re–enactors; and
5. Travel to synthetic sites at which evidence of the dead has been assembled, *i.e.* museums.

It is the latter category that pertains most to this research. Synthetic sites include, "...museums where weapons of death, the clothing of murder victims, and other artifacts are put on display". Synthetic sites include museums such as the Holocaust Museum Houston that displays such articles as clothing, photographs, and diaries from the Holocaust. In their work on heritage dissonance, Tunbridge and Ashworth touch on atrocity as a tourist attraction. They enumerate six qualities that make atrocity usable:

1. Nature of cruelty favours unusual or spectacular;
2. Nature of the victims characterised by innocence, vulnerability, and non-complicit;
3. Numbers only because human imagination has difficulties extending sympathies to small groups;
4. Nature of perpetrators should be unambiguously identifiable and distinguishable from the victims;
5. High profile visibility of the original event; and
6. Survival of records.

BLACK SPOTS

Finally, Rojek coined a third term affiliated with the concept of dark tourism. His expression, black spots, refers to the "...commercial developments of grave sites and sites in which celebrities or large numbers of peoples have met with sudden and violent deaths. He cites such examples as the stretch of California highway where hundreds congregate each year to remember actor James Dean's 1955 death and Pere Le Chaise in Paris where thousands flock to see musician Jim Morrison's grave, amongst others. As this research seeks to understand visitor motivation at the Holocaust Museum Houston, it will follow Seaton's 1996 model. For the purpose of this paper, the terms dark tourism and thanatourism will be used interchangeably and encompass a broad spectrum of sites. However, unlike Lennon and Foley's dark tourism definition, both will refer to travel to sites of death and disaster based on visitor motivation. Such destinations may be on-site, where the actual event took place.

For example, Mauthausen Concentration Camp, the Dallas Book Depository where John F. Kennedy was assassinated and Dakota in New York where John Lennon was shot. In addition, thanatourism destinations may be off-site. These are representations of the event, which are located away from the actual site. Such examples include The Maritime Museum of the Atlantic which houses artifacts from the *Titanic*; Pere Le Chaise Cemetery which is the final resting spot for a number of notables including Jim Morrison; and finally and most significantly for the purpose of this study, the Holocaust Museum Houston which is home to both Holocaust survivors and artifacts.

HISTORY AND HERITAGE

Two other cognate terms must be defined for the purpose of this study: history and heritage. This is especially important given the contention that often surrounds the two terms. Anne Faulkner defines history as an inheritance from the past and, "...carries a definite connotation of value, or importance, or fame".

Heritage on the other hand, is something, "...inherited from our cultural past: no judgement of good or bad is made". However, not all scholars and practitioners share these definitions. Lord Charteris, late Chairman of Britain's National Heritage Memorial Fund, believed the term history does not carry strong values, that it is analytical and factual. Conversely, heritage invokes emotional and psychological resonance, connected to values and a sense of obligation to one's ancestors and descendents. Zuzanek concurs with Charteris' definition.

History is defined as being a broad, chronological term, with non-personal connotations. On the other hand, heritage is associated with a subjective and emotional interpretation of the past. For the purpose of this study, the two terms will correspond with Zuzanek's 1998 definition: history will constitute factual data while heritage engenders a familial, personal connection.

POST-MODERNISM

Much of the literature on dark tourism invariably defines the phenomenon in the context of post-modernism. Therefore, it is necessary to understand the origins and chronology of post-modernism in order to fully comprehend the role dark tourism plays in today's society. A starting point is modernism, the movement from which postmodernism emerged. The beginning of the modern era is generally associated with the period of European Enlightenment, around the middle of the eighteenth century. At that time, societies were experiencing rapid transformations under the Industrial Revolution, and with it a transfer of power from the aristocracy and absolutist kings to the newlyemerging middle class.

Impacted societies became more urbanized, industrialized, and regimented. The Industrial Revolution and modernity spurred other significant changes in society. Firstly, with scientific and industrial advances, individuals were no longer dependent on the church.

Modernity broke down barriers between sacred and profane. This also influenced tourism. To illustrate, Rojek notes that, where society once viewed cemeteries with respect and dignity, modernity opened them for mass tourism thereby transforming them into tourist sites. MacCannell asserts modernity dislocated our attachment to work, neighbourhood, town and family. Where once the home was workplace, leisure space, and family hearth, our time and attachments were eventually dispersed across various locations.

Without these ties to the home, society became interested in the lives of others and began to simulate real life for tourists. Modernity was also a time of rationality, progress, and personal improvement, hence, the many forms of educative tourism which emerged in that era. Beginning with the Grand Tours of the 17th century through to Thomas Cook's 18th century excursions, individuals attempted to improve themselves and social conditions. Continued industrialization allowed for increased education through marketing, communications, and infrastructures. Modernity however, had consequences. Such strong beliefs in science, technology, and even humankind eventually led to disappointment on many fronts. Events once inconceivable in modern minds shook society to the core upon occurrence.

Lennon and Foley site numerous instances of the breakdown of modernity; the sinking of the *Titanic* brought into question the invincibility of technology; the deliberately–planned Final Solution brought into question the humanity of rationality; and presidential assassinations brought into question the effectiveness of liberal democracies. Riding concurs, quoting, "...all technological progress implies risk...The victim of the Chernobyl accident was science, knowledge, even consciousness...".

These disastrous events resulted in anxiety and doubt about, "...the key tenets of...modernity such a progress, rationality, science, technology, industrialization and liberal democracy". These changes have led to an emerging shift in society. Around the mid-1980's, a relatively new way of thinking arose as an area of academic study. It was termed postmodernism. Much of post-modern thought comes from a reaction to modernity. Pre-1980, post–modernism was determined an irrational reaction to modernist rationality. The 1990 Oxford

Dictionary defines it as a movement in reaction against that designated modern. More recently, it has been defined in part as a questioning of Victorian views. Tourism literature reveals significant impacts that post-modernism has had, and is having, on tourism products. Society has seen a continuous move away from traditional mass tourism and package holidays to what has been termed by Munt as post-modern tourism.

This genre of tourism is characterized by the pursuit of new destinations and experiences and by an increasing diversity of products ranging from ecotourism to heritage tourism. Such tourists in general, "...place an emphasis on 'other', non-western destinations...authenticity, truthfulness, contact with indigenous cultures, environmental concerns and the desire to partake in sustainable travel experiences.

They also show an increasing tendency to intellectualise holidays, with an emphasis on study and learning...". These tourists are looking to increase their cultural capital. Dark tourism is considered by some to be a product of post-modern society and a number of dark tourism sites illustrate this. French philosopher and writer, Paul Virilio, is currently attempting to create a Museum of Accidents in Paris.

He recognizes, "Accidents happen. In fact they have always happened, from the asteroid that presumably wiped out dinosaurs, to the great fire that razed central London in 1666...A good many...are unavoidable acts of nature. But many more are human accidents provoked by the very technology that we celebrate...". Although the museum has not been actualized, as a pilot project, Virilio has developed a temporary exhibit where photographs and movies of every imaginable nature and human-made disaster are shown.

Foley and Lennon document the relationship between anxiety and dark tourism. In their research on the attraction of death and disaster, the authors stipulate sites beyond the memory of the living do not count as sites of dark tourism for they do not incite anxiety and doubt about modernity. They compare sites of the Scottish Wars of Independence and the United States' Vietnam War Memorial.

The Scottish sites, due to their chronological distance, do not induce questions on modernity and its consequences. However, artifacts and messages left behind at the Vietnam Memorial suggest elements of anxiety and doubt over a controversial war. The rise of spectacle is another consequence of post-modernism found in tourism literature. As Rojek states, "Meaning has been replaced with spectacle and sensation dominates value". To illustrate, he points to private–sector initiatives like Robin Hood Country in Nottinghamshire, England and Catherine Cookson country in Tyneside, England, both of which are constructed around mythical and fictional themes. Pretes found in post-modern society, objects become representations and are commodified, packaged, consumed and eventually obscure reality; hence, commodity becomes a spectacle. He cites as an example, the Santa Claus Village in Finland.

He describes it as, "...a contrived tourism attraction...a city...built entirely on image". The difficulty of spectacle is that it blurs the distinctions between the real and the imaginary. Ignoring reality, "The spectacle presents itself as something enormously positive...It says nothing more than "that which appears is good, and that which is good appears"". Hence, visitors are satisfied with the spectacle and may assume the spectacle to be the truth and the whole story.

When television and other media outlets entered people's living rooms, previously unknown worlds were revealed; consequently, a number of authors attribute the media as being responsible in part for the rise of dark tourism as spectacle. Although Seaton notes that thanatourism has been a factor since the Middle Ages, he also recognizes the media's role in fuelling public interest in death and disaster. He notes, "Murder coverage in the...press produced stampedes of visitors to death locations for sightseeing and souvenir hunting".

Foley and Lennon also recognize the media's early role in publicizing disaster tourism, particularly with the 1912 sinking of the *Titanic*. "Newsreel companies filmed survivors landing in the USA while reporters wired stories around the world". However, they too note media's post-modern importance. As an example, they focus on the assassination of John Fitzgerald Kennedy and its aftermath as a watershed moment in post-modernism. "Television broadcasts were interrupted across the globe to break the news. In the USA, coverage took precedence over scheduled programming and announcers... extemporized on camera as news changed and events unfolded". Lennon and Foley continue, "Central and notable in the media coverage was the death itself which offered a spectacle of televisual images defining the 'reality' of that weekend for many viewers.

The viewing of the funeral itself constituted the heaviest day of TV viewing in the USA to date...". Furthermore, Neilsen report of 1963 reported that approximately 93 per cent of TV-equipped households watched the funeral procession to Arlington National Cemetery. This rise in spectacle strongly impacts public commemoration and memorials. As a consequence, today's architects and builders simply do not construct a memorial; they must also build to reach a generation, "...to which history has been spoon-fed as entertainment and spectacle". This is evident not only with the sites of fictional representation that Pretes and Rojek describe. For some dark tourism sites that emphasize their educational and remembrance missions, interpretation veers closely to spectacle. Foley and Lennon cite the Sixth Floor Museum, Dallas and the Arlington Cemetery, Virginia, as examples of sites that have difficulties delineating education, remembrance and spectacle. As Connally is quoted in Lennon and Foley as saying,

- I don't think the time has come when history will really look at the Kennedy administration with a realistic eye. And how could we? When you see a beautiful little girl kneeling with her hand on her father's coffin, when you see a handsome little boy standing with a military salute by his slain father, how can you feel anything but the utmost sympathy?.

Rojek uses Jim Morrison's grave in a Paris cemetery as an example, "...where the search for spectacle has replaced the respect for solemnity". Once a sacred site, Morrison's tomb is now a, "...defaced, urine stained Mecca". The literature reveals additional inherent problems with such significant dependence on the media. Often, the time relationship causes problems. The past appears to visitors a planet different than the one they inhabit. Using Treblinka concentration camp, Steiner articulates this issue.

- Precisely at the same hour in which Mehring or Langer were being done to death, the overwhelming plurality of human beings, two miles away on Polish farms, five thousand miles away in New York, were making love or worrying about the dentist. The two orders of simultaneous experiences are so different, so irreconcilable to any common norm of human values, their co-existence is so hideous a paradox....

Furthermore, constant repetition of the past through the media can cheapen, marginalize, or trivialize the magnitude of the events being interpreted. Steven Spielberg's production, *Schindler's List,* is often singled out for its historical flaws. Foley and Lennon and Lanzmann describe how the movie operates within the confines of a traditional Hollywood narrative: there is a well-defined plot and an easy-to-follow chronology.

Rather than offering an accurately- documented version of the events, the film renders a fictionalized account written for popular consumption. Repetition is another key consequence of post-modernism occurring repeatedly in dark tourism literature. "As far as tourism is concerned, the emergence of simulations, replications, and virtual experiences as part of a tourism product has been a critical factor in the emergence of dark tourism". In 2000, the authors elaborated, "The interpretation and re-telling of events surrounding...death have shaped perceptions of reality.

In projecting visitors into the past, reality has been replaced with omnipresent simulation and commodification". In his work on black spots, Rojek concurs, stating black spots contain signs of repetition and duplication, a sign of post-modernism. As a result, the real in the postmodern world is confined in pure repetition. Repetition leads into other post-modern characteristics: simulation and duplication. As Foley and Lennon note, dark tourism, "...embodies the simulation of experiences, the importance of reproduction, and the significance of the media".

Examples abound. At the United States Holocaust Memorial Museum, patrons are given an identity card that progresses with them as they tour the museum, "...imitating whether you have been arrested, imprisoned, transported to a concentration camp, gassed, etc.". Similarly, when visitors enter the Apartheid Museum in Johannesburg, they are arbitrarily assigned racial classification and experience part of the museum from that viewpoint. At the Imperial War Museum in England, you can experience first-hand a replication of life in England during World War I.

Their Trench Experience, "...commodifies the life, sights, sounds and smells of life in the trenches..." while the Blitz Experience, "...includes the replication of an air raid while sitting in an Anderson shelter...". At the Sixth Floor Book Depository in Dallas, Texas, visitors can relive repeatedly, via the media, all aspects of the Kennedy's assassination from the presidential entourage and the assassination to the funeral and Lee Harvey Oswald's murder. Furthermore, the JFK Presidential Limousine Tour offers a replication assassination for visitors.

"For $25.00 visitors retrace the route in a replica of the presidential limousine, with an audio commentary playing on the car tape deck that includes crowd cheers, gunshot sounds, comments of other passengers...and the news broadcasts covering the death of the president". The tour ends at the Portland Hospital with confirmation of the President Kennedy's death. Rojek notes how James Dean fans duplicate the actor's death each year, on the same date, at the same time, at the exact location of the accident. They go so far as driving period vehicles. "Mile for mile, and moment for moment they try to repeat the sights, sounds and experiences that their hero experienced on the journey".

Museums and historic sites are not the only dark tourism spots to repeat the past. In Halifax, The Warehouse Restaurant has turned its dining room into a,

- ...culinary shrine to the *Titanic*...For $60.00 per person...patrons partake of six of the 11 courses offered to the first-class passengers on the night the ship went down-including poached salmon and Waldorf pudding. As a violinist and cellist play period pieces, an actor assuming the character of the *Titanic*...works the room, encouraging diners to take on the identity of some of the ship's betterknown passengers....

There are undeniable consequences to the excessive use of replication, simulation and duplication. With a high dependence on virtual experiences in our post-modern society, "...reality is a matter for debate". They continue, noting since interpretation confuses history and utilizes techniques to maintain interest, it, "...will remove the real that much farther from the simulation". Another aspect of post-modern society related to dark tourism is the dedifferentiation of leisure.

Everything is now feasible as a leisure activity. As a consequence, all forms of leisure have become equal and all events and sites have become potential tourism destination. Two hundred years ago, cemeteries were sacred, yet the National Federation of Cemetery Friends in Britain promotes them as outdoor museums. Lennon and Foley also note the commodification of the sacred, this time at Auschwitz where a number of private retail enterprises have developed.

"Everything from hot dog stands, booksellers, postcard vendors, film stores and discount pottery warehouses are to be found. This, and the internal sale of concentration camp memorabilia, present the camp authorities with a clear dilemma". De-differentiation can also be seen in the rise of museums and attractions that may be classified as dark tourism sites. Tourism to society's back-regions has developed in areas traditionally off limits or obscured from view.

In Lothian, Scotland, two mining collieries have been repackaged as the Scottish Mining Museum. In his study on New York's Little Italy, Conforti researched ghettos as tourist attractions. Finally, "Under postmodernism, it might be said, everyone is a permanent émigré from the present". Nostalgia is then seen to be a key paradigm of post-modernism, and Lennon and Foley cite numerous examples as testimony: the regeneration of urban centers; the creation of conservation: museum villages; the protection of landscapes; the boom in retro fashion; and the academic process of quoting and citing.

History, time and space then become commodities for sale. This sense of nostalgia appears to come from several sources. First, the doubt and anxiety modernity has produced surfaces in post-modern tourists who are searching for a simpler past. The tourists are, "...yearning for a past they can no longer find in their own social settings. Unable to tolerate their present alienated condition, and ever fearful of the future, they seek solace in days gone by-a world where it was once possible to distinguish right from wrong...pleasure from pain". Similarly, individuals become nostalgic for a time they envision as more alive, more exciting, more romantic than present day society.

- There was also an excitement in the streets of New York in 1882 that is gone...[people]...were...interested in their surrounding...[and]...carried with them a sense of purpose...they weren't bored, for God

> sakes...Those men moved through their lives in unquestioned certainty that there was a reason for being...Faces don't have that look now.

The media has exacerbated romantic visions of the past. James Cameron's movie, *Titanic*, is perhaps the most notorious example of disaster-turned-romance. The movie, which glossed over the deaths of over 1,500 people, chose instead to focus on the love affair between two fictional characters, Jack Dawson and Rose DeWitt Bukater.

The movie does recognize the enormity of the deaths when Rose reminisces, "Fifteen hundred people went into the sea when *Titanic* sank from under us. Six were saved from the water, myself included. Six out of 1,500". However, the premise of the film is the true love between Jack and Rose. *Titanic* is not the only entertainment source to turn disaster and war into romance.

On November 23, 1987, *Designing Women*, a then-popular television show, aired an episode called *I'll Be Seeing You.* In it, one of the lead characters dreams of a soldier out of World War II for her birthday. She envisions the war as a romantic era of drama and unrequited love, and as the episode unfolds, Charlene actually meets her soldier and falls in love. Nostalgia also surfaces under the guise of remembrance.

"Like an individual approaching old age, Americans are increasingly looking backward, trying to extract from the past those things they want to preserve, those symbolic artifacts that reflect significant and proud moments in the development of their nation". Much of the literature conceptualizes dark tourism as being a post-modern phenomenon, a reaction to the doubt and anxiety imbued by modernity. With 17th century industrialization, came ongoing social change: rationalization, modernization, science, technology, and knowledge.

This progress however, had its consequences. Some authors cite the sinking of the *Titanic* as the embryo of post-modernism. An unsinkable wonder of man's ingenuity, when the ship sank it shook society's belief in technology. Soon after, the Holocaust instilled doubt about people's humanity while subsequent presidential assassinations produced anxiety about liberal democracies.

As a result, society, including the tourism sector, began a transformation. Several key points, which illustrated dark tourism's correlation with postmodernism, were identified in the literature review. Firstly, was a move away from traditional, mass tourism as witnessed by the recent emergence of specialized tourism: green, heritage, adventure, dark and eco- tourism. Post-modernity has also influenced a rise in spectacle, brought about in part by the increased dominance of the media. Such media as television, movies, and videos have blurred the distinction between reality and simulation. The repetition of dark tourism events makes it hard for visitors to differentiate between time and space. The past becomes another planet. With this distancing, comes a need for the past and a heightened sense of nostalgia. In sum, for many authors, dark tourism provides the context for a post-modern experience. A society filled with doubt and anxiety looks to a variety of outlets to recoup the past. Generations dependent on the media have difficulty separating reality and therefore become satisfied with simulation and duplication.

CULTURAL VALUES

To grasp tourist motivation at sites of dark tourism, it is essential to understand the memorialization process of such sites, the how and why they were initially erected. Not all sites of death, disaster, and destruction are memorialized, nor do all sites evolve into tourist destinations. Much of this commemoration is shaped by cultural values. As Foote reported, "...attitudes towards violence and tragedy are closely aligned with cultural values".

In his aptly named book, Shadowed Ground: America's Landscapes of Violence and Tragedy, Foote discusses at length the impacts cultural values have on forging both a nation's memory and its commemorative landscape. The memorializing sites seen today have all been shaped by political, social and/or economic factors, sometimes over a number of decades. According to Foote, when a site experiences a tragic or violent event, one of four outcomes results: sanctification, designation, rectification, or obliteration. Most relevant to this study are the former two, and they are discussed in detail below.

SANCTIFICATION

The most common motives for sanctification are to honour martyrs, fallen heroes, great leaders and community loss. The process involves the creation of a sacred place, often identified by a durable marker such as a statue, building, monument or memorial garden. It also involves some form of formal consecration, a ceremony explaining the site's history and significance. However, this is not always an objective process as illustrated by the sanctification of Abraham Lincoln. Bodnar explains, "...the shaping of a past worthy of public commemoration in the present is contested and involves a struggle for supremacy between advocates of various political ideas and sentiments".

Although today Lincoln is regarded by many as one of the greatest American presidents, his memorial in Washington D.C. was not completed until 1922, fifty-seven years after his death. Foote states that, "...the heart of the problem of building a larger memorial was that Americans did not agree on how Lincoln should be remembered". At the time of his death in 1865, Lincoln was considered a polarizing leader who was responsible for dividing the nation. His name was synonymous with the American Civil War and any efforts to commemorate him were overshadowed by the after-effects of the war. However, these aftereffects began to fade with time.

- Gradually, over several decades, the Civil War came to assume new meaning for Americans in both the North and the South. Whereas early assessments stressed only the issue of victory and defeat, by the late nineteenth century the war was being cast in heroic terms by both sides...both North and South could maintain that they had fought the good fight for causes each side held dear...Only a step separated this view from seeing the war as a struggle that tested-and strengthened-the nation.

As American cultural values began to alter the status of the Civil War at the turn of the 19th century, they also began to transform Lincoln's reputation. No longer vilified as the president who divided the nation, the Lincoln Memorial was dedicated in Washington, D.C., in 1922 to the *defender* of the nation.

DESIGNATION

Designated sites, "...arise from events that are viewed as important but somehow lacking the heroic or sacrificial qualities associated with sanctification". Due to a number of reasons, they omit the rituals of ceremony and consecration. For example, the designation of a site may be a transitional phase.

The site could, over time, either be consecrated or eventually obliterated from memory. The commemoration process of Martin Luther King Jr. illustrates this idea. After King's assassination at the Lorraine Motel, Walter Bailey, building's owner, marked the site to venerate the Black hero. However, the wider American population did not immediately accept King' as a heroic symbol, and therefore sanctification was not forthcoming. This is due in part because, "...commemoration is primarily enacted by former victims, survivors or relatives...Rarely does any state commemorate its own crimes...".

Young supports this idea. "Only rarely does a nation call upon itself to remember the victims of crimes it has perpetrated. Where are the national monuments to the genocide of American Indians, to the millions of Africans enslaved...? They barely exist". For a group that has suffered such negative images and stereotypes, or who simply has not molded into American ideals, preservation has been limited. It took twenty years before the Black struggle was integrated into American cultural values and therefore King to reach national recognition. As Foote noted, the changing political climate finally allowed such black minority sites to be commemorated. Changes included,

"...downsizing controversial divisive issues and instead stressing values and virtues held in common by parties on both sides... and canonizing heroes, and creating shared monuments...". Foote is not the sole academic to recognize the influence of cultural values on the commemoration of dark places.

Preservation is a selective process for Barthel and that which is selected often reflects the interests of those in power. Similarly, Tunbridge and Ashworth found motives behind some interpretation, which, "...may include the manipulation of...essentially sensitive heritage so that it contributes to a variety of contemporary goals even though these may historically have had little relevance to the original atrocity events". For Goodey, cultural influence does not lie solely in the hands of politicians: "There has always been those rich enough to create taste in landscape". Tunbridge and Ashworth reminded us that media is also highly selective in its choice of victims thereby influencing cultural values.

For instance, the British Broadcasting Company (BBC) was not in Rwanda and, "...world interest in East Timor was stirred only after the broadcast of a 1990's videotape, some 15 years after the violence had begun". A number of additional academic works have looked at cultural values and commemoration. Also using the Black example, Crew noted that interest in Black History did not begin until the two decades after World War II. While initial commemoration took place with local, grass roots movements, it was not until the early 1970's that mainstream America began to pay heed to Black History.

Much of this change came with the political activism of the 1960's. However, despite recent commemorations of Black History, certain parts of history remain vague, especially antebellum plantations and slavery: perhaps because this subservient part of history continues to diverge from overriding American values. Compare this to modern slavery commemoration Britain. Until the last century, Unite Kingdom perceptions of Britain's role in slavery were that of social reform. With an absence of physical evidence, a smaller Black population, and no watershed mark to signify slavery as being important, Britons until recently have been removed from their role in the slavery triangle.

It was easier to focus on the positive aspects of slavery that the historic sites postulated. For example, there is the abolition campaign led by William Wilberforce. The change came when a leading white, British philanthropist traveled to Barbados and discovered Britain's ignorance about slavery. He funded a permanent exhibit at the Maritime Museum in Liverpool, England, and today, all aspects of slavery in Britain are interpreted. Another illustrative example is to compare the sinking of the *Titanic* to that of the *S.S. Atlantic*, which sank in 1898, killing 562 persons. Until 1912, the *Atlantic's* sinking had the distinction of being the worst single-vessel maritime disaster. Unlike the

Titanic that carried a number of rich, influential individuals, the Atlantic was carrying mostly European immigrants to the United States. As a result, there is little commemoration to the victims except within the tiny Canadian fishing villages that played rescuers' roles in the tragedy. Another manifestation of conflicting cultural values is what Tunbridge and Ashworth define as heritage dissonance. As the authors noted, "All heritage is someone's heritage and therefore logically not someone else's". Hence, when individuals attempt to lay claim to a part of someone else's heritage, conflict can arise. Furthermore, conflict is exacerbated when one party is comprised of tourists and tourism providers. Lennon and Foley note,

- Viewing the past – as opposed to history – as a set of discourses aimed at a particular group highlights the suggestion that history is for someone and that the contemporary dominant power élites are most likely to play a significant part in shaping that reality when the target group is ordinary citizens in the guise of tourists. Thus those with the responsibilities for tourism promotion and development may have a previously unrecognized ethical dilemma – that of adjudicating in debates over 'whose history' prevails in interpretation.

This is well illustrated in a question posed by Tunbridge and Ashworth. Is a British bomber pilot or German U-boat captain a hero, villain, or both simultaneously? For the allies during World War II, the British bomber pilot was a hero; however, the citizens of Dresden did not likely feel the same way after their city was bombed in 1945 by allied air raids. The question becomes even more profound looking at contemporary interpretation of the events in Dresden.

Although Britain and the United States devastated the city in 1945, the issue today is often skirted in the retelling of the war for, "...fear of offending the English-speaking tourism market". Consequently, tourism creates dissonance as people cater to the tourism dollar rather than adhering to authenticity. The literature cites a number of additional relationships between tourism and heritage dissonance.

Foote discusses the 1889 Johnstown flood that killed almost 1,800 of the town's residents. Although a marker was erected in commemoration, little else was done. "Many residents felt that it was now time...to put the flood behind them and move forward with reconstruction, that further memorialization would only prolong painful memories". However, journalists and tourists continued to inundate the region in attempt to keep the story alive. Over one hundred years later, cultural values have changed, and now the town is the site of a flood museum and a national memorial. Rather than wanting to turn away tourists, tourism is, "...seen as a way to turn a past catastrophe into a present-day asset". Lennon and Foley discuss heritage dissonance regarding the Sixth Floor Depository in Dallas, Texas. Although a popular tourist site today, the Depository was not always seen in a positive light. "After the assassination, the building was clearly a difficult real estate proposition and state employees were understandably less than enthusiastic working on the sixth floor".

A former mayor of Dallas was quoted as saying, "For my part, I don't want anything to remind me that a President was killed on the streets of Dallas. I want to forget". However, tourists and other well-wishers flocked to the assassination site, leaving behind a collection of remembrances: flowers, madonnas, wreaths. Today a number of memorials commemorate the life of John F. Kennedy, including the Sixth Floor Book Depository, which is Dallas' number one tourist attraction. Dann and Potter noted that plantation and slavery tourism in Barbados often created dissonance by putting dollars first and people last. The island was,

- ...quick to realize that it cannot portray its history as it really happened, since the presentation of centuries of overt racism...is hardly a recipe for touristic success. There has consequently been a selective rendition of the past...[resulting]...in a loss of identification for the provider, and indigenous culture becomes reduced....

This premise is supported by Tunbridge and Ashworth who quote, "This shaping of past oppression, perhaps as a reaction to the perceived contemporary problems of these groups, creates obvious dissonance possibilities in the interpretation of this historical period...". While tourists and tourism-providers may not want to confront the island's history of suffering, for many islanders who endured slavery, telling their story may be vital. The Jersey Islands off the coast of England also illustrate a history at odds with tourism.

Today, "The 'ill wind' of the war years has been turned to the good. The relics and remains of Hitler's British stronghold have now taken their place...Jersey's German occupation is now big business, with more war museums per square mile than anywhere else in Europe". However, any reminders tarnishing the island's image during the war are sanitized or hidden: the collaborations, fraternization and compromises. Moreover, the whole issue of collaboration is dealt with in only one museum on Jersey in a minor display area.

This is because collaboration brings into question the belief that Britain stood alone against Hitler during the dark days of World War II, thereby hurting national identity and the tourism dollar. Light found dissonance to be alive and well in post-communist Romania. Like other Eastern and Central European nations, Romania has little desire to commemorate and interpret their communist past for, "...the physical legacy of Ceausescu's rule is an unwelcome reminder of a period of history which Romania is attempting to forget". As proof, after the 1998 revolution, statues of all communist leaders were torn down and streets were renamed.

However, there is considerable interest from tourists. In 1990, a year after the overthrow of communism in Romania, the country saw a 67 per cent increase in tourism. "Independent travelers took the opportunity to see for themselves the site and sights of Eastern Europe's most violent revolution, while travel companies hastily arranged packages for visitors wanting to see the locations associated with the collapse of communism". In Romania then, the desire to forget the past conflicts with the desire to maximize the economic benefits of tourism. Such heritage dissonance between survivors and tourism has possible ramifications aside from direct, human conflict. Firstly, as Henderson points out, "There is potential conflict between the functions of education and entertainment...".

If hosts ignore the interpretation that is being offered to guests, the line between education and spectacle may easily be crossed. Secondly, host sites may be missing opportunities to tell their stories. Using Light's Romanian example, tourists are left uninformed about the meaning of communism to the country and why they are so unwilling to share their stories. Conversely, tourism may be rushing the country to confront a past they are not yet ready to face.

Cultural values dominate history, heritage, and the memorialization process. Frequently, those in power manipulate which stories are told for political, economic, and nationalistic purposes. This alone can create conflict between the prevailing forces and victims and survivors as they battle for the ownership of the past.

Survivors and victims themselves do not always agree on the shaping of memory. However, the situation is intensified when tourists and tourism dollars enter into the equation. The literature was clear in outlining the conflict between hosts' wants and guests' demands. Unfortunately, the tourism dollar often triumphs over victims' wishes and historical fact.

There are severe repercussions to this situation. As illustrated in Dresden, Germany and Jersey, England, some historical facts were disregarded in order to satisfy tourists. In Dallas, Texas, there was a division in the community. In Romania, educational opportunities were lost due to the impatience of the tourism industry. Some sites may even be threatened with spectacle as tourism operators' rush to capitalize on tragic events. Dark tourism sites are particularly susceptible to heritage dissonance given the gravity and sensitivity of their origins. For those who have undergone such traumatic events, forgetting may be an instinctual reaction. Yet given the pervasiveness of the media, touristic interest is often immediate. It follows that these sites must be managed with heritage dissonance in mind in order to reduce conflict.

CULTURAL VALUES AND THE HOLOCAUST

The commemoration of the Holocaust is no different from the previous examples in that it, too, is impacted by prevailing cultural values. As Gourevitch notes, "In America...we recast the story of the Holocaust to teach fundamental American values...pluralism, democracy, restraint on government, the inalienable right of individuals, the inability of government to enter into freedom of religion". The USHMM in Washington, D.C. provides a highly illustrative example of this.

In the years following World War II, the world tried to come to grips with a number of conflicting emotions, especially regarding the Holocaust. Veterans who liberated concentration camps endured, "...an almost unbearable mixture of empathy, disgust, guilt, anger and alienation". Bystanders experienced guilt for not having taken a more active part, while perpetrators attempted to forget their actions.

The implications of the events were simply too threatening for public examination. In America, reactions to the Holocaust were similar, and the reactions of survivors who had come to the country were equally as mixed. Some simply wanted to forget, while others did not want to identify with the victims. Others starting a new life, "...were more concerned about acting as Americans than as Jews".

The political climate of the decades following World War II proved conducive to sustaining these conflicting emotions. Post-war America had allied itself with Germany against Cold War communism. Holocaust perpetrators had suddenly become the allies, while some liberators such as the Soviet Union were now considered the enemy. "Active memory of the Nazi past was considered a needless complication in the struggle to win the Cold War".

A number of international and national events began to change American opinions towards the Holocaust in the 1960's. May of 1967 saw the Six-Day War in Israel, with the ultimate Egyptian goal of annihilating Israel. For Jews in both the United States and abroad, this awakened dormant memories of the Holocaust and brought about a 'collapse of complacency'. The Jewish struggle for 'Never Again' was born.

On another foreign shore, America was fighting a losing battle against North Vietnam. As the conflict began to erode the American belief in the, "...righteousness of the American fighting man..." the Holocaust provided a foundation for good versus evil after the, "...disorientation of Vietnam...". Americans were forced to reconsider their values. On the home shores, the late 1960's saw a rise in ethnic particularism as an accepted form of cultural expression. It became acceptable to be different and to express those differences; therefore, many Jews became less reserved about demonstrating their Jewish identity in public. In the late 1970's, a number of additional events transpired. There were proposed anti-Semitic marches in Skokie, Illinois by American Nazis.

The American Office of Special Investigations began prosecuting war criminals. The NBC aired a miniseries on the Holocaust, and in 1978 then-president Jimmy Carter commissioned a presidential report on the Holocaust. Finally, and pointedly, the changing political climate was in Washington, D.C. directly influenced the commemoration of the Holocaust in the capital. As Linenthal relates, "The motivation to build a Holocaust memorial was linked with a clear message of the administration's support for the State of Israel". This was desperately needed as Carter wanted to appease the Jewish constituency after the sale of F-15 fighter jets to Saudi Arabia.

President Carter was using the, "...power of the government to do something many would perceive as good, and at the same time, reach out to an increasingly alienated ethnic constituency". In 1980, the Carter administration created a Campaign to Remember, a mail-out fundraising campaign targeting the American Jewish population. Throughout the 1960's and 70's, the above factors combined with others to bring about the genesis of a Holocaust museum in Washington D.C.

However, this museum would not only commemorate the Holocaust, it would be a, "...repository of American identity". The story, instead of focusing solely on the Jewish experience, would have to be told in a way that would be significant to an American audience: it needed to move beyond the limits of ethnic memory. To do so, the museum would reinforce, "...American identity by graphically revealing what America is not", "...through stark presentation of their antitheses in Nazi Germany".

Krauthammer reinforces this idea. Located in the Washington Mall, "...home of the monumental expressions of core national narratives", the museum provides excellent views of the Washington Monument and Jefferson Memorial. Here, "...juxtaposition is not just redemptive. It is reassuring. The angels of democracy stand watch on this temple of evil. It is as if only in the heart of the world's most tolerant and powerful democracy can such terrible testimony be safely contained". Outwardly, the commemoration process appears to be an easy practice. Americans flock in droves to the Sixth Floor Museum, the Lincoln Monument, and Gettysburg to venerate their heroes.

However, these heroes and events, which we take for, granted were likely once victims of debate and conflict over what accurately represented a national identity. The enshrinement of disaster and tragedy is not accidental: it is shaped by prevailing cultural values that forge and maintain a national identity. 'Remember the Alamo', the 'Maine' and 'Pearl Harbour' have all served as rallying cries to rouse patriotic fervour in the pursuit of justice. These words conjure up visions of freedom, bravery and liberty. Rarely does one hear reminders of unpopular events such as 'Remember Kent State' or 'Remember Saigon'. This is because shame and loss are not values governments want to instill in their constituency.

Therefore, the commemoration of dark tourism sites must be looked at under this light. Violence and tragedy are widespread in society; however, not all sites and events are memorialized. Social and political forces have moulded much of what is seen. Similarly, interpretation at sites of death and disaster must be viewed with skepticism. The truth may not be the ultimate ideal because it is more important to shape displays and exhibits into a marketable commodity.

UNDERSTANDING THE HOLOCAUST

For many, the scope of the Holocaust is beyond belief: that one state sponsored regime could systematically annihilate mass populations is unfathomable. Beginning in 1933 with Hitler's investiture as German chancellor, the Third Reich eventually exterminated approximately eleven million individuals before the 1945 Nazi surrender. Those targeted included, but were not limited to, communists and other political prisoners, Gypsies, homosexuals, and the mentally disabled.

Of those eleven million, however, over half were of Jewish origin. In Poland alone, 90 per cent of the Judaic population was wiped out. Pre-1933, there were 3.5 million Jews living in the country: approximately 300,000 survived. In Czechoslovakia, the ancient fortress city of Terezin was converted into a transit camp where 138,000 Jews died. Jewry in Austria, France, Holland, Belgium, Denmark, Norway, Luxembourg, Ukraine, Hungry and Lithuania suffered similar fates.

All totaled, 6 million Jews lost their lives during the Holocaust, including 1.5 million children. Whether termed Shoah or Holocaust, the remembrance and commemoration of such events are also overwhelming and are as varied as the individual experiences themselves. Much of the literature on memorializing the period emphasizes a deep divergence in commemoration, particularly between countries; for it is there cultural values dictate public memory. Furthermore, the stakes of remembrance are high for those involved. Holocaust commemoration not only involves veneration, but also perceived ownership of the events and subsequently the sculpting of a nation's identity.

To illustrate, two countries are examined: Israel, and most importantly for this study, the United States.

ISRAEL AND SHOAH

Today, Israel is a nation indelibly tied to Shoah. For some, the events of 1933- 1945 were precursors to the establishment of a Jewish state. The Israeli army's Informational Guidelines to the Commander on Yom Hashoah goes as far as quoting, "By standing under these conditions and refusing to surrender to despair the Jews made it possible the continuation of the Jewish people even in the inferno of the Holocaust and thereby helped created the State of Israel".

This form of recognition however, was not always the case, for Israel, like all nations, remembers according to national myths and political will. In the years immediately following the war, Israel had an ambiguous relationship with the destruction of the Shoah, particularly after statehood in 1948. Native-born Israeli's could not understand the mass extermination and did not care to commemorate the powerlessness of their people.

Similarly, many of the 350,000 survivors that settled there after the war found the past too painful to confront. There was little desire to commemorate what was perceived to be victimization and as a result, remembrance was greeted with silence. This silence was shattered with the 1961 trial of Adolph Eichmann. Hundreds of survivors stood to give testimony and emotion to their Holocaust experiences, and this soon opened dialogue between varying Israeli factions.

"The trial created a climate of opinion in which the Holocaust...became the central topic of conversation... [it]...ceased to be a taboo, and instead assumed an increasingly central – if contestedposition in Israeli society and politics". The trial brought together the dueling reactions to the Holocaust, thus reconciling Israelis with their past. Furthermore, it brought about the genesis of modern remembrance in Israel: that of rebirth. Today in Israel, memory is devoted to heroism and yesterday's victims have become modern martyrs. Where European museums focus on the annihilation of the Jews, at museums such as Yad Vashem in Jerusalem, the Holocaust links a, "...millennium of Jewish life in Europe before the war...to Jewish National Rebirth afterwards".

THE UNITED STATES OF AMERICA

Like Israel, both native-born Americans and immigrant survivors sought to put the past behind them immediately after the war. For Americans, Germany had become an ally in the Cold War; for survivors, the memories were too painful. Attitudes have changed dramatically in the past 60 years, and today the United States embraces the events. Now, what is, "...beyond dispute is that in the 1990's the 'Holocaust' is being made in America".

Holocaust history has become American history, justified by the country's roles as bystander, liberator, and haven for survivors. As a result, the Holocaust has become Americanized and the numerous Holocaust museums and memorials dotting the country exemplify this. From Dallas and Boston to Miami and Tucson, America remembers. Yet, America remembers through American ideals.

Perhaps no other museum illustrates this better than the United States Holocaust Memorial Museum in Washington, D.C. Where European sites focus on victims and Israelis on rebirth, in the American focus in on what it means to be American. As the USHMM's Memorial Council stated during the museum's inception,

- This museum belongs at the center of American life because as a democratic civilization America is the enemy of racism and its ultimate expression, genocide. An event of universal significance, the Holocaust has special importance for Americans: in act and word the Nazis denied the deepest tenets of the American people.

A number of other sources endorse this doctrine. Max Kampelman, Ronald Reagan's chief arms negotiator felt that,

- ...Europeans probably should have built such museums in their capitals, but they haven't and most probably won't...But our building will demonstrate the tolerance of our culture, its ability to empathize with the suffering of all its people. Or decision to build such a museum says something about our commitment to human rights and to the kind of nation we want to be.

Michael Berenbaum, director of the museum, commented that, "When people leave the U.S. Holocaust Memorial Museum, the monuments to democracy that surround it – to Lincoln and Jefferson and Washington – will taken on new meaning". For Cole, this indicates the museum's ability to affect all Americans. For him, "...the museum just off the Mall...gives an 'Americanised' telling of the 'Holocaust' to a target audience of non-Jewish mom, dad and kids from Iowa...[it]...talks of 'victims'/'survivors' and 'liberators'". Ownership of the Holocaust, then, must be understood in the context of this research.

The paper's focus is an American Holocaust museum and its American visitors, hence, an Americanization of the events. Should someone initiate a similar study in Israel, Poland or Germany, the results will likely differ, for each country comprehends the Holocaust differently. The events will be interpreted according to each country's own unique cultural value systems.

For visitors to the Holocaust Museum Houston, according to the literature, their experience will revolve around key American tenets. As bystander to many of the events, America will reach out through such museums to promise Nie Wider – Never Again. Exhibits will stand, "...as an explicit judgement on past inaction, and an implicit call to America (as self-styled 'policeman of the world') not to stand idly by in the future".

Via Holocaust museums such as in Houston, America may also overlay this inaction through her roles of liberator and haven for survivors. Once again, national cultural values such as pluralism, democracy, liberty and heroism are interwoven with other stories from the Holocaust. While Jewish death and destruction is commemorated, it is done so in an American context. Therefore, visitors to the Holocaust Museum Houston are not just experiencing the Holocaust, they are experiencing an American version of the events.

PUSH/PULL FACTORS AND TOURIST MOTIVATIONS

Researchers have long been commenting on the lack of research on tourist motivation, and much of this research to date on the subject identified the concept of equilibrium. In other words, research was focused on the theory that individuals travel to satisfy a need. Kim and Lee noted there are, "...psychological needs which play a significant role in causing a person to feel disequilibrium that can be corrected through a tourism experience". One of the conceptual frameworks that consider this need is Dann's push and pull theory where tourists are motivated by a push or pull to a destination Dann noted that past tourism research has indicated that the distinction between push and pull factors has been generally accepted practice.

He then went on to define the two concepts. Push factors as a motivation, "...refer to the tourist as subject and deal with those factors predisposing him to travel". Pull factors are motivators, "...which attract the tourist to a given resort...and whose value is seen to reside in the object of travel". Dann also noted that pull factors, to date, had taken precedence in tourism research and that there had been a lack of enthusiasm for push factors. This is supported by Crompton and Taylor who note the travel industry has also been conditioned to focus on pull factors.

The industry's, "...*modus operandi* is based on the assumption that people go on vacation to do and see things". Visitors then, are attracted to destinations by the cultural offerings and/or special attributes the site might offer. MacCannell supports this in his discussion on the language of tourism. For him, a tourist attraction is a sign; it represents something to someone. Hence, dark tourism sites use markers with language to pull tourists to the site. "The rhetoric of tourism is full of the manifestations of the importance of the authenticity of the relationship between tourists and what they see: this is a *typical* native house; this is the *very* place the leader fell; this is the *actual* pen used to sign the law; this is the *original* manuscript...". To compensate for this lack of push focus, both Dann and Crompton sought to understand the push factor more thoroughly. In his study of tourists in Barbados, Dann suggested that anomie and ego-enhancement created a push factor within travellers.

He argued, "...the presence of such factors is conducive to the creation of a fantasy world, one to which he plans a periodic escape". Dann's anomie refers to a society, "...whose norms governing interaction have lost their integrative force and where lawlessness and meaningless prevail". This lack of meaning has evolved into possible push factors, where the desire to, "...transcend the feeling of isolation obtained in everyday life..." pushes people to get away from it all. The study of anomie as a motivator juxtaposes with the current studies of postmodern society.

Today, where there is conflict in, "...wars, strikes, football hooliganism, muggings, highjacking and guerrilla violence", people continue to seek meaning in their world. Thus, anomie continues to push visitors almost 30 years after Dann's initial study. Dann also found ego-enhancement to be a push factor. He states that man needs to be recognized, to feel superior to those below him. One means of this advancement is via travel. "A tourist can go to a place where his social position is unknown and where he can feel superior by dine of this lack of knowledge.

Additionally, on his return a further boost can be given to his ego in the recounting of his holiday experiences". Crompton also deviated from traditional means of looking at push and pull. Previously, socio-psychological motives explained the initial decision to go on a vacation but the subsequent destination choice was a function of the pulling power of the destination. Crompton felt not only are socio-psychological motives useful in explaining the initial push or arousal to take a vacation, but "...they may have directive potential to direct the tourist towards a particular destination".

Crompton found nine motives for pleasure travel, including novelty and education, which were noted to be, "...at least partially aroused by the particular qualities that a destination offered". However, the other seven motives (escape from a perceived mundane environment, exploration and evaluation of self, relaxation, prestige, regression, enhancement of kinship relations and the facilitation of social interaction) were found to be unrelated to destination attributes. Indeed, Crompton found respondents in his study traveled for socio-psychological push factors unrelated to a specific destination.

More recent studies have had similar findings. Uzzell found, "Tourists are not motivated by specific qualities of a destination; rather, they match a destination's attributed to their psychological needs. Poria, Butler, and Airey also noted that, "...heritage tourism is a phenomenon based on tourists' motivations and perceptions rather than specific site attributes". The literature review also revealed a wide variety of push factors. Kim and Lee, in their research on visitation to National Parks in South Korea, found 12 motivational items that pushed visitors to a destination. Factors included escaping from everyday routine, adventure and building friendships, and family togetherness. Meanwhile, Botha, Crompton and Kim noted intrinsic push factors include escape, social recognition, socialization, self-esteem, learning, regression, novelty, and distancing from crowds.

Finally, Dann notes the language of tourism, while pulling tourist with good marketing, also pushes individuals to a destination. For the author, "...language of tourism gently talks to them about possible places they can visit by introducing various pull factors or attraction of competing destinations...By addressing them in terms of their own culturally predicted needs and motives, it hopes to push them out of the armchair and onto the plane...". As a result, although not the sole motivators for travel, push-pull factors provide a simple, concrete division that is easily understood. Therefore, for the purpose of this study, the factors provide manageable categories of motivations.

Furthermore, the factors found in the literature review lend themselves to this natural, albeit porous, division of internal push and destination pull factors. It must be noted here that the literature and this study recognize that factors do not always stand alone. For example, an individual might be pushed to visit Vimy Ridge because a close relative was killed there during World War I. However, the site itself may be commemorating a special anniversary and be offering conducted tours, which pulls the individual to the site. This individual might experience both push and pull factors simultaneously. Furthermore, an individual is not limited to experiencing just one push factor, nor is a site limited to offering one pull factor.

Many Holocaust museums affirm both education and remembrance in their mandate. The literature indicates that a number of individuals visit sites of dark tourism for personal reasons. Some visit such sites as a socially feasible way of expressing interest in death and disaster. Some come to learn about the history behind an event, like those who visit Gettysburg because of an interest in military tactics.

Some visit to commemorate family, friends or their own experience, such as war veterans and their families. Similarly, those affiliated with the site may also come to affirm their cultural identity. Some come because of feelings of guilt, and finally, some may come to simply out of morbid curiosity. These are being construed as push factors.

Conversely, dark tourism destinations can themselves pull visitors to their facilities, with the most common explanations being education and remembrance. Some sites feel a need to justify or rationalize their identity as a tourism attraction, while others incorporate education and remembrance into their public identity and mission statements. The Dallas Sixth Floor Book Depository Museum recognized this even before its inception. "It was created to meet the widespread visitor demand for information and understanding about a tragic but important event...". However it is approached, sites of death and disaster do pull people in order to learn and to remember. Two additional pull factors surfaced in the literature. Firstly, artifacts also supply a pull factor for visitors to visit sites of death and disaster.

For instance, some individuals might be attracted to Holocaust museums to see remnants of the events such as boxcars, human hair or Zyklon B gas canisters. Secondly, sight sacralization may pull tourists simply because the society has deemed that site to be of some touristic significance. While the media was discussed at length in the dark tourism literature as both a push and pull factor, this study sees modern communication technologies as being a mediator between the varying dark tourism components.

HERITAGE AND IDENTITY

It is not uncommon for individuals involved with death and disaster to return to the site of the event. Some individuals, such as war veterans or survivors, are directly related to the event; others are descendents and friends of victims and survivors, perhaps even relatives of perpetrators. Others are not related whatsoever, but rather identify with the event, such as movie star fans or those tied through race or religion. It must be noted those motivated by heritage and identity do not solely visit the exact sites of death and disaster: they might visit representative sites such as museums and reconstructions. Paying homage to someone they identify with can help formulate their heritage. Numerous examples can be found in the dark tourism literature.

VICTIMS AND SURVIVORS

Smith goes as far as attributing American mass tourism to the World War II experiences of American soldiers. She states, "Of those who returned home as victors, many were imbued with a desire to see the war-time sites under peaceful conditions". Today, veterans are still traveling to Europe to revisit the sites of their nightmares.

In November of 1998, 17 veterans of World War I traveled to France to commemorate the 80th anniversary of the armistice. South Africa has recently seen a deluge of sites open to help locals acknowledge, understand and cope with their painful past. Sites include the recently opened Apartheid Museum in Johannesburg and the District 6 Museum in Cape Town.

These sites are of particular importance given the recency of events. Apartheid did not end until 1994 and survivors of apartheid forma large majority of the population of South Africa. Beech found in two separate dark tourism studies, a definitive division in people visiting the sites. In his study of Buchenwald concentration camp in Germany, he noted that was the division was in two parts, "...visitors with some connection with the camp, that is survivors...and general visitors with no direct or indirect connection". Although he adds relatives and those with a shared heritage to the former category, it is important to note he defines survivors as a body of visitors. Beech's second study, which focuses on relatives not survivors, will be discussed later in this chapter. There is a potential problem with victim and survivor visitation: it will likely fade with time.

Beech compares the 1746 Battle of Culloden to the 1066 Battle of Hastings. He notes, "...there is still a residual group of Scots who feel drawn to the battlefield of Culloden with some sense of identity, whereas there are probably rather fewer English people drawn to Battle near Hastings with similar feelings of identity". This visitor decline is a feasible concern for visitation at concentration camps. Although visitor numbers at Auschwitz-Birkenau fluctuate from year to year, there are some telltale trends.

FAMILY AND RELATIVES

The impacts of death and disaster reach much further than concentration camp survivors and others directly involved in death and disaster. In the aftermath, large numbers of people are affected by the repercussions of the event. For some, it is the tragic enslavement of a distance African ancestor. For others, it is a relative that fought and was killed on the beaches of Vimy Ridge. For others yet, they have a heritage kinship through religion, race or gender. Consequently, visitors are attracted to sites of dark tourism because they have some personal affiliation with the event or someone who was involved in it.

The literature provides numerous studies and examples of sites where friends and relatives journey to actual or representative sites of death. However, it must be noted here that Foley and Lennon do not feel that friends and relatives visiting sites fulfill their definition of dark tourism. Nonetheless, for the purpose of this study, friends, relatives and descendants visiting sites of death and disaster will be considered dark tourism. Holt's Battlefield Tours organizes excursions to a myriad of 20th century European war sites, including the Menin Gate, Vimy Ridge, and Thièpval.

Aware that some of their guests have family that fought in the wars, the organizers also attempt to, "...accommodate the possibility of visiting the graves of relatives for those on the coach". Lennon and Foley continue their discussion on war cemeteries. They note, "...transnational tourism, especially cultural tourism, in the postwar period was spearheaded in Europe...and the sights of Europe became attractive and...relatively inexpensive to those from North America...Many visitors to Europe...had either fought in these wars or had lost friends and relatives in it". As in his Buchenwald study, Beech also found a division in tourist taxonomies at slavery sites in Britain, this time with a racial difference: White Britons and Black Britons. White visitors tend to be in unconscious denial and rarely identify with slave traders. However, Black Britons, "...born and brought up in Britain...identify with the slaves and see them as part of their heritage". In her study of Ghana and slavery, Essah found the country is turning the darker aspect of its past into a tourism commodity. Much of its marketing efforts are focussed on the United States and the Black diaspora.

American tourists in particular are targeted because they are thought to be journeying to Ghana in search of their African roots. The focus on the Black diaspora can especially be seen in the festivities surrounding the PANAFEST (Pan-African Historical Theatre Festival). In 2001, PANAFEST saw a record number of African Americans who, "...combine attendance at the festivities with their thirst for knowledge about their heritage". In his study of a New York City Italian ghetto, Conforti found individuals visit such areas because of a sense of nostalgia created by the need to connect with their heritage. He notes, "...Italian-Americans who have never lived in or near such neighbourhoods...visit...in an effort to underscore their identity, discover their ancestral roots, or at least come closer to them while in cities like Boston or New York".

He expands this discussion by citing other ethnic groups that have implemented cultural centers in order to educate such visitors. For instance, the historically Jewish section of New York contains a restored synagogue and a tenement museum. Representations of death and disaster also provide those with heritage ties a place to affirm their cultural identity. Beth Hatefutsoth, the Jewish Diaspora Museum in Tel Aviv is an ideal example. For Goldmann, the function of the museum is to forge the identity of Jewish people around the world who are living in quite different, and at times, antagonistic spheres. It provides a bridge for Jewish youth to comprehend the meaning of their Jewish ancestry.

Kovner concurs, adding the museum was to serve as a, "...contribution to the covenant...of the modern Jew with himself, his own identity, the covenant of the Israeli with the Jewish people". Weinberg reports the museum has succeeded in its goals. Many Jewish visitors attend for very personal reasons: to fulfill a sense of identity with their cultural past. "Beth Hatefutsoth is a warm museum: most of its Jewish visitors respond in a strong emotional way…their sense of identification with the past is vigorously awakened".

IDENTITY MOTIVATORS

Finally, a number of people who have neither a direct nor an indirect connection to the dark tourism event visit the site because of heritage motivations. They gain a sense of identity from such visitation. Rojek refers to the James Dean fans that recreate the actor's 1959 fatal car crash. Their annual procession to the death site acts partly as, "…a monument to the dead hero". Lennon and Foley extend this sense of identification by noting, "…the erection of a memorial to Dean's death by a Japanese businessman, rather than a local touristic imperative". A similar event is the annual vigil at Strawberry Fields each December 8th, the anniversary of singer John Lennon's death outside the Dakota apartment building in New York City. Lennon's fans lobbied to have a memorial garden erected, and today, Strawberry Fields provides a shrine for all Beatles fans.

In sum, the impacts of death and disaster leave lasting impressions, not just for those individuals involved but also for their family members. With such events come mixed feelings but an inevitable tie to the site and/or event. One consequence is dark tourism visitation, and as the literature articulates, this is a common phenomenon. Victims, survivors, and their loved ones often return to the scene of tragedy for a number of reasons. Some individuals who directly experienced events return to see the destination under peaceful circumstances. Others yet go to confront a painful part of their past. By returning to the past, understanding and closure are possible.

Visitation by this segment poses a challenge for dark tourism sites, however. As time passes, this population ages and eventually this segment will fade away. Family members and friends also comprise a population that visits due to heritage affiliation. Some visit to honour and pay tribute to family members whose lives were lost. Others visit to help forge their identity, to discover their roots and where they came from. Visiting sites of death and disaster allow these visitors to understand their heritage. Others yet will visit due to nostalgic feelings of the past. Finally, heritage motivated visitors may also visit due to an indirect affiliation with the events and/or the individuals involved.

This is especially common in relation to celebrity deaths, where individuals formulated their identity in part around their hero. The works of musicians and actors often touch the lives of individuals who feel connected to it. The messages relayed in songs and movies connect viewers, listeners and readers to their visions of themselves.

HISTORICAL MOTIVATIONS

As Smith notes, "Battlefields are of particular interest to two diverse groups: history buffs and military strategists, both real and armchair, who tramp over the area with books in hand, studying such details of the battle as it relates to terrain, to ground cover and to troop movements". Consequently, visitors do not need to be directly affiliated with a death or disaster site or event to be attracted to it: some are simply interested in history. A number of academics have found cultural interest of some sort, including history, to be a motivation for general pleasure travel. Using unstructured interviews of 39 adults, Crompton found two-culturally oriented variables that motivated individuals to travel: novelty and education. Pearce and Caltabiano, in their study of visitors to Florida, studies the benefits sought by visitors in their holiday. Included was attending cultural events and visiting historical sites. Taking part in educational programmes was also on their list and, under certain circumstances, could be construed as being a cultural motivator.

Anderton developed a nine-category taxonomy of tourists based on motivation. On this list were learning holidays and cultural tourism. There is however, very little research on dark tourism motivators in general, let alone history as a motivator. One of the few authors to touch on the subject is Beech. In his research on Buchenwald as a tourism product, he discusses the division in visitors at the German concentration camp. "Within a short time of arriving at Buchenwald as a tourist, one is immediately struck by a division among the visitors…visitors with some connection to the camp…and general visitors with no direct or indirect connection".

He continues his discussion by commenting both types may be on a learning holiday, although he does question whether that is the motivation. This limited research is augmented by the number of dark tourism products discussed both in the literature and in marketing brochures. For instance, the Smithsonian Institute has sponsored excursions to battlefields for a number of years. Their 1994-1995 brochure offered a four-day, Civil War trip through Virginia, from Petersburg to Appomattox.

The itinerary traced, "…the longest siege campaign in American military history…and features battlefields, private homes and museums associated with this decisive campaign…". The year before, Holt's Battlefield Tours offered lectures on Waterloo and the Zulu, Boer and Crimean wars. For the 2002 season, Holt's offered such tours as Eagles On The Danube, where participants visit sites of Napoleonic battles, and Battle Of Bosworth Field, where participants visit sites of the 1485 battle between Richard III and Henry VII. It is important to note as Smith did, these battle years, "...preclude veteran attendees and the tours are historical commemorations".

Ghostwalks have recently risen in popularity and are now seen as being more than merely fun and entertainment. Says interpreter Kyle Upton of the storytelling behind ghostwalks, "...[it]...is well suited to the study of history because it brings people and events to life for young people who might never see them as anything more than a collection of facts and dates". Cemeteries have also become more than just places of veneration and commemoration. Lennon and Foley note, "Now tourists rather than mourners visit and undertake cemetery tours". For some, these burial grounds are,

- ...enigmatic histories of social patterns, settlement patterns, diseases like smallpox or influenza, childbirth mortality, storms and weather, ethnic bonds. Social distinctions-class, money and family-are re-enacted, families clustered together, the affluent in the choice spots, accident victims embracing mass graves and, in the past, suicides and atheists outside the sanctity of the enclosure.

Hamscher supports this idea of cemeteries' being repositories of historical facts. As an educator at Kansas State University, he utilizes cemeteries as a research source for many of his courses, including one on death and dying in history. For Hamscher, the sites are a, "...valuable source for investigating a broad range of subjects concerning the collective values and attitudes of generations past...they...provide important insights into views of death, the relationships between the living and the dead, religious beliefs, and gender and class distinctions".

The National Park Service also caters to the increasing demand in dark history tourism. In 1992, they published a brochure, *Visiting Civil War Battlefields: How to Have A Quality Experience.* This was followed by a string of books to guide people through the battle sites and their histories. In 1993, National Geographic published their *Guide to the Civil War National Battlefield Parks.*

It includes maps showing troop movement and terrain type, statistics on the number of casualties, and summaries on each battle. Despite the increasing interest in the historical aspects of dark tourism and the availability of dark tourism sites, there are inherent difficulties with history as a dark tourism motivator. The National Park Services claims, "We've learned, you don't take sides, you don't moralize, you tell what happened from a historical perspective. And we do that here...too...here's the people involved, here's what happened, when it happened, how it happened, why it happened. You can draw your own moral conclusion". The literature illustrates that this is difficult to achieve. Sites can purposefully or inadvertently take sides, particularly when the negative aspects of history are being interpreted.

As Lennon and Foley comment, "...to retain only the positive aspects of one's past and to obliterate all trace of evil is to present a cultural and historical landscape that is, to say the least, incomplete". Yet, the literature abounds with sites that ignore the negative. Early in 1995, the Smithsonian Institute in Washington cancelled a proposed exhibition entitled, *'The Last Act: The Atomic Bomb and the End of World War II'*. In the exhibit, the museum questioned why the bomb had been dropped.

Bowing to lobbying by veterans' groups, the Smithsonian agreed to changes in the exhibition, "...resulting in criticism from historians that 'known facts' were being ignored and that the exhibition was being 'historically cleansed'". The Jersey Islands off the coast of England were the only geographic part of England to be occupied during World War II and also ignore critical facts of the occupation. Today on the islands,

- The 'ill wind' of the war years has been turned to the good. The relics and remains of Hitler's British stronghold have now taken their place, both chronologically and commercially, alongside the older and more venerable attractions of the islands' heritage. The sightseeing circuit of war curiosities is now well established. Jersey's German occupation is now big business, with more war museums per square mile than anywhere else in Europe.

The museums however, do not provide a full historical perspective. Images that could tarnish the islands' during the war are sanitized or hidden: the collaborations, fraternization and compromises. In fact, the whole issue of collaboration is dealt with in only one museum on Jersey in a minor display area because collaboration brings into question the ideal that Britain stood alone against Hitler.

In his study of southern American plantation brochures, Butler comments on how the term plantation appears to be undergoing a 'major revision'. In his textual analysis, the word slave occurred less frequently than all other keywords. Where once the term was automatically analogous with slavery, today the slavery aspect is being overlooked in marketing because, "By presenting slavery, too much of the ugly, historical reality of daily life in the past would be brought into the picture".

As a final example, Japan is notorious for ignoring some of the uglier moments of its past. At the Hiroshima Peace Memorial any, "...contextuality concerning Japan's conduct during the war is noticeably absent". Similarly, at the Nagasaki Atomic Bomb Museum, there is a strong nuclear deterrence message with little said on Japanese aggression towards China and Korea. While ignoring aspects of dark history appears to be prevalent in the literature, so too is the changing nature of history.

As society changes, so does history and so does the interpretation of that history. Changing cultural values of a society have tremendous impact on which histories are interpreted. Events such as the, "...Jewish Holocaust in Germany, Vietnam and Black Civil Rights in schools in the USA...and the Irish Question in Ulster and mainland UK have all been reappraised recently as elements of the students' education about aspects of their national heritage which may have been suppressed, or represented differently in the 'approved' version". In sum, empirical studies on historical education as a dark tourism motivator are non-existent. However, by looking at the wide range of products available to visitors, it can be understood that history does incite visitation to sites of death and disaster.

Furthermore, to paraphrase Smith, the fact that many of these sites predate any chance of survivor visitation illustrates historical commemoration and learning. One reason for the popularity of these products is that they provide experiential learning. Through first-hand experience, these events can be brought to life. To trace actual path of the underground railway has a much bigger impact than to simply read of it in a book. The literature also reveals that sites of dark tourism can act as research sites. They act as archives for social conditions, political climates, and environmental hardships. One of the difficulties associated with this however, is the manipulation of history by prevailing cultural values and the powers that dictate them. Hence, dark tourism sites provide learning experiences but visitors must be wary that the whole story is being communicated.

SURVIVORS' GUILT

The fact that survivors and victims' families return to scenes of death and disaster are shown by one war veteran who, on a visit to France, stated, "...those of use who have been in combat share something very special...I simply had to be here to honour those men". For many who experienced the horrors of war, atrocity and disaster, returning to the scene is cathartic, a way to honour those who did not make it home. Alternatively, it may be a way to unburden a sense of guilt endured simply because they survived death and disaster.

It must be noted that this discussion focuses on guilt as opposed to shame and the literature defines the two concepts separately. Todd comments that guilt, "...connects the self to the social world...[and is]...concerned with how the self is perceived". Shame however, "...remains confined within the self's parameters of selfidealisation...[it]...involves something that one cannot bring oneself to articulate to another". Todd then studies the concept of guilt. In her research on the ways in which students confront the suffering of others, the author found three possible methods they identify with guilt.

Some experience guilt because, "...they believe they have not done enough to help out those who suffer". Others compare and call into question their own lack of suffering. Finally, some claim they are made to feel guilty, focusing on how they are not responsible for the past. The literature illustrates how the former two are often experienced today by people in relation to the Holocaust. The literature supports a variety of definitions of survivors' guilt, particularly in terms of Holocaust survivors. Carmelly distinguishes two types of survivors' guilt: guilt about surviving and guilt about certain acts. Niederland partially concedes with Carmelly.

He suggests that survivors' guilt is a reaction to simply having survived. Lifton, in his study on Hiroshima survivors, coined the term death guilt. Garwood has written perhaps the most detailed and decisive work on survivors' guilt and the Holocaust.

As both a psychoanalytic psychotherapist and a child survivor of the Holocaust, he offers a unique perspective of survivors' guilt. He feels the aforementioned classic theories of guilt are unsatisfactory; they are too clinical. They, "...direct thinking away from the actual experience and towards the phantasies generated in the unconscious".

Although not all survivors experience guilt, its incidence, intensity and persistence is high. To explain, Garwood describes four essential components of Holocaust survivors' trauma in light of a primal-development theory. The four elements are threat of annihilation, powerlessness, object loss, and torture: however, feelings of powerlessness in the face of annihilation are of greatest importance. Garwood explains,

- In the post-partum period the neo-nate is totally dependent on its carer for its survival...All significant discomforts...will be experienced as possible abandonment which will provoke instinctual fear of annihilation with attendant instinctually driven anxiety derived from the self-preservation instinct...Powerlessness in later life evokes unconscious memories of this earliest vulnerable state...accompanied by overwhelming emotions...often self-blame and consequential guilt.

The entire Final Solution proposed by Hitler to liquidate Jews and others, sought to make individuals, particularly those in concentration camps, feel powerless. Humiliation, enslavement, and ultimately annihilation were the goals of the Nazi Socialist regime. Leon, Butcher, Kleinman, Goldberg and Almagor comment that individuals who survived were made to feel they had more than their fair share of luck.

As Garwood points out, "...the price of their survival was the death of their loved ones and fellow Jews. It follows that self-blame and guilt surface. A number of authors utilize the primal-development theory regarding guilt and the instinctive fight or flight response. For Holocaust survivors, fight and flight were next to impossible: both would likely end in annihilation. As survivors, the anger towards this powerlessness could not be expressed; hence, the anger directed at one's self resulted in self-blame and guilt. Lack of grieving also contributes to the persistence of survivors' guilt. Although often difficult, it is understood, "The effective mourning of loss has long been ... fundamental to mental health".

However, for many survivors, guilt persists because they are unable to grieve and mourn their losses. This is particularly true for Holocaust survivors. In addition to feelings of powerlessness and fears of annihilation, "Mourning at the time of the losses was impossible as survivors were in their own life and death struggle. On liberation the understandable priority was to rebuild their lives; and they were encouraged to look forward and put the past behind them", Lipstadt and Linenthal both support this statement. In post-war America, survivor reactions to the Holocaust were similar. Some simply wanted to forget, while others did not want to identify with those victimized.

Others who were starting a new life, "...were more concerned about acting as Americans than as Jews". It was easier to ignore the memories and attempt to get on with life. Other individuals may have experienced guilt for their inaction during the Holocaust. This may be particularly true for some Americans. In 1942 the SS St. Louis, a Jewish refugee ship landed on the shores of the United States. However, America, like other countries, did not grant passengers refuge. All 1106 individuals were sent back to Nazi dominated Europe. The Holocaust Memorial Museum in Washington, DC delineates the potential guilt Americans might have experienced. One of their aims is to provide an, "...encounter with American indifference to the plight of Nazi victims, would force museum visitors to weight the cost of being a bystander...one of the 'lessons' was that the indifference of the bystanders was critical to the success of the aggressors". Marion Pritchard, despite saving approximately 150 Dutch Jews during World War II, articulates that she, too, feels guilt over her experience. "I never wanted to talk about the war, perhaps because I had some guilt that I didn't do enough.

There were times that I had to choose the safety of...the children over going to help someone else". Veterans who liberated concentration camps might also experience survivors' guilt about the Holocaust. Abzug found liberators lived with, "...an almost unbearable mixture of empathy, disgust, guilt, anger and alienation". Many experience what Thomas calls, "...the tension of living in the present with the baggage of the past...".

One liberator recalls, "I was not prepared for what I saw at Buchenwald. I think that made it more traumatic...I didn't talk about it for years. I didn't want to remember the ugliness of it". One of the ways for survivors to reconcile their feelings of guilt is through memorialization. As Garwood maintains, "Memorials are of the greatest importance...Memorialization and naming of perished families gives them a permanence that combats the fear that they will be forgotten and lost forever".

For many survivors, carrying on the names of victims is one way to purge themselves of guilt. Museums such as the Holocaust Museum Houston provide an outlet for this healing. Although not all survivors experience guilt after surviving an atrocity, its incidence and persistence is high, particularly with Holocaust survivors.

Therefore, a great deal of literature has been written on the subject, much of it focusing on the reasoning behind the guilt. Academics cite two major reasons for this remorse. There is guilt for surviving, for a lack of suffering while others feel guilt over their actions, for not doing enough. Concentration camps were breeding grounds for such perceptions. The feelings of powerlessness instilled in camp prisoners brought about helplessness and feelings of guilt for not being able to do anything.

This was furthered by a lack of traditional fight or flight options, both of which would result in death. There was also a lack of grieving opportunities in regards to the Holocaust. In the camps, people were caught up in their own life or death struggles, while in the post-war years people wanted to forget and put the past behind them. Memorialization and interpretation are two ways of assuaging guilty feelings. Remembering the fallen keeps their memory alive, thereby giving survivors a purpose. Furthermore, as illustrated in previous pages, dark tourism visitation provides additional means of understanding and coping with the past. Returning to the site of the event allows people to put the past to rest.

CURIOSITY AND NOVELTY SEEKING

CURIOSITY

Academics and pop culture proponents alike have long realized humanity's undeniable attraction to things morbid. Seaton reaches back in time to an 1827 essay by Thomas De Quincey, *On Murder Considered as One of the Fine Arts.* It, "...purported to be a paper which had been delivered to a wholly fictitious Society of Connoisseurs in Murder.

It developed a premise that closely resembles...Dark Tourism – that an act or event which might be deplorable or repugnant from a moral point of view could have considerable attraction as a spectator sport". In the paper, De Quincey himself wrote, "Murder...when tried by the principles of Taste, turns out to be a very meritous performance". Thomas also reaches back in time to the American Civil War to describe how some individuals are simply motivated by a sense of curiosity.

At the Battle of Manassas, "There were even spectators that day in 1861. People had packed lunches and driven in their carriages from Washington to watch the battle...". The author also recounts his own experience of seeing a photograph of a dead Civil War soldier, and subsequently visiting the site of the soldier's death. "I like to think it was respect for the young man's life and life itself that made me want to see where he died".

He confesses however, that he is not completely sure this was his reasoning. Previously, Steiner noted the attraction of Holocaust museums because many find the subject matter 'darkly fascinating' and 'seductive'. He quotes, "Not only is the relevant material vast and intractable; it exercises a subtle, corrupting fascination. Bending too fixedly over hideousness, one feels queerly drawn. In some way the horror flatters attention...". Uzzell also found people's curiosity about atrocity is insatiable; they are motivated by empathy, excitement and other psychological stimuli of varying moral worth.

Lennon and Foley add, "Horror and death have become established commodities, on sale to tourists who have an enduring appetite for the darkest elements of human history. Rojek concurs, suggesting, "The interest in catastrophes and disasters might seem to be distasteful. However, it would be foolish to deny that it is widely shared".

In pop culture, hundreds are attracted to the Massachusetts' town and house where Lizzie Borden is thought to have murdered her father and stepmother. Sullivan found this interest perplexing, "...that the American public, swimming as it is in a sea of contemporary violence, still finds the trial of Lizzie Borden in the early 1890's the most continually absorbing case in the annals of this nation's homicides". When asked what brings these tourists, one bed and breakfast operator replied, "From the simply curious to the morbidly fascinated, the "Lizzie buffs" are legion. They are amateur sleuths, college professors and otherwise unremarkable folks who are – to a sometimes disturbing degree – fascinated with one of America's most infamous murder cases". This last quote highlights the hazard of curiosity as a motivator: its potential transformation into spectacle.

For, as Walsh comments, curiosity can be exacerbated by the idea of spectacle. Lennon and Foley agree, stating, despite other mandates such as education and remembrance, there is a, "...fundamental difficulty of delineating education and entertainment/spectacle and an uncritical approach to history".

The work of Debord supports this relationship between spectacle and curiosity, noting both are staged and both are sensational. The literature abounds with examples of sites that walk the fine line between education and spectacle. At the turn of the 20th century, Luna Park on Coney Island, New York, used spectacle to induce curiosity in visitors for touristic enjoyment: they provided simulations of the eruption of Mt.

Vesuvius, the flooding of Johnstown Pennsylvania, and the 1900 destruction of Galveston. They even went as far as simulating a hurricane, citing education as a justification.

- The city and harbour were recreated in miniature with model buildings. Then through a combination of real and fake water, large sheets of painted cotton fabric, intricate lighting and mechanical effects, the city was transformed into a state of utter destruction. A lecturer explained the sequence of events to the audience.

Sing Sing Prison in New York State, in the quest to build a museum in the stillactive prison, often espouses education as one of its primary goals. However, as one author recognizes, there is no ignoring the fascination with the place itself, including the death chamber. In addition, as Lennon and Foley acknowledge, such sites often become both famous and notorious, thus inducing spectacle. On Sunday April 28, 1996, a gunman killed 35 people at a popular historical site in Tasmania, Australia. Today, visitors at Port Arthur, "...include Port Arthur on their itinerary for two reasons. Overtly for all the traditional reasons of history but I suspect that many visitors want to see for themselves where those terrible events actually occurred. I think it's normal human reaction". Holocaust sites are particularly vulnerable to curiosity's transformation into spectacle, given artifacts often displayed. At Auschwitz-Birkenau concentration camp, "...there are rooms full of clothes and suitcases, toothbrushes, dentures, glasses".

Yet, the authors comment on the lack of explanation, orientation, and historical documentation to back the display of such disturbing objects. Without proper interpretation, these exhibits may become spectacle. When deciding on exhibits and displays at the National Holocaust Museum in Washington D.C., there was concern that the Zyklon-B cans used in concentration camp gas chambers would attract the ghoulish. Linenthal remarks on the debate surrounding their exhibit.

- Was it impossible not to fall victim to some ghoulish desire to 'see' one of these cans? What was the purpose of seeing it? Of displaying it in a museum...Or was it precisely because these canisters had been used to kill millions of people that they carried a power, a fascination that made it impossible not to include them....

NOVELTY SEEKING

To understand curiosity as a motivator, it is necessary to look back to early research in the psychology and sociology fields. Montgomery was among the first to combine curiosity and the concept of novelty. In his experiments with laboratory rats, Montgomery found that novel stimuli evoked an exploratory drive, otherwise known as curiosity. The more novel the situation, the more curious the rat became.

Other studies found humans exhibited similar behaviour and correlated it to tourist movement. Berlyne observed stimuli gradually loses power to raise arousal through repetition; however, novelty increased exploratory behaviour. For tourists then, a change in environment may be a manifestation of a desire for novelty. Similarly, Smock and Holt noted unusual or novel objects aroused curiosity, while monotonous and routine objects galvanized the individual to encounter new aspects of his or her environment.

This premise is supported by Mayo and Jarvis who assert tourism is one of the most common means of alleviating or escaping boredom. Novelty seeking as a tourist motivator subsequently emerged as an area of academic study, albeit not a well researched area. As Lee notes, "As tourism research has evolved, it has moved from focusing on describing tourism behaviour patterns, to identification and categorization of the motivational and socio-psychological forces which explain those behaviour patterns".

One of these forces is novelty. Jenkins defined novelty as a function of the degree of contrast between present perception and past experiences. For Judd novelty is simply the state or quality of being new. Something is considered novel if, relative to previous experiences, it is new or different. The novelty of an object or experience can be expressed on a continuum, varying from completely novel to very familiar.

This directly corresponds to Cohen's typology of tourists. Cohen found that novelty is an essential element of tourism experiences; however, he also noted that many tourists preferred a bubble of familiarity in order to appreciate the novelty of their experiences.

From this study, he proposed a typology of tourists based on their need for novelty and familiarity. Other studies have looked at the role novelty plays in motivating tourist behaviour. Mehrabian and Russell found the degree of novelty sought is closely related to the individual's preferred arousal level. An individual who is aroused by new environments often looks for novelty, complexity, variability, and other associated stimuli. Like Cohen, they report some tourists seek to satisfy high arousal levels by seeking the unfamiliar. Some researchers, however, attribute this desire for novelty to genetics.. Overall, the literature review revealed five relevant novelty dimensions that tourists may use when evaluating the novelty potential of a destination. They include change from routine, escape, thrill, adventure and boredom alleviation.

CHANGE FROM ROUTINE

Change is defined as altered or different conditions of environment, psychological outcomes, and/or lifestyles. Travel provides the ideal opportunity for change. Pearce accedes, stating a change from routine includes a search for new experience and the quest for adventure and excitement. Crompton found pleasure-travelers to be motivated by seven sociopsychological motives. The first, escape from a perceived mundane environment, complements the idea that a vacation is an equilibrium-restoring break.

For tourists, the overriding necessity was that, "...the pleasure vacation context should be physically and socially different from the environment in which one normally lives. Crompton also cited novelty as a pull factor in cultural tourism, along with Smith and Turner. The role of novelty recognized by these researchers in explaining the pull of a destination suggests the tourist's desire for new and different experiences is a fundamental motivator in the destination-selection process.

ESCAPE

Hornby defines escape as a temporary distraction from reality or dull routine, while McIntosh and Goeldner add that tourism provides opportunities to escape life's problems. McIntosh suggested four categories of travel motivation, including interpersonal motivators. This category expressed a need for novel experiences in terms of escape from routine and meeting new people.

THRILL

Hornby defines thrill as an experience in which excitement is the essential element. Mayo and Jarvis found the concept of thrill in their study on arousal in tourists. They found people may try new things, even at some risk, and a novel environment may represent unpredictability for a tourist. This unpredictability is then viewed as a source of arousal from thrill that may attract novelty-seeking tourists.

ADVENTURE

Adventure is defined as an exciting experience obtained through the medium of strange and unusual happenings. For some travelers in Crompton, novelty was analogous with adventure. "Novelty was defined by respondents in a variety of ways. Synonyms included curiosity, adventure, new and different". A new destination should then possess large amounts of novelty, uncertainty, and complexity to have high adventure potential, hence high arousal.

BOREDOM ALLEVIATION

Boredom alleviation is defined as the removal and/or reduction of the perception that experiences available in the home environment are not sufficient to satisfy the need for optimal arousal. In our urbanized and industrialized society, life is often reduced to an organized routine, thereby increasing boredom. Escaping boredom is a basic human impulse, and researchers believe travel is an optimal way of relieving boredom.

Nunnally and Leonard proposed boredom leads to exploration in order to increase arousal that in turn results in selecting novel experiences. Mayo and Jarvis asserted tourism is one of the most common means of alleviating or escaping boredom. Academics unanimously agree tourists have a fascination with death, atrocity and horror. Furthermore, this is not a recent observation: historically, curiosity has played a significant role in travel and tourism.

From early religious pilgrimages to 19th century examples, most notably the American Civil War, people have traveled to view sites of death and disaster. This curiosity continues today as illustrated by the variety of dark tourism products being offered. Early research on curiosity took place under the auspices of sociology and psychology. In controlled laboratory experiments, rats were found to be attracted to novel situations.

The newer the stimuli, the greater the rats' exploratory behaviour, otherwise known as curiosity. So too humans. Repetition increased boredom while novelty increased curiosity. Travel is understood to be a manifestation of curiosity. As people grow bored of their home environment, the motivation to see something new and different increases. Yet, research reveals varying levels of curiosity and novelty in individual tourists. Some seek almost complete familiarity in a new environment while others envelop themselves in exotic environments, purposefully shunning anything familiar. Academics attribute these differences to the individual's arousal level.

The literature highlighted five key elements tourists might use when evaluating the novelty potential of a destination: change from routine; escape; thrill; adventure; and boredom alleviation. Individuals looking for new experiences seek these elements and judge a destination accordingly; hence, the attraction of dark tourism sites. For people with high arousal levels, they offer any number of combinations of the five factors. One danger of curiosity is its potential transformation into spectacle. A number of academics voiced this concern in the literature in addition to providing concrete examples of sites that vacillate between education and spectacle. There is the risk of people being attracted to a site because of gruesome details rather than visiting sites for other, more socially acceptable reasons. This is especially relevant to Holocaust sites whose mandates focus on education and remembrance. While such sites stress learning, curiosity may turn such artifacts as gas chambers, Zyklon B canisters, and human hair into spectacles.

DEATH AND DYING

Death and dying are natural occurrences; however, the concepts themselves are socially constructed. "The fears, hopes, and orientations people have towards [them] are not instinctive, but rather are learned from such public symbols as the languages, arts, and religious and funerary rituals of their culture. Every culture has a coherent mortality thesis whose explanations of death are so thoroughly ingrained that they are believed to be right by its members". Variances in cultural attitudes towards death and dying can be observed today. For many Western Christians, heaven, or the end of death, is the ultimate goal. Yet for Eastern Buddhists and Hindus, "...the arch-ordeal envisioned is not death but rather the pain of having to undergo another rebirth.

It is the end of rebirths that is their goal...". In addition to variances between cultures, one culture may approach the concepts differently from generation to generation; time and cultural mores often influence individuals' reactions during the death process. Historically, reactions to death have changed dramatically over the past fifteen hundred years. O'Gorman's *Stages in Development of Current Attitudes to Death and Dying*, and Aries' *Five Models of Death* exemplify this change. Stage One begins in the Middle Ages, circa 500 AD. At this time, death was, "...regarded as the deliberate personal intervention of God".

The church readily sanctioned this idea in its eagerness to maintain control over the masses. The, "...inculcation of the fear of death in general encouraged dependence on the consolations of religion and the church which -controlled it". To encourage this dependence, the church 'stage-managed' representations of death in paintings, monuments, morality plays, and sermons, thereby keeping death in the forefront of awareness. Two incidents in the 14th century coincided to initiate change in social attitudes towards death and dying. In 1358, the Bubonic Plague struck Europe, killing up to twothirds of the European population.

The disease brought changes in attitudes towards life, death, and religion. At the same time, the Renaissance developed a foothold in European society, also bringing dramatic changes in attitudes towards life, death, and religion. With a growing collective sense of the demise of the old feudal order, dying became the time when the true essence of oneself was assumed to be revealed. Circa 1460, the treatise, Ars Moriendi, was published to instruct individuals on the art of dying. During the 16th and 17th centuries, the Scientific Revolution once again shook belief systems previously guided and guarded by the church.

Tentative and disturbing questions, "...about the theories of ancient authorities, whose views had been accepted for centuries...created a completely new way of looking at nature and a new way of thinking and arguing about physical problems".

These questions included queries on death and mortality. Death became independent, a break from life rather than part of a continuum. This attitude paved the way for the rise of the 'bourgeois' death in late 1600's. By the turn of the 17th century, the Industrial Revolution again changed social perceptions of death. The newly-created bourgeoisie sought health into old age, and when death came to those not old and infirm, it was deemed untimely.

Those who could afford to were in some ways increasingly able to pay to keep death away. The rise of the bourgeoisie and the ability to defy death brought a consciousness of scientifically-trained doctors, and subsequently, an elevation in the medical doctor's status and role. Subsequently, doctors took center stage, "...struggling against the roaming phantoms of consumption and pestilence". Death in the 19th century became the outcome of diseases specified by the scientifically trained physician who now held life-giving powers. The doctor's role continued into the 20th century, this time with doctors themselves taking the initiative to prevent death.

Health, death, and dying became commodities to be purchased. Many researchers see this era as the end of human ability to deal with death intimately. As O'Gorman sums, "By the middle of the 20th century...health [had] become a commodity undermining the unique spiritual and intellectual strength of the human race which enables them to rise to the challenges of dying and death". This commodification of death can be observed in the increase of businesses affiliated with death and dying. Sudnow and Walter point to the rise of such services as funeral parlors, headstone makers, counseling services, and flower shops. More recent additions include cryogenic services that aid in preservation of life for the future.

These sentiments reveal the death-defying attitudes of some segments of Western society. American health care values mandate that life is sacred and must be preserved at all costs. The aged are institutionalized so that they are hidden from sight. Kearl comments, "Gauging from their increasing segregation from other age groups, the elderly are our culture's...lepers". All this brings about an increase in hospitalization, where in the United States, 70 per cent of terminally ill patients die in institutional settings. There are serious ramifications for western society in regards to these attitudes. Barley, Illich and Helgeland state that society has repressed any meaningful acceptance of, or preparation for, death because of our preoccupation with youth, good health and longer lives. Lennon and Foley note that death has become privatized and rituals have become increasingly less community-oriented. Kagawa-Singer et al. further this statement, "The United States lacks a richness of rituals to mark significant life transitions".

Hamsher in her study of cemeteries found there have been significant changes in the meaning of death. Looking at modern 'memorial parks', the author observes, "...the dead themselves are the least intrusive element in the landscape. The dialogue between the worlds of life and death is muted". She concludes by noting how the living have disengaged themselves from the dead. With this disengagement and reduced death rituals, some sectors of society may lack healthy outlets for expressions of death and dying. Few people know how to understand dying let alone deal with death directly.

One implication of this may be an interest in sites of dark tourism. As Seaton identified, 20th century Britain, "...has tended to conceal death and to regard any dwelling on it as morbid and pathological. Yet death continues to exert a fascination and motivates travel in ways which are rarely openly admitted". Without valid outlets of expression, people may turn to death that is removed from them in order to express interest in the outcomes of death. Since they cannot get close to death via their own personal experience, perhaps understanding comes from substitution. Dark tourism destinations may provide these substitutes.

They may offer socially viable ways of expressing an interest in death and may push visitors to a destination. Kagawa-Singer suggests memorials can provide essential rituals to aid in the death processes for the living. Using the Vietnam War Memorial in Washington, DC as an example, she notes it is a symbol of death and continuity, allowing public acknowledgement of private grief, thereby initiating healing. To do so, the memorial helps people accept the reality of loss; allows them to experience the pain of grief; initiates adjustments to new roles; and draws the emotional energy form the dead and turns it to those who are left. Attitudes towards death and dying have changed dramatically since the Middle Ages when church and God controlled the life course.

Today, death has come under the auspices of institutions. Doctors fight to prevent death and life can actually be bought and sold. When death does appear on the horizon, the dying are shuffled into hospitals and nursing homes. Individuals themselves attempt to defy aging and death, emphasized by our social obsession with youth. All this affects how some sectors of contemporary society deals with death. The living have become separated from death and there has been a decrease in death rituals to aid in acceptance and healing. Few people have a comprehensive knowledge of death. One means of understanding is via dark tourism visitation. Memorials can play healing and coping roles. Visiting memorials can increase understanding for survivors, victims, and others. Perhaps then they can manage dealing with the tragedy. Similarly, by visiting dark tourism sites, perhaps people can understand and cope death and dying.

NOSTALGIA

NOSTALGIA DEFINED

Nostalgia was originally conceptualized as a painful yearning to return home. In recent decades, it has been viewed as a normal human reaction. However, there is little consensus on a unanimous definition. Davis defined it as, "...a positively toned evocation of a lived past". Belk suggested it is, "...a wistful mood that may be prompted by an object, a scene, a smell, or a strain of music". Holbrook and Schindler expanded the definition to entail, "...a preference towards objects that were more common (popular, fashionable, or wider circulated) when one was younger (in early childhood, in adolescence, in childhood, or even before birth)". For the purpose of this paper, nostalgia will imply a wistful mood that results in a preference or fantasy for something from the past.

NOSTALGIA AND POST-MODERNISM

For many authors, nostalgia is a key characteristic of post-modernism. Pretes sees post-modern society as being filled with uncertainty and stress, with escape and illusion strategies for coping. He furthers this idea by stating, "Society takes on the characteristics of a perpetual present, leading to nostalgia for ideas of the past...History, time and space become commodities". Lennon and Foley concur, citing nostalgia and society's commemorative environment as being key to post-modern culture. They acknowledge the importance of monuments as evidence of post-modern nostalgia.

- A central element for retention of a museum/monument as opposed to its replacement with the television/media image is the centrality and primacy of the object. Museum objects...take on a key role in a culture that is dominated by moving images and fleeting visions in modern technology. Permanency of monuments, ruins, preserved spaces, can serve to attract a public dissatisfied with constant simulation and media culture of the modern age.

Other academics, however, attribute modernity as being responsible for the 'cult of nostalgia'. For Rojek, modernity helped shape nostalgia as people yearned to go back to simpler times. "The constant revolutionizing of the instruments and relations of production", which the 19th century established as normal, made the, "...flight into the calmer, resplendent, pre-modern past seem like a magnetic attraction for large numbers of the Victorian intelligentsia". MacCannell also sees modernity lending itself to nostalgia. He writes, "The progress of modernity depends on its very sense of instability and inauthenticity. For moderns, reality and authenticity are thought to be elsewhere: in other historical periods and other cultures, in purer, simpler lifestyles. In other words, the concern for modern...are components of the conquering spirit of modernity...".

Finally, Golden also sees modernity as being key to nostalgia. He notes, "...some museums reveal nostalgic yearning for what is seen to be the simple life of other times and other places...In this view, museum, as a facet of tourism, manifests a response to and an attempt to assuage the fragmentary disconcerting quality of modernity".

NOSTALGIA STUDIES

Several studies have delved into the concept of nostalgia as a tourism motivator. Conforti cites nostalgia as one of the keys to the regeneration of Italian ghettos for tourists. These areas serve, "...Italian-Americans who have never lived in or near such neighbourhoods, but visit them in an effort to underscore their identity, discover their ancestral roots, or at least come a little closer to them...".

On any given weekend afternoon, probably half the tourists in New York's Little Italy are Italian- Americans: suburbanites coming into the city for the nostalgic ethnic experience. In her study of war tourism, Smith recognizes, "Old soldiers do go back to the battlefields, to revisit and to remember the days of their youth...one graying veteran summed it up well, "those of us who have been in combat share something very special...I simply had to be here, to honour those men"". This sense of nostalgia is underscored by Smith's vernacular when describing war tourism.

Such terms as, "the heroic past...remember the fallen...lest we forget...when we were young...reliving the past..." all denote a romantic yearning for the past. Lowenthal adds, "...age lends romance to times gone by" and the more time passes, the more mystical it appears. This illusion of romance to instil nostalgia is also seen in Barbados, where tourism authorities, rather than looking at scholarly data, have chosen instead, "...to caricature both host and guest within the romantic feudal framework of the 17th century Great House". Instead of interpreting the dark side of antebellum plantation life, marketers focus on the romantic side.

Hence, people yearn to experience a more gracious, genteel past. Dann and Potter continue this discussion. The success of Bajan plantation tourism is dependent on four things: the post-modern ethos of Bajan visitors; the related appeal of dark tourism attractions; the effectiveness of promotion; and nostalgia pervading their motivation. The authors describe this nostalgia as a quest for an absent order, a, "...playful hankering after a differentiated premodern world by tourists from a post-modern de-differentiated home environment". They further develop this description. The tourists are, "...yearning for a past they can no longer find in their own social settings. Unable to tolerate their present alienated condition, and ever fearful of the future, they seek solace in days gone by-a world where it was once possible to distinguish right from wrong...pleasure from pain".

Therefore, the visitors' need for nostalgia must be satisfied in countries they assume retain a natural system of justice. Ioannides and Ioannides is one of the few studies directly looking at nostalgia and travel in the Jewish context, albeit Jewish-American specific. Although the Jewish religion has no mass pilgrimage destination similar to Mecca or Lourdes, the authors point out Jews travel for reasons of history. By visiting such places as old Jewish neighbourhoods, synagogues and homes of famous Jewish personalities, "...Jews can discover the Judaism of their ancestors". Eisen calls this the "mitzvah of nostalgia".

This visitation also includes graveyards and Holocaust death camps, for it is here that Jews can reconnect with their past and reassess their religious identities. Ioannides and Ioannides maintain, "These nostalgic tours also allow the visitor a chance to see the 'graves' of their forebears and perform, with others who have the same need, the required acts of public mourning for martyrs who are not necessarily family members". As a result of their study, the above authors identified 22 separate categories of Jewish attractions. Of particular interest for this study are five attraction categories: shrines of Jewish history; monuments and memorials to Jews; places of general historic importance having some Jewish connection; historic places and buildings preserved for or donated to the public by Jews; and interfaith shrines. As a public building donated by Jews, commemorating Jewish history, the Holocaust Museum Houston falls under Ioannides' and Ioannides' conceptualization of an attraction that Jews visit because of nostalgia.

NOSTALGIA AND MARKETING

Marketers have long been in tune with the power of nostalgia. "Consumers are encouraged by marketers to experience nostalgic feelings through the use of nostalgic themes and images in advertising, the marketing of nostalgic products, and the utilization of consumer products to capture or create nostalgia through fantasies and memories". Dann found war sites also employ nostalgia to promote their attraction, mainly through the glorification of battle. This however, is dependent on whether, "...the country in question emerged victorious...". He cites a 1992 British Imperial Museum advertisement that stated, "Visit Britain's war museums and you'll see, feel and even smell what life was really like in the two world wars...After all, the experience of war was shared by everyone. And now we'd like to share it with you...". Similarly, Britain at War Experience plays on people's feelings of nostalgia. One of their promotional brochures reads,

- Britain is at War...and YOU can be in the midst of it. Come back with us on an unforgettable journey back in time to wartime London and the Blitz...its [sic] the experience of a lifetime...Britain at War is more than just a tourist attraction...its [sic] a unique trip down memory lane for those who lived through these bittersweet days and is an educational must for all those too young to remember.

This notion is underscored by an endorsement by famed singer Dame Vera Lynn, who believes, "...all children should visit this nostalgic and moving experience". Marketing nostalgia, however, is not always an easy task given the complexity of the concept, with both positive and negative emotions feeding into the reaction. While the positive components of nostalgia are easy to market, products with negative connotations can also be marketed (those feelings of desire stemming from loss).

Therefore, to assist in marketing nostalgia, yearning should be coupled with attempts to minimize that loss. One way to accomplish this is to explicitly, "...portray the product as a means of recapturing enough of the past to avoid an overwhelming feeling of loss". The consumer is more likely to, "...limit the sense of loss when the purchase can actually allow him or her to recapture much of the original feeling ...The present experience is likely to be perceived as a reflection of the past, not as a true recreation of it". For Dann, this sense of nostalgia is accomplished by, "...screening out unpleasant vistas while retaining colourful places and people in the memory forever".

While the lineage of nostalgia remains unresolved, the literature is clear that it is a condition of yearning for the past: notably, a purer, simpler time when life was not so complicated, unstable and fragmented. Contemporary society seems to have evolved into the latter state, and many look back to the past as a magic time. Some of this yearning is a result of marketing, as illustrated previous.

The literature also recognizes nostalgia is a complex concept, especially given the gravity of some parts of history. While love, joy and happiness are easier to market, nostalgia is also a powerful tool at sites of death and disaster. The literature reveals a number of reasons for this. Firstly, dark tourism sites often provide answers in a search for heritage. They provide a place of identity for those nostalgic for their family's history. Secondly, dark tourism sites may romanticize and glorify the past thereby attracting visitors; conversely, individuals may romanticize and glorify the past, seeking out sites of death and disaster. As time passes, this becomes easier to do as negative memory fades and nostalgia for the positive grows.

Thirdly, education may be used in conjunction with nostalgia. As it is important to remember the past, so too it is important to teach the next generation. Finally, sites of dark tourism may influence nostalgia by minimizing the loss and/or screening-out the negative. By emphasizing the positive side of history and ignoring or minimizing the negative, individuals may in turn be more attracted to the site.

EDUCATION

In the aftermath of death or disaster, the need to understand why the event occurred manifests itself in many ways. Some individuals turn to higher religious or spiritual forms, seeking answers to why loved ones were killed. Others take legal action in order to place responsibility for the event's occurrence. Dark tourism sites can offer understanding through education and knowledge.

Tourism as a form of educative enterprise is strongly associated with the key principles of modernity and has age-old roots. With 17th century industrialization came advancement and increases in education, marketing, communications, and infrastructures, all of which in turn lead to educational travel. Witness the 18th century Grand Tour undertaken by wealthy aristocrats and the 19th century temperance tours organized by Thomas Cook. At the turn of the 20th century, dark tourism exhibits were being promoted and justified with an educational component.

At Luna Park on Coney Island, exhibits included such simulations as the eruption of Mount Vesuvius, the destruction of Martinique and the 1900 Galveston flood. One exhibit even featured the fabrication of a hurricane, accompanied with simulated lightning and water and a lecturer explaining the sequence of events to visitors. Today, individuals continue to travel for knowledge, understanding and educational opportunities, and dark tourism sites continue to promote their educational mission. Most notable is the Smithsonian Institute.

The Smithsonian Associates, the educational arm of Washington D.C.'s museums, offered a number of educational tours for the 2002-2003 season. These ranged from *The Civil War at Chancellorville* to the *Philadelphia Campaign and Valley Forge*. One of the more interesting tours, *Booth's Escape Route*, traces John Wilkes Booth's escape route and reveals the, "...personalities, intrigues, and dramas surrounding the assassination" of President Abraham Lincoln. A number of sites emphasize their educational mandate in order for people to learn from past mistakes. The Brown Foundation, which administers the Brown VS. Board of Education National Historic Site in Topeka, Kansas, also considers education as part of their mission.

They strive, "...to improve the quality of life for individuals and strengthen our overall sense of community by furthering educational equity and multicultural understanding". By learning from the past, it is hoped future generations of Blacks will live improved lives. Similarly, at Pearl Harbour, Hawaii, there is the feeling that education will aid in producing a more secure tomorrow, that future generations will learn from past mistakes. In speaking of the Japanese attack and its aftermath, one visitor acknowledged, "If a visit to this memorial leaves visitors with a better understanding of why the attack took place and with the strong feeling that we must not let this happen again, then surely those entombed will not have died in vain". The Oklahoma City National Memorial also seeks to educate the public against future events, this time terrorist attacks. In addition to the 168 chairs erected to remember each victim of the 1997 bombing, the memorial is also comprised of a museum and a terrorism institute.

Here people can understand the events in hopes of preventing further terrorism. Other sites have used an educational focus to cope with an increase in their popularity. To meet public demand and as an education service, in 1992, the United States National Park Service published a brochure, *Visiting Civil War Battlefields: How to Have A Quality Experience.* In Fall River, Massachusetts, where visitors flock to see Lizzie Borden paraphernalia, city officials have reacted in a similar way.

"If your claim to fame is a murder case, you want to about it in the most educational way possible". Finally, the literature reveals education can offer a form of catharsis. Seaton, in his study of thanatourism, related that the study of death for catharsis is not a new concept. Thanatopsis (the Aristotelian contemplation of death) provided relief from death for early Christian societies. The author noted, "...by experiencing the pity and terror of representations of Death, a person could be inoculated against, or purged of its terrors in real life". Seaton uses the example of pilgrims traveling to sites of martyrdom and interment as early forms of thanatopsis.

Here enters the tourism component. Pilgrims ventured to sites of death and disaster to pay homage and more importantly, to learn and understand death. More recently, Lennon and Foley, in their discussion on the renovation of Dachau, Germany concentration camp, noted, "...when the renovation...of the camp began...the level of local resistance was considerable. It was part of a past that many wanted to leave behind yet, for the victims, their relatives and others, understanding required interpretation and rediscovery". Baudrillard expanded this.

"Forgetting the extermination is part of the extermination itself". Foote observes similar occurrences with the memorialization of sites of death and disaster. The process of erecting memorials and monuments, many of which include some element of education, "...is...a way for communities to come to terms with a disaster". And like Holocaust sites, these memorials help, "...to assure survivors that victims did not suffer alone, that their deaths meant something more...".

DIFFICULTIES WITH EDUCATION

While the majority of researchers recognize that sites of dark tourism incorporate education into their mandates and missions, many academics also recognize the issues and dangers surrounding such incorporation. One of the more controversial dark tourism sites promoting education in their mandate is the Sixth Floor Museum in Dallas, Texas. "It was created to meet the widespread visitor demand for information and understanding about a tragic but important event...documentary films and interpretive displays help...[to]...educate younger audiences about the meaning of an unforgettable chapter in American history".

Curators, managers, and project directors have iterated this educational justification often since the museum's inception. As far back as 1970, the educational mission has been stressed.

When Nashvillian, Aubrey Mayhew, bought the building, he sought to develop it as a historically significant museum as opposed to a tourist trap. Much of this was done to, "...capitalize on the 'dark' interest evidenced at a site of assassination...and in... public defence of the development". Other justifications included the absolution of communal guilt and coming to terms with history. Then-mayor, J.M. Shea Jr., stated that Dallas could not carry on into the future until it confronted its past. Conover Hunt, then-project manager for the museum, clarified this by stating,

- Dallas is joining other cities that have had to confront the problem of stewardship of a tragic part of history...and like Washington DC, Pearl Harbour, Gettysburg and Manassas, Dallas has dealt with the demands for information by creating a prominent educational display for the public.

There are several reasons for controversy over this mandate. Firstly, there has been significant commercial development at the site. A retail outlet operates from within the Sixth Floor while a corporate facility is open to rent. Lennon and Foley report the debate over catering facilities at the site. The museum bookshop sells a child's cutout book where the reader can dress and undress the entire John F. Kennedy family.

One vendor defends these actions by observing that when individuals visit a historic site, they want a memento or something to remember the trip by. Education at the Sixth Floor is also made controversial by the expressed opposition of the Kennedy family who see Boston's John F. Kennedy Library as the primary education and research center. Further distancing themselves from the Sixth Floor Museum, the family went as far as issuing the following statement.

"The family has taken the position that the only memorial should be the Kennedy Library...with its outreach capabilities in terms of inspiring people to service". Henderson recognizes that visitors at sites of dark tourism may have such motivations as a search for knowledge or novelty. However, for some sites, the educational mission veers closely to spectacle. This is another difficulty of an educational mandate. Mestrovic attributes this to the fact that museums are obliged to win and reward the attention of visitors and often do so via entertainment. For Lennon and Foley, a heavy dependence on media reveals a, "...fundamental difficulty of delineating education and entertainment slash spectacle and an uncritical approach to history".

Interpretation on the Channel Islands in Britain illustrates an additional dilemma regarding dark tourism and education: education can be selective, and biased history is therefore reinforced through interpretation. There were significant anti-Jewish measures and sentiments on the islands before and during the German occupation during World War II; however, this is neglected in interpretation and these omissions are significant. Visitors are not being told the whole story, perhaps even misguided in their information. Additionally, "...no public memorial has ever been erected on either island in commemoration of the deaths of slave labourers...This is even more disturbing since Alderney was the site of the UK's largest mass murder".

The brutality exhibited by the German occupiers left a death-toll in the thousands. The dark side of occupation is ignored; rather, the focus is on liberation and the ensuing celebrations, leaving an incomplete history.

EDUCATION AND THE HOLOCAUST

Despite the aforementioned educational dilemmas, education at Holocaust sites is regarded as being especially important. As Levi reminds, Holocaust sites are not, "...mistakes to efface. With the passing of years and decades, their remains do not lose any of their significance as a warning monument; rather, they gain in meaning". Society has an obligation to commemorate those who lost their lives in the Holocaust, "...not just to ensure their continued existence 'lest we forget' but to ensure they occur 'Nie Wieder'". One way to ensure that it never happens 'Never Again' is through education.

At the United States Holocaust Memorial Museum in Washington D.C., education is a primary component for a number of reasons. For Weinberg, "...it was to make visitors understand how attempts to annihilate an entire people came to be and how this was executed". Linenthal comments on the museum's mandate.

"People would need to be convinced that the museum would be more than a horror story before they could be persuaded to visit. Each of these impulsescommemorative sensibility and educational imperative, appropriate institutional civility, and public reassurance-became part of the interpretive mix in exhibit planning". For the USHMM, education centers on ensuring such horrific events are never repeated. Much of the education is aimed at the general public so they understand and learn from the past; however, some education is also geared towards heads of state so that they too can prevent these kinds of atrocities from happening again. "The Holocaust museum not only was a crucial memory for survivors or members of the public; but also might help those entrusted with affairs of state to navigate through troubled waters". As Riding supports, "...recalling...is the best way to avoid...". Educating against future events is a common theme found in the literature on the USHMM.

Linenthal observed that the museum would, "...stand as warning against hatred and dehumanization whoever the victim is". Discussing the exhibit on ethnic cleansing in the former Yugoslavia, Lennon and Foley commented, "Such exhibitions clearly reaffirm...Museum's mission to relate the history of the Holocaust to world events". To underscore this education, the museum is a reminder to the dangers of the outside world. Eskenazi, museum's Director of Public Information concurs. The museum acts as,

- ...a counterpoint to all of these other museums and memorials that you see, they all celebrate humans-their technology and art and creativity and we're saying watch out there is another side to humankind and to what humans are also capable of doing...I think people are interested in seeing things and learning things they feel they should see and that's part of it, this is actually something people feel they should see or learn something about or have a responsibility to learn about.

The Beth Hatefutsoth Museum of the Jewish Diaspora in Tel Aviv also states that education is an integral part of their site, and this importance is emphasized in the programmes offered. For adult visitors, their education department runs, "... a variety of study days, workshops and seminars". The museum's educational component for youth is detailed programmes that cater to, "... approximately 50,000 schoolchildren per year between the ages of 12 and 18". Furthermore, these visits are usually, "... structured around a particular topic designed to coincide with the history being taught at school". The history of the death-education/tourism relationship spans hundreds of years.

Beginning in the Middle Ages and still prevalent in today's society, education has provided interpretation of death and disaster for over 700 years. Much of this understanding necessitates travel. This is one of the key themes that emerged from a perusal of dark tourism literature: travel to try to understand death is not new.

A second theme is that education seeks to prevent similar events from occurring. If present and future generations can experience past tragedies, they will hopefully learn from their forebears' mistakes. As one interpreter at Washita Battlefield National Historic Site explained, "...we become keepers of the stories. It is up to us to make the intangible connections. We can help them form a deep connection to the story and the place so that future generations do not forget what happened at these tragic sites, ever". A third observable theme is that education may be a reaction to popularity, and may be introduced to offset such notoriety. Some sites of death and disaster draw attention from other sources much as media exposure, hence attracting hordes of visitors. However, without some form of interpretation, visitors may not understand the event. As a result, the dangers discussed previously might eventuate. Catharsis is a fourth theme that emerged from the literature. Education is often a means for a community to come to terms with the tragedy that touched them; it provides a means of understanding an event and subsequently provides relief. Keeping the past alive helps some survivors and victims keep the memories of other victims alive.

This is not to say that education as a pull factor lacks inherent dangers. Some sites use education as a justification for their existence. Other sites focus on their educational mandate while providing what some consider unsuitable products and services. This in turn can lead to controversy and conflict, particularly when heritage dissonance arises, as exemplified by the Kennedy families' experiences in Dallas. With education also comes the danger of spectacle. Most sites attempt to provide education in an interesting, entertaining way.

However, spectacle can overshadow meaningful interpretation. Much of this is attributed to an overdependence on the media where constant repetition collapses reality. Finally, an additional dilemma with education found in the literature is that telling the whole story is difficult. Community leaders, popular opinion or touristic demand on what is wanted may dictate exhibits and interpretation. Despite these dangers, education at Holocaust sites is revealed to be critical, correlating with many of the aforementioned themes. Key to Holocaust education is the hope of prevention of a repeat of past atrocities. Sites focus displays, programmes and outreach on teaching present and future generations the horrors of the Holocaust in hopes they learn not to let it happen again. Humankind has a dark side and by revealing it, individuals may be taught to heed it.

REMEMBRANCE

Remembrance is a vital human activity that connects us to our past and our future, and the ways we remember define us in the present. Remembrance helps cement our identities through an understanding of what has shaped us thus far. It allows us to learn from past mistakes and go forward with clear vision of the future.

"As individuals and societies, we need the past to construct and anchor our identities and to nurture a vision of the future...". Given many sites of dark tourism are warehouses for memories, it is not surprising they also mandate remembrance, in addition to education, as a factor in their planning. The literature review revealed a number of sites that cited commemoration and remembrance as their raison d'être. This is especially true for, but not limited to, sites of the Holocaust. When the Beth Hatefutsoth Museum of the Jewish Diaspora was proposed in 1959, its primary purpose was commemoration. The museum's originator felt that, "Following the…Nazis…and the establishment of the State of Israel, the 2,500 year old chapter of the history of the Diaspora is, in a certain sense drawing to a close. Thus the museum was to 'create a living memorial to the Jewish Diaspora'".

Today, one of the main themes in the permanent exhibit is a commemorative section simply called, Remember. Similarly, the United States Holocaust Memorial Museum also works on an educational-remembrance doctrine. Museum creators believed that a failure to remember those who died would, "…mean to become accomplices to their murders". The museum then would, "…stand in commemoration of the destroyed Euro-Jews and their civilization…". Hence, the inclusion of a Hall of Remembrance, "…where people can reflect on what they have seen".

A visit to the Holocaust Museum Houston emphasizes their commitment to remembrance. One of the first things one encounters is their permanent exhibit entitled, *Bearing Witness: A Community Remembers*. Elsewhere in the museum, in the *Lack Family Memorial Room* visitors can reflect on their experience at the Wall of Remembrance or Wall of Hope. Outside is the *Eric Alexander Garden of Hope*, memorializing the 1.5 million children that perished in the Holocaust. Sites other than those related to the Holocaust also espouse remembrance as a mandate.

At the Oklahoma City National Memorial, the inscription on the Gates of Time reads, "We come here to remember those who were killed, those who survived and those changed forever. May all who leave here know the impact of violence. May this memorial offer comfort, strength, peace, hope and serenity". The Menin Gate in Ypres, Belgium does not simply stand in commemoration to the war dead. It trumpets its remembrance loudly, every day stopping traffic. The Gate is located on one of the busiest roads in town and acts as a constant reminder of sacrifice. At 8 p.m.each night, buglers from the local fire brigade sound the last post as a living tribute from the people of Ypres The literature also revealed reverence is a key feature at many of these sites of remembrance.

At Pearl Harbour, a number of steps are taken to ensure respect. Visitors must first view an interpretive film before they are able to board the skiffs to the memorial. Once there, "...reverence is encouraged by staff present upon the Memorial structure. Beach-style clothing is not permitted upon the memorial...Visitors...are required to lave aboard the next-arriving small craft from the shoreside". This is done so visitors approach the structure as a memorial rather than simply a tourist attraction. Lennon and Foley also found reverential contemplation to be desirous in interpretation at Auschwitz-Birkenau.

- The interpretation assumes a knowledge of the camps and their purpose. Explanation, orientation and historical documentation are limited. In the larger barracks entitled 'Jews', the displays are reverential as opposed to historical or sequential...The aim of interpretation is to stimulate reflection and contemplation rather than an historical/literal interpretation to catalyse an understanding and appreciation of the past.

Some of Holt's Battlefield Tours also attempt to adopt an atmosphere of reverence. One of their key tours encompasses World War I battle sites, including affiliated cemeteries of the Commonwealth War Graves Commission. Here, "The tone is, not unexpectedly, reverential with customers encouraged to bring items of remembrance and, where this is feasible, to lay flowers at the graves of family members, etc.". The review of the literature also suggested remembrance is done in a large part to educate society so that such events are never repeated. As Beech warns, society has an ethical obligation to educate visitors. Lennon and Foley concur, noting,

- From Honolulu to Hiroshima and from Saigon to Singapore conflicts of the twentieth century are offered as part of touristic fare, most

> often as...a salutary warning from whatever is being represented should never happen again. It is not unusual for parties of schoolchildren from home and abroad to be seen at sites of infamy, degradation and death alongside the elderly on coach tours, historians on theme vacations and the merely curious on a day trip on extended tour.

Butler, in his discussion on whitewashing slavery in contemporary plantation tourism, recognized the dangers of not remembering slavery. Without such remembrance, "...the result is a lost opportunity for a nation to learn from its past mistakes...so that when confronted with similar evil in the present or future, they can challenge it before it becomes...". The erection of the U.S. National Holocaust Memorial Museum fulfilled similar beliefs. Through, "...this act of remembrance, Americans would not only memorialize Holocaust victims, but would instil caution, fortify restraint, and protect against future evil or indifference".

Without such remembrance, survivors would be accomplices in murder and prevent the lessons from being disseminated. This is not to say remembrance is devoid of controversy. Cultural values often dictate what is and is not commemorated. As Henderson observed, "Truth is the first casualty of war".

What is offered under the guise of remembrance may not be the full story. Smith noted, "Victory reinforces group identity and national pride, self-worth, belonging to a winning team, knowing you've done something right". Inevitably, the victors create monuments and memorials to commemorate their success. However, some governments may control such messages to suit their own agendas rather than attempting to reach any level of authenticity. Barthel supports this idea, noting heritage often lies in the hands of governments who present their own versions of the past that corresponds with their own interest. In some instances, this manipulation becomes outright propaganda. In Vietnam, current governments have promoted war tourism using message of solidarity, a heroic struggle against outside aggressors.

At the Cu Chi Tunnel complex where Vietcong ran supplies to forces in South Vietnam, certain interpretations appear geared specifically towards locals. Although some film footage at the visitors centre is original, "...the rustic atmosphere and local heroes who were honoured as 'Number One American Killers'". Remembering defeat is also difficult. Yet as Mayo recognized, "...defeat...cannot be forgotten and a nation's people must find ways to redeem those who died for their country to make defeat honourable. This must be done by honouring the individuals who fought rather than the country's lost cause". This is not an easy task.

The Vietnam War Memorial is black granite and below street level. Some veterans have labeled it the Ditch of Shame while Smith identified it as a monument of defeat. Foote found defeat is not the only event difficult to commemorate and remember. "Shame can be a powerful motive to obliterate all reminders of tragedy and violence". He cites such instances as places of mass murder, events caused by human negligence, and accidental tragedies that reflect badly on a group or community.

Under such circumstances, the shame and grief may be too hard to bear and as a result, no public remembrance takes place. Holocaust remembrance brings with it its own difficulties, especially given the urgency of remembrance. However, here too controversy exists in regards to interpretation of such sites. Some believe the scope of the Holocaust is too big for interpretation. Steiner argued that it is best, "...not to add the trivia of literacy...to the unspeakable". Conversely, others have argued, "...silence brings with it the problem of displacement and may encourage further generations to forget or ignore the incidence of this terrible period of human history".

Survivors fear they again will be victimized through the murder of memory and there is a need, to fulfill, "...victims' wishes to defeat the conspiracy of silence".

For Baudrillard, "Forgetting the extermination is part of the exterminating itself". A common cliché states that to know where you are going you must know where you have been. In other words to move forward, the past must be remembered and understood. Therefore, as places of commemoration and remembrance, dark tourism sites can play a significant role in this understanding.

They allow for the forging of identities, the mapping of the future, and the reading of contemporary society. For many such sites, their primary purpose is remembrance, particularly remembrance for education. By venerating the past, individuals and society can learn from previous mistakes. Holocaust museums in particular operate under this agenda. In order to prevent further genocides, they offer places of learning and reflection through remembrance. There are dangers, however, to remembrance. As iterated throughout this paper, prevailing cultural values often dictate what is remembered and commemorated.

Therefore, important and relevant stories may be ignored for political, economic or social gain. This applies also to sources of shame. Significant events and stories may be obliterated because of the shame and grief they cause. The Holocaust provides a unique set of dilemmas, particularly in how the remembrance is undertaken. While some feel monuments and memorials can stand on their own, others appeal for accompanying interpretation. What is clear, is that the Holocaust is an extraordinary event that demands remembrance: for survivors, relatives, and a strong tomorrow.

ARTIFACTS

The literature is not inundated with empirical studies on the ability of dark tourism objects to pull visitors to specific sites. However, there are a number of ancillary studies that must be noted. In his categorization of thanatourism, Seaton recognized one relevant classification: travel to view material evidence or symbolic representations of death in locations unconnected with their occurrence. These include, "...museums where weapons of death, the clothing of murder victims and other artefacts are put on display".

He cites such examples as the Museum of the Revolution in Cuba, which exhibits blood-spattered, bullet-riddled clothing of heroes of the Revolution and instruments of torture used by the Battista regime; and Madame Tussaud's in London where wax effigies of famous murderers are displayed. Tunbridge and Ashworth also cite Madame Tussaud's exhibits as an attraction. They note the wax museum where, "...the tourists' appetite for...artefacts relating to tragedy is substantial". Opening in London England in 1846 to house gruesome relics of the French Revolution, today the museum boasts 2.5 million visitors a year. Smith in her research on war and tourism, found military victory may lead to tourism, and she acknowledges the pull of artifacts found at some sites.

She notes, especially, the British Museum with its, "...countless...valuable curios that were incidental to colonial expansion...and many gold altars of Spain, and the gold chalices and jewelled cross that are booty from the conquest of Peru". However, she does recognize, "Tangible elements of war can be described in tourist brochures and serve as incentives for tourism...but that alone is not sufficient motivation to attract large numbers of pleasure-seekers to sites of carnage". Uzzell however, makes a case for the presentation of the display of certain controversial artifacts. He emphasizes that museums and interpretive sites should relate all aspects of human history, including that of atrocity because, "We are deceiving ourselves if we think that when we stand in front of a case of...photographs of mutilated bodies we are looking at the past. We are also looking at the present and the future". Hence, Uzzell promotes hot interpretation.

By displaying such artifacts as glasses and identity cards, museologists and interpreters provoke reactions. Without such reactions, people may adopt a cool and detached attitude to history. Aside from the above studies, there is little empirical research in this area. To supplement this dearth of academic work, heritage industry publications and popular culture literature were also considered. It was revealed in a number of articles and marketing brochures that artifacts are often employed to attract visitors. Artifacts from the *Titanic*, particularly, have been used to pull visitors to sites; and these efforts have been extraordinarily successful.

Up until 1997, the Maritime Museum of the Atlantic had, as part of its collection, a deck chair from the *Titanic* along with a few other pieces of wood from the ship. "Each year, even this modest display [drew] visitors from around the world". However, with the 1997 introduction of an entire exhibit about the *Titanic*, including additional artifacts, the museum saw its visitation increase 2.5 times from the previous year.

Similarly, when the National Maritime Museum in Greenwich England opened an exhibit about the ship in 1994, it was the, "…most popular exhibition the museum has ever staged, helping to attract some 720,000 people…". Central to its exhibit were some 150 artifacts salvaged by RMS *Titanic* Incorporated, the team that located the wreck in 1985. Pieces ranged from parts of the ship to passengers' belongings. In Kansas, remnants of the 1931 plane crash that killed Notre Dame's legendary football coach, Knute Rockne, continue to attract visitors. As one state publication advertises, "Up the road at Cottonwood Falls, the Chase County Historical Museum houses pieces of the plane and other items related to the crash".

Meanwhile, other sites import relics of dark tourism to emphasize their message and draw additional visitation. The New York Battery Park City Authority has as its centrepiece an actual stone cottage from potato-famine-era-Ireland in order to provide the city's large Irish population, "...something tangible to connect us with the past". The author notes similar relics found throughout New York City.

These include a tablet cast from metal from the USS Maine sunk in Havana Harbour in 1898; a tablet containing nine coins from an eleven-year-old victim of United Airlines Flight 1049 1960 air crash; and a 15-foot statue brought from Hiroshima, one of the few surviving structures after the 1945 bombing. Numerous brochures of dark tourism sites offer artifacts in their marketing campaigns. At the National Civil Rights Museum in Memphis, you can walk into a Montgomery city bus or a Greyhound bus similar to those used in the 1961 Freedom Rides. You can see the salvaged mast of the USS Maine, sunk in 1898, at Arlington National Cemetery in Virginia. At The Second World War Experience Centre in Leeds, England, you can see wartime letters, diaries, photographs, and official papers. In the context of the Holocaust, artifacts bring with them their own controversial dilemmas, particularly in the kinds of artifacts displayed.

Foley and Lennon detail the debate surrounding almost two tons of human hair on exhibit as Auschwitz. While some argue preservation is vital for remembrance, others argue this type of remembrance is ineffectual. Young argues, "These artefacts...force us to recall the victims as the Germans have remembered them to us: in the collected debris of a destroyed civilization...In great loose piles, these remnants remind us not of the lives that once animated them, so much as of the brokenness of lives". Linenthal concurs, stating hair is, "...not a commodity to be shipped, transported...and crafted for dramatic displays". However, he does note the location of such artifacts plays a role in its display.

While hair, bones, and ashes do not belong in an American museum where no concentration camp stood, if their appearance was in a museum such as Treblinka or Auschwitz, it would be acceptable. The Imperial War Museum in London described its own dilemmas when assigning artifacts to be displayed in their recently opened Holocaust Exhibit. Museum staff wanted objects that would, "...bring the reality of the subject home...give some tangible sense of the...conditions of those imprisoned...and...offer visitors the special interaction which only fabric genuinely of the period can offer". However, consensus over these objects was difficult to achieve.

While some felt *not* displaying such items as a marble dissecting-table would sanitize the subject, others felt it would upset survivors and encourage 'prurient' interest. In other words, people might be attracted to the horrible and obscene as opposed to the subject itself. The exhibition of such controversial items has additional consequences. Lanzmann feels such displays have the capability to harden the visitor, to make them less sensitive to the topic. Meanwhile, Lennon and Foley already believe society may be hardened, "...that the artefacts and attitudes of modernity have reached a stage of ambivalence and ambiguity which continues to be present in some public consciousness".

The latter authors highlight this idea with an example from Auschwitz-Birkenau where, "Groups of schoolchildren were taking photographs of each other, parents were photographing their children at the gate of Birkenau and, indeed, school parties were sitting on the ruins of the crematorium eating sandwiches". A further, indirect consequence of exhibiting artifacts to attract visitors, is the ensuing emergence of souvenirs. Lennon and Foley continue their discussion on Auschwitz.

- In the vicinity, a range of private retail units have developed. Everything from hot dog stands, booksellers, postcard vendors, film stores and discount pottery warehouses are to be found. These, and the internal sale of concentration camp memorabilia, present the camp authorities with a clear dilemma.

Similarly, the Imperial War Museum operates a number of commercial ventures at their many sites, including a retail shop and franchised café at their main branch. At the Duxford branch, "...income generation is to the fore with cafés and a large shop offering a range of possible purchases consistent with a day out in the countryside". This author entered the Imperial War Museum web site to view the array of souvenirs offered.

All memorabilia is said to be associated with any current special exhibits while each branch specializes in products connected to its particular theme. Such mementos include replica war posters for children with suggestions how they could help with the war effort; replica certificates issued to children by King George VI for the Victory Celebrations; and model aircraft sets. All are reproduced from artifacts found within the museums. Empirical research on artifacts as motivators is limited.

However, popular culture and ancillary academic studies illustrate the attraction of such objects. Some authors goes as far as propagating the use of artifacts to provoke reactions and emotions from visitors. Controversy can force individuals to take a stance. The review of related dark tourism literature enumerates a number of sites that actually use artifacts to promote visitation. Much of this was found in site brochures and other marketing materials. Therefore, sites appear to use concrete evidence of dark events as attractors. Furthermore, the literature revealed the success of such promotion. Two sites in particular found a significant increase in visitation after the introduction of tangible objects from the *Titanic*.

The display of artifacts at Holocaust sites proved to be a controversial undertaking. Some academics and museum professionals strongly advocate the display of such things as hair, bones, and spectacles. They cite the need for tangible objects to bring home the scope of the Holocaust. Other professionals disagree, claiming such exhibitions are useless, that they are improper remembrances for the dead. A final note on the attraction of artifacts is their commodification through souvenirs. Although some items serve as appropriate reminders of the trip, the resulting retail commercialization is troublesome. While books and replica posters may be pertinent to the history of the site, the ensuing cafes, postcard vendors, and hotdog stands can deteriorate the sites and take away from their gravity.

SIGHT SACRALIZATION

As mentioned previously in this study, cultural values often dictate what sites and events are commemorated, including incidents of death and disaster. However, MacCannell continues this discussion in terms of tourist attractions and the processes of sacralizing sights for tourism. As Seaton quotes, "It is not that tourism creates more things to see - although it does that too - but that is constructs new meaning structures by which existing things can be seen and revalued". MacCannell likens tourist travel to religious pilgrimages. When tourists travel, they are searching for the authentic, and this search becomes like a sacred journey or religious pilgrimage. In this search for authenticity, some objects go through a process of sacralisation where they are marked, making them separate and different from other sights, and so branding them meaningful. The first stage of sight sacralization involves the naming of an object, where attractions are marked worthy of preservation. This involves some form of authentication testifying to an object's aesthetic, historical, monetary, recreational, and social value.

Such authentication might include restoration of a period home or the photographing and x-raying of an object. The second stage is the framing and elevation phase, where an object/sight/site is put on display and official boundaries are set around the object/sight/site. Official boundaries include markers that make the sight recognizable as an attraction: plaques, interpretive displays, spotlights, additional protection, and hanging silk cords. All can confer importance upon a site. As Dann noted, "Markers speak.

They convey messages to tourists, and…in turn relay messages to other tourists and potential tourists". Without markers, the site would be meaningless. MacCannell's third stage of sacralization enshrinement takes place when, "…the framing material that is used has itself entered into the first stage of sacralization".

As an example, the author chose the Sainte Chappelle church in Paris, originally built to house/frame/elevate Christ's Crown of Thorns. Today, while the object is still a major tourist attraction, the church has become an attraction in its own right. Next, a sight enters the mechanical reproduction stage where the sacred object, or one associated with a sight or site, is reproduced. Reproductions include souvenirs, prints, or photographs. As MacCannell notes, this phase, "…is most responsible for setting the tourist in motion on his journey to find the true object". The final stage of sight sacralization is social reproduction. This occurs when such entities as groups, cities, and regions begin to name themselves after the famous attraction. For example, while in Memphis, one can drive down Elvis Presley Boulevard, camp at KOA Graceland, or eat at Elvis Presley's Memphis.

SIGHT SACRALIZATION AND DARK TOURISM

There are limited studies on sight sacralization within the context of dark tourism. Foley and Lennon state the way a dark tourism sight develops as a tourism attraction is systematically and socially organized, designed to be different from everyday. However, Seaton's definitive work on the sacralization of the 1815 Battle of Waterloo is perhaps the only one of its kind. Waterloo's historical significance is achieved by its ranking as one of the 15 most decisive battles in the world.

Its importance however, does not account for its success as an attraction, for modern tourism is unconcerned with other battlefields examined in Creasey's book. Marathon, Blenheim, Chalons, and Pultowa, once pivotal battles, remain relatively obscure today. For Seaton, "The answer lies, rather, not just in the historic importance of the battle, but in the nature of the tourism process itself-how it is constructed, influenced, and sustained". By studying Waterloo under the umbrella of MacCannell's five-step sacralization process, Seaton is able to explain the rise of the battlefield as a major tourism destination.

Naming

The actual battle of Waterloo was fought by six different armies and took place over four continuous battlefields; thus, its geographical space had no precise name marked on a map. However, it was the English general, Wellington, who chose to name the battle 'Waterloo' after the hamlet and inn at which he stayed the night previous. In doing so, Wellington venerated his own role, and England's, in the battle. This socially-constructed name has had a direct impact on tourism at Waterloo.

- In the first action at Ligny the Prussians fought an important if unsuccessful...operation...while Wellington was...fighting at Quatre Bras. At Wavre two days later...the Prussians fought another diversionary action...However, by being categorized individually...as minor skirmishes preceding the great battle, Ligny and Wavre became marginalized as "warm-ups" to the main show....

This marginalization continues today. Ligny, Quatre Bras and Wavre are visited much less than Waterloo because of the pre-eminence of the name Waterloo.

Framing and Elevation

MacCannell defined framing and elevation as, "The putting on display of an object – placement in a case, on a pedestal or opened up for visitation. Framing is the place of an official boundary around an object". Yet Seaton noted that battles are ephemeral and that it is not possible to put them in cases or on pedestals.

Seaton did note, however, that it is possible to elevate and frame a battle through monumental markers. Witness what occurred at Waterloo. Eight years after the battle, the Belgian people constructed the Butte de Lion, a massive bronze statue to the allied forces at Waterloo. It touristic impact was enormous. "Once the monument was built, it was inevitable that it would become a tourism spectacle…and that restaurants, museums and hotels would spring up as they did and still do (along with a panorama, housed in a rotunda and built just before the First World War; a modern visitor centre built in the last 20 years; and numerous gift shops)". Today over 135 monuments and markers stand in remembrance of the Battle of Waterloo.

Enshrinement

Enshrinement, refers to the point at which, "…the framing material that is used has itself entered the first stage of sacralization". As one example of enshrinement, Seaton cites the Waterloo Church, "…where the British deposited battle standards, military pendants…and placed memorial plaques to the dead". Prior to the battle, the building was relatively unimportant; however, it was subsequently rebuilt on a grander scale.

Mechanical Reproduction

According to MacCannell, mechanically reproducing tourism sights or objects elevates them as significant touristic attractions. The media played, and still plays, an important role in these reproductions, ranging from Hollywood blockbusters to comic strips. Seaton concurs, "The sustained reproduction of Waterloo through the printed word and graphic image was one of the reasons it achieved a unique place in public imagination". The litany of mechanical reproductions that surfaced about Waterloo is wideranging and Seaton attributes this to the coinciding advances of technology; poems, books, and ballads were written and distributed; caricatures, lithographs, and photos were developed; and equally as important, guidebooks were enhanced. These reproductions served to secure Waterloo's importance in culture and tourism.

Social Reproduction

MacCannell's final step in sight sacralization is social reproduction: the representation of cultural objects in everyday life, away from their places of origin. Notable examples include the naming of roads, pubs, streets, bridges, and monuments. According to Seaton the name Waterloo,

- …was disseminated in an astonishing variety of manifestations…Virtually every town had its Waterloo or Wellington street, road, or terrace…Furthermore, as the Empire expanded there were towns called Wellington in Canada, New Zealand, and Australia…In summary, Waterloo entered the popular psyche of the British at home and overseas...".

Although Seaton's Waterloo example correlates with MacCannell's sight sacralization process, the author recognizes the original concept was developed for objects as tourism attractions rather than destinations. He cites as examples di Vinci's Mona Lisa, Napoleon's hat, and the Moon rock. Therefore, due to MacCannell's object-oriented focus, Seaton offers a number of modifications to the original concept. Firstly, Seaton believes the sacralization process can be abbreviated to just two phases: naming and mechanical reproduction.

To illustrate, he details the sudden rush of visitation to the site immediately after the battle, "...before any significant framing and elevations, enshrinement or social reproduction had taken place". He attributes this to the media onslaught to report the victory. Furthermore, the guidebooks and other reproductions that took place before sight elevation indicate the predominance of mechanical reproduction.

This leads to Seaton's second modification: there is no evidence the marking stages occur in any particular order, except for the initial naming phase. He states sacralization is not a linear process with a final end point nor does the process uniformly affect everyone. The process is influenced heavily by the powers that place the sight on offering and those who gaze at it. Sights may be rethought or redrawn by those, "...presiding over the process". As an example, he cites the erection of new markers at the site, particularly the more recent additions occurring over 150 years after the battle.

These include a plaque installed by the French at Hougomount as late as 1990. Seaton also believes framing, elevation, and enshrinement are less important for tourism generation than naming and mechanical and social reproduction since it is the latter three that propel visitors in the first place. Both reproductions may, "...well be the key sacralization factors in the success of major international attractions". Finally, Seaton observes that what was once seen as remarkable can mutate, thereby dimming demands for the sight, a process he calls sight secularization or sight desacralization.

While Waterloo is still considered a major tourist attraction, "...it rarely provokes the kind of euphoric triumphalism that it did a hundred years ago- even among the British". In sum, not all sites of death and disaster develop as tourist attractions. One reason for this as previously discussed, is the influence of prevailing cultural values. If those in authority do not deem an event or site important, then it is largely ignored. Sociologist Dean MacCannell formulated another possible cause for the development of tourist attractions: sight sacralization.

While tourism physically develops new attractions, so too it develops destinations through the construction of new meaning structures. Using MacCannell's 5-step process, Seaton demonstrated the sacralization of the site of the Battle of Waterloo. The *naming* of the battle Waterloo, gave that specific site pre-eminence and therefore a recognition factor to the public at large. Since the name sounded familiar, it must therefore be important. The *framing and elevation* of Waterloo followed with the erection of monuments and markers to the fallen. With something concrete to now gaze at, tourists began to arrive. Phase three, *enshrinement,* came with an unimportant church rebuilt after the battle. While the artifacts inside the church are still important attractions, people now come to see the building itself. Finally, *mechanical and social reproductions* of Waterloo are still prevalent in society. Guidebooks continue to direct tourists to the site while pubs, streets, and cities can be found across the British Commonwealth.

Seaton does note however, that MacCannell's original concept was object based rather than destination based. Therefore, he offers a number of modifications to the process, which in turn influence the sacralization of dark tourism sites. Feasibly, dark tourism sites can be sacralized in just two stages: naming and mechanical reproduction. Given the prominence of the media in contemporary society, naming will attract visitors with or without any markers being erected. For instance the hordes of visitors travelling to Lockerbie, Scotland after the crash of Pan Am Flight 103. There are no social reproductions of Lockerbie. One does not find a Lockerbie Street or Lockerbie Park named after the tragedy. Seaton also comments that the process can occur in any order, citing the continuing erection of monuments at Waterloo as an example. Conversely, there may be a reversal of sacralization as time passes and memory fades. In the same article, the author notes the declining popularity of the Battle of Hastings.

ROLE OF THE MEDIA

Contemporary media has an undeniable influence over public consciousness. Individuals regularly turn on their televisions and radios for weather, news and entertainment. In turn, public opinion and behaviour are informed by these sources. From what to wear on any given day to who to vote for, society depends on the media for information and answers. Furthermore, this influence has expanded as communications have become a global commodity.

The media also has undeniable influence over pubic interpretation of the landscape including sites of dark tourism. According to Lennon and Foley, "...global communication technologies are inherent in both the events which are associated with a dark tourism product and are present in the representation of the events for visitors at the site itself". Hence, the relationship between dark tourism and the media is thoroughly interconnected.

The authors further this statement by noting the development of mass media, "...has changed the relationship between the public and world events.

Thus, an event represented as 'dark tourism' is likely to have taken place in the last hundred years and been brought to the public via modern mass media. The scale and scope of the tourism product are likely to be driven by the media". The 1912 sinking of the *Titanic* is considered to be the genesis of global media. Although television did not exist and communications were slower than today, newspapers and newsreels were quick to report on the tragedy. Forty-six years later, the media again brought the *Titanic* to the forefront of public consciousness with the release of the film, A *Night to Remember.* The film, "...effectively turned the relatively impersonal and largely forgotten sinking into a series of individuals 'stories' of fictional characters upon the vessel.

In 1998, the *Titanic* once again rose onto the big screen with the release James Cameron's *Titanic* While the *Titanic* represents the advent of global communication, the life and death of John F. Kennedy perhaps represents the watershed.

Even before his assassination he was referred to as the 'television president'. "From the initial 'great debate' with Nixon through the regular live televised news conferences to his ultimatum on US television demanding that Russian missiles be removed from Cuba, he showed an early mastery of TV". It was after his assassination however, that the media influence began to dominate his life and death. White noted, "Television was at the centre of the shock. With its indelible images, information, immediacy, repetition and close-ups, it served to define the tragedy for the public". Connally furthered this. Not only did the media define the tragedy, it characterized Kennedy's entire administration.

- I don't think the time has come when history will really look at the Kennedy administration with a realistic eye. And how could we? When you see a beautiful little girl kneeling with her hand on her father's coffin, when you see a handsome little boy standing with a military salute by his slain father, how can you feel anything but the utmost sympathy? It's a scene of pathos, of remorse, of tragedy, and that's the way we now view President Kennedy.

MEDIA AS A PUSH AND PULL FACTOR

The media has a unique place in dark tourism in the fact it acts both as a push factor and a pull factor. Through its mass appeal to audiences, it has the ability to bring dark tourism sites to public consciousness (and conversely, keep other sites out of public perception). What the public reads and hears through the media is brought to the forefront of the awareness thereby creating destination awareness and an aware set for potential visitors. Furthermore, through its extensive use in the actual interpretation at dark tourism sites, the media can pull people to a site. People who want to hear and see specific information may be attracted to the tools used at such sites.

As Lennon and Foley note, "Technology and particularly multimedia have been used to relate the visitor experience to the individual". As will be illustrated further in the paper, dark tourism destinations often rely heavily on technology to convey their messages.

MEDIA AS PUSH

Even before the advent of electronic communications, the media has played an integral role in relaying information to the public. Such mediums as, "...broadsheets, poems, songs and political speeches were essential instruments in stimulating popular indignations...". For instance, when Abraham Lincoln was assassinated in 1865 it was, "Newspaper headlines and telegrams [that] spread the news of Lincoln's death". However, modern communication technologies have extended the range, immediacy and impact of such events.

This increase has also resulted in an increase in the popularity of dark tourism sites. Media coverage appears to have the ability to both push and pull visitors as illustrated in the literature review. In Fall's River, Massachusetts, there is an undeniable interest in all things Lizzie Borden, but as one local tourist operator noted, travel "...seemed to pick up in recent years after a string of television documentaries".

The Sixth Floor Museum in Dallas also reports visitation increases after media focus. "Recording approximately 0.5 million paying visitors a year this remains Dallas' premier paid attraction with an average annual increase of visitors in excess of 15 per cent. Attendance fluctuations are noted during times of media focus on any aspect of the Kennedy story". According to the Dallas County Historical Foundation, visitor numbers increased significantly upon the release of Oliver Stone's movie JFK while anniversaries also lead to increased media and increased visitor numbers. Other media have served to tantalize visitor interest in all things Kennedy.

For Foley and Lennon, "...novels and film treatments such as the *Parallax View, Executive Action* and *JFK* have all contrived to feed the growing interest in the events of the Kennedy death". In 1992, the National Parks Service in the United States reported every national battlefield and cemetery reported a, "... significant increase in attendance, as much as 75 per cent in the last ten years for the Fredericksburg, Virginia Memorial". Park staff attributed some of this to the influence of the media.

Two years earlier, the Public Broadcast System aired the Ken Burns miniseries, *Civil War*. This coverage was accompanied by a, "...surge of Civil War tourism interest ...supported by numerous travel articles in the leading magazines, Travel Holiday, National Geographic Traveler...as well as travel sections in newspapers such as the Boston Globe, New York Time etc.". Since the release of James Cameron's, *Titanic*, Halifax has also been basking in surreal popularity. Hard Copy, People Magazine, The Boston Globe, Bangkok Post and the Sunday Times of London have all featured Halifax and the *Titanic* in their publications.

As a result, affiliated sites saw a tremendous increase in popularity. Countless mementos were, and continue to be, left at J. Dawson's grave at Fairview Cemetery by movie fans believing he was Jack Dawson of the movie fame. The Maritime Museum of the Atlantic saw an increase of triple the visitors. Ironically, at the time of the movie's release, the museum was about to open a permanent exhibit on the *Titanic*. The response was immediate.

- As it turned out, as we were putting the final touches on our exhibit, we learned that Cameron's move, which, by this time, had received an extraordinary amount of worldwide media attention ...was to be released on Dec. 18, 1997. Taking advantage of this fact, on Dec. 17 we put a release out on the newswire which began "Coincident with the release of James Cameron's movie Titanic, the Maritime Museum of the Atlantic is please to announce the opening of its new permanent exhibit...". Within 24 hours, we began fielding calls from local, then regional, then national, then American and then other international media.

Holocaust sites are not immune to the power of the media. Dachau was not a major extermination camp yet ironically, it remains one of the most visited, stemming in part from media influence. Much of this is because it is often featured in media portrayals of liberation and the reporting of the on-site war crime trials of camp guards and other Nazi party members. Lennon and Foley cite Krakow, Poland as another dark tourism site impacted by media exposure, this time after the release of Steven Spielberg's movie, *Schindler's List.* The,

- ...popularization of Thomas Keneally's book Schindler's Ark [sic] by the production of...[the]...film...caused tourism to increase significantly in the 1993-4 period. In effect, 'Schindler tourism' developed, focusing on the remaining cluster of synagogues, cemeteries, and strongest of all, the disused film sets for the...production. The film sets located near to Krakow became a Schindler tour in the years 1994-5.

MEDIA AS PULL

Modern media not only plays a role in disseminating information to the public off-site (thereby pushing visitors to the destination); it also plays an important role in the development of on-site interpretation. Sites associated with the Kennedy assassination and the US Holocaust Memorial Museum in Washington, D.C. all exemplify this reliance on media for their interpretation. Lennon and Foley note that central to interpretation at the Sixth Floor Museum are pictorial images including, "Upwards of four hundred photographs, [and] six documentary films (heavily based on contemporary TV coverage).

As a result, since its opening in 1989 the museum has been presented with numerous awards for its use of video. Other communication mediums are used extensively in and around the Sixth Floor. Inside the museum, visitor can hire audio tours to heighten their experience. While outside, limousine tours retrace Kennedy's last steps accompanied by an, "...audio commentary playing on the car tape deck that includes crowd cheers, gunshot sounds, comments of other passengers...and the news broadcast covering the death of the President". The New Museum at the JFK Library in Boston also utilizes media in its interpretation at the site. "In each of the White House rooms and other locations there are screens located as a primarily element of exhibition space...[along with]...TV screens...used to show television clips in an attempt to give the visitor the 'impression' that someone at the time would have had when watching their own TV".

Interestingly, the authors also noted that displayed artifacts are not authenticated, signifying the secondary role they play to the media tools offered. At the US Holocaust Museum, technology also defines the visitor experience. "Central to the interpretation is the use of newsreels, radios broadcasts, and papers.

The reality of the 1930's and 1940's is recreated in the way US citizens were actually informed of the rise of Nazi Germany and the progress of the war". This includes interviews with witnesses and film footage of camp liberations. Also central to the interpretation is a passport given to each individual on entering the permanent exhibit in the museum. Visitors are asked to,

- ...type their age, gender, and profession into a computer, after which they will be issued an identity card of someone like themselves who was caught up in the Holocaust. At three stages of the exhibit, visitors will have their cards updated, so that with every passing year in exhibit-time, the personal history of what might be called our phantom-guide will be revealed. At the end of the permanent exhibition, visitors will insert their cards into a television monitors and meet the companion face-to-fact through oral history – or if the phantom-companion died, the memory of the deceased will be conveyed by surviving family and friends.

This use of passports attempts to link visitors directly to the Holocaust. The museum goes as far as allowing visitors to print their updated passports as they progress through the exhibit thereby allowing them to take their experience outside of the museum. In addition to the permanent exhibit, the museum also houses a learning center where people can learn more about the Holocaust. Here visitors can access the 24 computer terminals from which they can, "...call up articles about Holocaust-related topics; watch film clips of or hear taped interviews with survivors of the Holocaust; look at maps or photographs; and listed to related music".

A CONCEPTUAL MODEL

The literature clearly illustrates the influence the media has on dark tourism. It has the ability to inform and therefore attract people to dark destinations. By placing such events and destinations in the forefront of communications, visitors are made aware of these kinds of travel options. Whether they are pushed because of heritage, history, guilt, curiosity, death, dying or nostalgia will vary with each individual tourist; however, the media offers the information to satisfy these factors. In other words, it acts as a mediator between push factors, visitors and the destinations.

Furthermore, on-site interpretation relies heavily on media and therefore is able to use such technology as a pull factor. People can 'hear' tapes of survivors or the commentary of news correspondents; they can 'see' the liberation of concentration camps or even the death of a president. By offering such sensory and provoking experiences, museums are able to pull people to their exhibits.

Whether they are pulled because of education, remembrance or artifacts again vary with each individual; however, the media at dark tourism sites offers ways to satisfy these pull factors. In other words, the media can also act as mediator between pull factors, visitors and the destinations.

2

Research Methodology, Data Analysis and Results in Dark Tourism

RESEARCH METHODOLOGY

Due to the limited research on visitor motivations to Holocaust museums, this study takes an exploratory approach. Two separate methods were chosen; a qualitative focus group and a questionnaire administered to a sample of tourists and resident visitors.

The principal method used in this study was a survey administered to museum visitors; however, it was determined that a preliminary focus group with museum staff would enhance the survey content. It was believed staff might provide first-hand insights on visitor trends and related observations given their front-line work with the public. It is museum staff that encounter dark tourism visitors on a daily basis; therefore, they are the most likely individuals to hear comments and observe reactions to the museum. Although the literature is largely based on empirical study, researchers may miss some experiences that front-line employees may notice. Furthermore, the public may be more relaxed and unguarded in front of staff as opposed to academics.

The second method of study was a mixed questionnaire. Due to the potentially sensitive nature of the Holocaust Museum Houston, a mail-out survey was selected as the means of obtaining information, as opposed to administering the survey on-site in person. This was done out of respect for visitors who might have experienced trauma or distress immediately after visiting the site. Approaching individuals leaving such an emotional experience could be construed as insensitive. Furthermore, the magnitude of the experience may have biased survey responses.

FOCUS GROUP DESIGN AND ADMINISTRATION

A focus group was utilized as a first step to the survey design. The literature on thanatourism and dark tourism gives limited understanding of why individuals attend such sites; therefore, it was important to gain a broader perspective on visitor motivation. Krueger comments how focus groups are useful under such circumstances. A focus groups is a,

- ...carefully planned discussion designed to obtain perceptions on a defined area of interest in a permissive, non-threatening environment. It is conducted with approximately seven to ten people by a skilled interviewer. The discussion is relaxed, comfortable, and often enjoyable for participants as they share their ideas and perceptions. Group members influence each other by responding to ideas and comments in the discussion.

Management at the museum organized for six staff members to participate voluntarily in an informal focus group to discuss visitor motivations to the museum. As museum staff encounter visitors on a daily basis in an intimate manner, it was believed they would provide additional insights into why visitors come to the Holocaust Museum Houston specifically and sites of dark tourism in general. It was presumed the ideas generated in the focus group would provide useful insight for the survey.

A meeting was arranged and a series of questions were then developed with the theoretical framework and research questions in mind. On February 22, 2002 the six staff members participated in a group discussion focusing on why they believe visitors visit the Holocaust Museum Houston and other sites of dark tourism. Staff make-up was comprised of one weekend docent, one weekday docent, one volunteer, the museum's executive director, the museum's visitor service coordinator, and the museum's education coordinator. This composition was arranged to capture the maximum range of visitor encounters.

Each member of the group was given a cover letter explaining the purpose of the meeting. To encourage Krueger's relaxed and comfortable atmosphere, a general interview guide approach was used whereby a set of topics were outlined although the order and wording were not predetermined. A series of structured questions were asked, augmented with open-form probing questions to obtain additional information. Appendix F details the initial focus group questions, and during the interview probing questions where applicable followed. Focus group results were transcribed into a Microsoft Word document and then transferred into Atlas Ti for qualitative analysis.

SURVEY DESIGN AND ADMINISTRATION

Upon entering the Holocaust Museum Houston, one member from each visitor group is asked to fill out an information card for the museum's visitor database. Over a four-week period during March and April 2002, a sign was posted above the information card drop-off box in the museum, indicating that when visitors filled out that card, they might receive an off-site, detailed survey. Respondents were broken down into voluntary and non-voluntary. If visitors chose *not to* accept the detailed survey, their information cards went into one response box.

If visitors did choose to participate in the detailed survey, their information cards went into a separate response box. These voluntary response cards were set aside from non-voluntary response cards, thereby providing the database from which the sample was randomly chosen.

A database of 1,318 visitors to the museum during the four-week period was accumulated. From this, a sample of 500 individuals was chosen by systematic sampling, where every nth person in the population is selected for the sample. To calculate *n,* the population number is divided by the desired sample number. Hence, for this study, the population was divided by the sample to get 2.636. From there, every third person in the population database was chosen for the study sample.

As this is exploratory research, the survey consisted of both of open-ended and closed-ended questions. Closed-ended questions were asked in relation to possible motivations to the site to establish if their motivations reflect the literature. Open-ended questions were asked about motivations in order to establish motivations that might not be included in the survey. Close-ended demographic questions were also asked in order to differentiate between local residents who visit and tourists from out of town, and to establish a profile of visitors to the site. This design of the survey was drawn from a number of sources.

First, questions reflect motivations found in the literature review. Secondly, information garnered from the focus group was incorporated into survey questions. Finally, questions and design were adapted from two previous surveys at dark tourism sites: The National Holocaust Memorial Museum, Washington, D.C., and a National Park Service survey at the USS Arizona Memorial.

SURVEY INSTRUMENT

Five broad research questions were formed in order to guide this study, and provide direction for both the focus group and survey questions. Under the umbrella of these questions, ten specific questions were developed to further the broad categories. These questions were based on personal experience and extensive reading, therefore drawing upon major factors identified in the literature review on dark tourism.

The questions also sought factors and motivations specific to the Holocaust Museum Houston. The theoretical framework behind the research questions was Dann's Push and Pull Theory. The author recognized two different types of traveler motivations: push factors, or internal motivations that come from within the visitor; and pull factors, or motivations that emit from external sources such as the site itself. It was believed the Holocaust Museum Houston, as a destination for visitors, created both visitor push motivations and site pull factors. Chapter II discusses the theory in detail in addition to site-specific push and pull factors. The media figured prominently in the literature on dark tourism; however, as a factor, it did not fit under either push or pull. A model was then developed to understand how the media acted as a mediator between push and pull: it is what moves people from push to pull.

SURVEY METHODS

Upon completion of the survey instrument, steps were then taken to distribute the survey to the sample. Respondents had two options for responding to the survey: they could mail back their survey or respond on-line at the author's web site specifically created for this research. At the beginning of the study, the Holocaust Museum Houston confirmed there was room on the card for e-mail addresses on the initial information card they handed out.

Therefore, the sample was divided into two: those with a postal address alone and those with both postal and e-mail addresses. With the web site operational, postcards were developed in order to pre-contact individuals, informing them of upcoming contact from the researcher. A pre-contact was undertaken, as it has been found contacting respondents before sending a questionnaire increases response rates. The postcard informed individuals they would be receiving either an e-mail or a mail survey within the next two weeks. Postcards were sent out June 13, 2002.

One shortcoming of this research is that e-mails and survey were not sent out until seven months later. Two hundred and eighty-three surveys were mailed out January 21st 2003 to those with only postal addresses. The following week, from January 27th-29th, two hundred and seventeen e-mails were sent to the remaining sample with e-mail addresses. Attached to all surveys was a cover letter informing visitors of the purpose of the survey, their rights in regards to responding, and any contact information should they have questions. Postal service respondents were given three weeks and e-mail respondents were given two before postcard reminders were sent out on February 11, 2003.

An identical postcard was sent out to both sets of respondents for two reasons. Firstly, it gave postal service individuals the opportunity to respond via the Internet should they have lost the initial survey. Secondly, I felt that repetitive e-mails might be harassing to respondents. In the end, participants completed a total of 188 surveys; however, two responses were almost identical using the same respondent number. From the answers, it appears a husband and wife each filled a survey out. Because of this, both responses were deemed inadmissible, bringing the total number of usable surveys down to 186 out of a possible 500.

Specifically, there were 88 e-mail respondents and 98 mail-back respondents. This represents an overall response rate of 37.2 per cent. The survey itself consisted of a combination of both open and closed-ended questions; therefore, analysis was carried out in three parts. Firstly, data was inputted into a Microsoft Access database. Those surveys answered on-line went directly into the database, while mailed back surveys were inputted manually. From there, descriptive statistics were formed using Atlas Ti.

The software was utilized to evaluate the qualitative data procured from the fourteen open-ended questions. Data from each question was inputted into the software package in order to ascertain any commonalties. A number of significant themes emerged and are described in a chronological basis further in the paper. Additionally, some qualitative data is supplemented with basic quantitative statistics. For instance, where visitors were asked to list other Holocaust destinations they have recently attended, percentages were added for additional insight.

RESEARCH LIMITATIONS

Before any analysis or discussion can take place, it must be understood certain limitations exist in this research, thereby influencing any observations and conclusions. Firstly, dark tourism is an emerging field and there is limited prior research on the topic, particularly in the area of motivation. Therefore, there are no precedents by which to compare. Findings are exploratory and stepping-stones for much needed additional research.

Secondly, there are limitations in the methodology of the study. The sample was taken from a specific population: it was collected over a one-week period in March 2002, during spring break. Therefore, given it was a holiday period, the incidence of vacationers, students and other specialized populations may be higher than during other times of the year. During the compilation of the sample database, datum was taken from handwritten information cards. Given the use of handwriting, mistakes in addresses (particularly e-mail addresses) were possible and some therefore may have not received surveys.

Furthermore, as previously mentioned, there was a significant time gap between the initial pre-contact postcard mail out and the mailing/e-mailing of the actual surveys. During the interim, potential respondents may have moved, lost interest or forgotten information. E-mail surveying is also a relatively new method. While almost half the sample reported e-mail addresses, not everyone is comfortable using computers and may have been too intimidated to use technology. Furthermore, given potential fears of computer viruses, some respondents may not have opened the e-mail although pre-contact postcards were sent. Thirdly, author bias may exist.

Having a personal interest in dark tourism lead to this study, and although an extensive literature review was undertaken, some of the initial motivators came from the author's own assumptions. Hence, additional motivations may exist that the author is unaware of. Fourthly, although this research attempted to understand visitor motivation, it is recognized that the survey was administered post-visit and responses are likely influenced by the museum experience. As a result, there may be mixing of the concepts of motivation and experience, and while this research is exploratory this overlap is seen as a limitation. Finally, this study looks only at the Holocaust Museum Houston as a case study and therefore results may not necessarily apply to other sites of dark tourism.

One of the initial aims of this paper was to see if motivations at the museum reflect overall dark tourism sites. Yet it must be kept in mind, the study did only look at one site and results must be seen in that light. The above limitations must then be taken into consideration when reviewing the following chapters. While information is based on an extensive literature review, a museum focus group and a detailed survey analysis, conclusions and inferences are influenced by study limitations and the author's own biases. To assist in substantiating this work, further research is needed in the area of dark tourism.

DATA ANALYSIS AND RESULTS

Research for the study occurred in two interrelated steps. First, a focus group took place where six museum staff members were interviewed regarding their thoughts on visitor motivation. Information garnered from the meeting was then applied to a survey mailed out to the sample. Subsequently, analysis of the data took place in two separate steps: of the focus group and the survey. In this chapter, results from the focus group and survey are discussed on a basic level. Observations are made simply on the findings: Chapters V and VI however, do go into more detail. Chapter V provides a discussion of the results while Chapter VI summarizes the conclusions of this study, the implications for further research and the implications for dark tourism managers and administrators.

FOCUS GROUP ANALYSIS AND RESULTS

A focus group was utilized in this study as an integral step in the survey design. The literature on thanatourism and dark tourism gives limited understanding of why individuals attend such sites; therefore, it is important to gain a broader perspective on visitor motivation. Museum staff, docents, and volunteers encounter visitors on a daily basis in an intimate manner. Hence, it was believed that they could provide additional insights into why visitors come to the Holocaust Museum Houston specifically and sites of dark tourism in general.

These insights were then woven into the survey questions. From the focus group discussion, sixteen themes emerged. These themes were recurrent topics discussed by focus group participants. Given their repetition by a variety of individuals, they were considered to be important concepts and therefore analyzed. Much of what was discovered correlated to what was found in academic and popular writings. Of the sixteen major themes, ten were found in the literature review: death and dying, education, exhibits, media, personal connection, morbid curiosity, remembrance, history, survivors' guilt and catharsis. This reinforced the original variables intended for the survey and therefore they were included as questions. Furthermore, motivation, an eleventh and separate theme, was found during analysis; however, participant discussion in that area focussed on previously mentioned themes. Three of the remaining themes were considered site specific and were not included in this survey.

These included visitor types, visitation dates and visitation duration. While each theme could provide insight into motivation, in themselves they were not actual motivators. Finally, two additional themes surfaced during analysis: hope and change. Change was expressed as a post-visit response versus a motivation to come to the museum, and was therefore not included in the survey. However, hope was expressed as a motivation during the focus group. Meeting survivors and witnessing others in a worse predicament could provide individuals with hope that they could survive their own, personal ordeals. Due to this potential motivation for visitation, hope was included in the survey.

Visitor Types

The results were unanimous that the Holocaust Museum Houston attracts a diverse composition of visitors. As one docent commented, the museum attracts, "All kinds of people". From gang members and sociology students, to nurses and quilters, visitors from all walks of life visit the museum.

Visitation Dates

Although the museum's clientele varies widely, spring is reported to be the busiest time of year for visitation to the museum. This is in part because Holocaust education takes place in the spring. Elementary school groups visit the museum on field trips while older students make use of the museum's library as term papers come due. Spring is also reported to be the busiest time of year due to spring break. The 2002 break saw 2,500 visitors come to the museum. In addition to spring break, museum staff also report other holidays as being busy periods. Memorial Day and July 4th report high visitation, as does Mother's Day. In the amazed words of one staff member, "And another funny thing, odd thing, is that on holidays, for instance. Well not real holidays, but Mother's Day for instance. It's packed. And who would think you would come to take your mother to the Holocaust Museum. But there are".

Visitation Duration

Although some visitors stay three hours, the majority of people at the museum visit for two to two and half-hours.

Death and Dying

Although the literature on visitor motivation does not directly maintain that death and dying influence visitation to sites of death and disaster, the author theorizes that it does play a role in people's interest in the subject. Furthermore, the literature on death and dying supports the notion that some sectors of North American society may not have a deep understanding of either process. Some segments of contemporary society have placed dying individuals into hospitals and nursing homes, away from friends and family. Pietroni, reported that 70 per cent of the terminally ill die in institutions.

As a result, some individuals may feel separated from death and lack understanding. Insights from the focus group discussion further supported the idea that visitors may be interested in sites of death and disaster because of a lack of understanding. One participant stated that, "...in our culture we're so separated from death and most destruction that there's a fascination with seeing that". This opinion was seconded by another participant, who felt that,

- ...in the United State people don't like to talk about death. Europeans they're more used to it and if you start thinking on the way you should think, I think, the minute you're born you start dying. So it's, it's a, no way out. Can't do nothing about it. You have ten thousand dollars, you can be frozen and wait two hundred years. But the United States is bad about it. They just don't like to talk about it.

With this additional insight, it was decided to include a question on death and dying on the survey. Rather than ask outright if they thought sites of dark tourism provided an outlet for understanding death, respondents were asked to report what mechanisms contemporary society has to deal with death and dying. Included on this list were Museums and Other. From this question, we can garner an understanding how society copes with death and disaster and if museums play a role.

Interestingly, the discussion revealed one group who currently uses the museum as an education center for death and dying: student nurses. With a number of hospitals located in close proximity to the museum, it is reported that, "Nurse groups and groups of student nurses who are studying death and dying" often come into the Holocaust Museum Houston. The museum then, does provide a forum for understanding death and dying. Although these specific visitors come to the museum for the specific purpose, they are still motivated by a want to understand death and dying.

Education

Within the broad spectrum of education, two major subthemes emerged. First, is the use of interactive, sensory programmes to stimulate visitors and make the exhibits more relevant to the lives of the visitors. The museum takes a highly sensory approach to their education programmes and activities. Staff gave one instance of an artist who constructed a large butterfly out of six million plus soda tabs, one to represent each of the six million Jews who lost their lives in the Holocaust. This artwork subsequently came to the Holocaust Museum Houston as a temporary exhibit. For visiting students, it was a useful illustration using something they could relate to.

A child may not comprehend six million deaths, but he or she can grasp six million pop tabs. One focus group participant recounted when a child dropped a soda tab and the other children chastised him for dropping a real person. Another illustrative example of a sensory, relevant programme that the museum offers is the gang programme the Executive Director developed. She developed a three-day programme for gangs with the Holocaust as a backdrop for teaching as some gang members might see the parallels with the Holocaust and their lives. One participant noted these parallels.

"I just think because they, they can relate to a lot of this cause you know. But we have kids that've had their heads split open, some much worse than that, they have gun shot wounds. In the beginning, we had hard-core gang members in here and they brought everybody back because they could relate to this". Even with gangs, sensory, relevant programmes can make a difference. The second subtheme to emerge was the types of students that make use of the programmes.

Although they receive a variety of students, they predominantly see school groups, "...who have in some way been touched by the Holocaust in their education, their curriculum". From the discussion with museum staff, it is evident their programmes pull in visitors with interesting, interactive, and relevant activities. Furthermore, these programmes are integrated with the school curriculum to attract large numbers of school groups. Education appears to a key motivator to individuals coming to the museum.

Hope

Hope emerged as an unexpected topic of discussion. As a visitor motivation, it did not appear in the literature, yet it was discussed by a number of participants. However, it must be noted that the museum's proximity to a large number of hospitals may be an influencing factor. Focus group participants noted that a number of patients from nearby hospitals come into the museum. One volunteer expressed her admiration,

- And it's amazing that they would come because I've had people who have their little marks where they're going to radiation and here there. You know I can't give a tour when I am feeling bad, when I'm sick because it's just too much. But here they're in a horrible place in their lives and they choose to come here.

This visitation was explained by the fact that perhaps people felt better after a visit, that they felt hope. The fact that people have the opportunity to meet Holocaust survivors also provides a forum for hope. For those in less fortunate circumstances, "Perhaps, you know they meet a survivor...and ...that...gives them hope that they can be, grow up to be a normal being, laugh at jokes that are personal". Therefore, although the museum's proximity to numerous hospitals may influence hope being a motivator, it was included in the survey. A number of key points were raised as to the survivors themselves providing hope, and this could induce visitation.

Museum Exhibits and Displays

The museum houses a permanent exhibit that functions as the core attraction; however, it also features a number of temporary exhibits that serve to promote repeat visitation among other things.

As with the education component, experiential exhibits are reported to be the most successful. Furthermore, visitors often sight the people behind the voices as some of these individuals can also be found working in the museum on any given day. The temporary exhibits appear to have even more pull for the visitors.

Museum staff report that people come in and ask what exhibit is being featured. "And the changing exhibits believe it or not bring repeats back to an exhibit. People who have been here before, they just want come into to see what we have in our changing exhibit". Therefore, in accordance with the literature, exhibits do have the ability to pull visitors to the museum.

Media

During the discussion with the focus group, the media emerged as a tremendous influence on people's knowledge of the Holocaust, although it was recognized that this influence is both positive and negative. This knowledge in turn has the capacity to both positively and negatively impact visitation. For many school children, The Diary of Anne Frank is their first encounter with the Holocaust.

Today however, the influence of the media has expanded as more mediums become available. The movie *Schindler's List* provides a useful example. One participant revealed that, "...they used to say that Anne Frank has made, I think it was Anne Frank, there's been fifty million copies made of Anne Frank, I can get the fact number. But on one night alone, 64 million people sat down and watched *Schindler's List* uninterrupted...". This exposure impacts museum visitation, for awareness brings in visitors. Yet exposure does not necessarily have to be good.

One staff member recognized the old adage that bad press is better than no press. "It's like movie stars and they say no press is bad press because it keeps your name up there. Even during the whole Enron thing, people kept say it's not bad that y'all are so closely related to the Lay's and Enron. Your name is splashed in the *New York Times* and *Newsweek* and *Time Magazine*". Another illustration of good media exposure occurred when the museum was exhibiting quilts and giving quilts to school classes to give to a needy child. Quilters from the Houston Quilt Convention caught wind of this and immediately responded. "It's the biggest convention we have, and they heard about this, and so they gave us hundreds and hundreds of quilts so that we'd have a stack of quilts all day".

Another positive media influence to emerge from the discussion was the rise in popularity of the History Channel. The participants felt that the History Channel has opened the doors to history that were previously shut. Through its entertaining yet informative formatting, the channel has given individuals a unique perspective to the past. "You just read the words and it doesn't mean anything and you make it come alive and people are interested. The history channel cinched the deal.

You start to see history from a different point of view than just the names and dates you got in school". Discussion however, also centered on the negative effects of the media as an influencing factor for museum visitation. Although media can increase visitation, some feel that too much exposure creates the opposite effect; people are inundated with information and lose interest.

- I guess from the other side there, I know for a while there, there were a lot of Holocaust movies were coming out. Right around when

> Schindler's List came out. That was before I had been to the museum and I remember thinking that's that last Holocaust film. I know about it, I've heard about it, and I understand about, and that's all. I don't want to see anymore. So it can have the opposite effect.

Another participant went as far as to say that this over exposure in effect turned the Holocaust into a cliché. Insensitivity may also be another negative side effect of increasing media exposure. The more people see of the horrors and grim reality of the Holocaust, the less sensitive they become to it. One participant felt that, "Living in the information age and people are just bombarded with more information than I know I can hold. And it's easy to be insensitive you almost have to be.

This was seconded by another participant who explained that, "I think our world, our world is, I mean, communications, the media, you know everything has made us a little more, you know insensitive. Just watch television and they've made that would have never been made twenty or thirty years ago. Five years ago. I think the media plays a large role.

Motivation

Although museum staff can only surmise what visitor motives are, three potential motives were discussed during the focus group. First, as has been hypothesised with a personal connection, visitors come because they want to understand their connection to the Holocaust. Descendants of survivors come in looking for information because their parents will not tell them. Secondly, as presumed from the education standpoint, people come in because they want to know more, to understand.

As one participant stated, "I think a lot of time history has dark endings and you, and your education, you're teased a little bit with the history and you become inquisitive and you just want. You know the results, you already know what's going to happen but it's just going through that process of getting it down I think. I think a lot of history is dark". Thirdly, as also surmised from the literature, people are interested in exhibits, particularly the changing exhibits.

Personal Connection

Establishing a personal connection plays a large role in the operations of the museum and a number of instances were revealed during the focus group where a personal connection to the Holocaust was a motivator. One participant found that, "Second-generation survivors, you know kids of survivors, which come to the survivors' organizations to ask about where their parents were because the parents won't tell them". Many of these adult children are seeking answers to their family's history.

However, it is not just a personal connection to Holocaust survivors that motivate people to come to the museum. Some come because they had husbands, fathers or grandfathers that fought in the Second World War. The museum even receives war veterans as visitors.

One focus group participant noted, "And a lot of veterans that come in here army veterans. They come in here just to see, and probably most of them have never been here before.

They say, I'll just look in here and they want to see how they present it". Focus group participants revealed that the personal connection is key in getting their message across. By offering experiences with a personal connection they are able to make it personal and immediate.

One individual felt that the stories in the *Voices* video are the most powerful messages they have. They recounted a time when a group of children actually met one of the people behind the voice.

- And then it's really neat when one of the survivors is out there like Walter was out there today, he was walking around waiting for me, he's a survivor from the video, and the kids that came out of the movie, and there's Walter, and they were just. They thought he was their long lost brother. So emotional. Walter came in crying.

The gang programme that was implemented in the museum also works on the premise of personal connection.

Many of these children and teenagers come from violent backgrounds and able to identify with the pain of the Holocaust. More importantly, the connection is made how dangerous gangs can be. The Nazis represent a gang with ideals that almost destroyed a culture.

Catharsis

Catharsis was not a common topic in the visitor motivation literature, nor was it a common topic in the focus group. However, the literature dealing with survivors directly discussed how different people coped with their experiences. Some World War I veterans returned to battle scenes to commemorate fallen comrades and to confront their own experiences. The focus group touched on this idea.

One Holocaust survivor quoted, "Everybody gets it out from the system different ways, you know, it doesn't bother me. It bothered my brother so he start writing books so he got it out of his system. Everybody, some of them still won't talk about it". Consequently, a question was included in the survey on catharsis. Should the museum get a high number of people visiting because they have personal connections to the Holocaust or related events, perhaps then a question on catharsis may be relevant to their experience.

Morbid Curiosity

There was little consensus from the focus group on the topic of morbid curiosity, although all agreed people visit because of it. Visitors at the Holocaust Museum Houston have expressed morbid curiosity. Individuals in the Memorial Room where victims' ashes are displayed often wish to see the ashes, but are embarrassed for fear of appearing morbid. Similarly, some individuals want to meet survivors and occasionally request to see their tattoos from the concentration camp.

Although one of the volunteers was offended by the seeming insensitivity of individuals looking to see the tattoos, the survivor in the focus group did not find this morbid or disturbing. There was a divergence in the group on what causes morbid curiosity. One camp feels that morbid curiosity stems from a lack of exposure, particularly visual exposure. One participant felt that, "...there is an attraction to just to the, the morbid aspects. Because that's not something we usually see. And to read about these kinds of things, and know that these things happened.

It's a totally different thing to see a picture of it than". Conversely, other participants believe that morbid attraction occurs because we are over exposed to the morbid. One woman thought, "... there's a lot of morbidity around. September 11 and television and I'm just amazed at the things that you know, that five children drowned.

I think that children hear that from the television over and over and over. To me the morbidity is around everywhere". This was furthered by another participants who stated that, "I think it's around everywhere, but I think that part of it too, that there's so much gratuitous violence, in the movies, and in your head...". Although there is little agreement as to what morbid curiosity is and where it may come from, participants agree that it does indeed motivate individuals to visit the Holocaust Museum Houston. Hence, it was included as a survey question.

Remembrance

The idea of remembrance at sites of dark tourism appears to be especially poignant when discussed in the context of the Holocaust. Contemporary society has innumerable ways of remembering victims of tragedy: family members; oral history; photographs; cemeteries; videotapes; audio tape recordings; television footage; newspaper clippings. However, for many Holocaust victims, there is little if anything to remember them by. One focus group participant recognized,

- ...we have photographs of a tenth of the people who were related to Houston's survivors that died in the Holocaust. There's nothing to remember those people. No cemetery and no photographs. That would be ninety per cent of them. It's as though they never existed. And to think in sixty years it would be as though you never existed. Coming here, at least I have grandchildren someday that will pass this museum and say that place a lot to her. And so, it's something about being remembered that people go to.

Abraham, a Holocaust survivor and a focus group participant supported this idea, testifying, "I tell people sometime go to the memorial room it's my grandparents' cemetery. Two flags over there for my mother, my sister, my father.

And my two pairs of grandparents". Therefore, from the focus group, a consensus appears that people need a place of remembrance, a concrete symbol of what was lost, a place to pay respects and to remember. The idea of remembrance at the Holocaust museum was also highlighted by the importance of living witnesses.

It is vital that these survivors are given a voice in order to keep the memories alive, and sites such as the museum provide these voices. Museums such as the Holocaust Museum Houston are repositories for people who help keep the memory alive.

This will become increasingly important in the next twenty years as one participant noted.

- I think as survivors are getting on in the twilight of their years, I think you have a lot of people who come in just because they realize a lot of these witnesses and survivors won't be here thirty years from now...And then it's up to institutions like this to keep the memory alive because we won't have these great eyewitnesses, the Bob Dole's, the Abraham's of this world.

From the focus group discussion it becomes clear that remembrance plays an important role in Holocaust Museum Houston. It provides not only a place of remembrance for the generations directly affected by the Holocaust, but equally as important, it provides a place of remembrance for generations to come.

And with remembrance comes understanding and learning and the hope that such events will never happen again.

History

Contrary to the literature, little was said in regards to if visitors come to the museum because of an interest in history. However, participants recognized unanimously that a good teacher can spur an interest in history. Teachers that stimulate and encourage students provoke learning.

One participant noted that, "...they'll remember something they really enjoyed learning about in school and they'll come back just because of the teacher". More recently, the history channel has provided that stimulation to learn. One participant recognized that, "There are lots of people that are just more interested in history. They have the History Channel. You start to see history from a different point of view than just the names and dates you got in school". Another participant furthered this idea, stating, "You just read the words and it doesn't mean anything and you make it come alive and people are interested. The History Channel cinched the deal".

Change

One of the surprising themes that emerged from the focus group discussion was that of change. Neither the literature nor the author supposed that change would be a factor in the visitor's experience. However, a number of participants made note of how people change from when they enter the museum to when they leave.

As one individual simply stated, "They change. From beginning to end". Some felt that people were more sombre when they left and this was because, "...the museum makes it all so real. Living in the information age and people are just bombarded with more information than I know I can hold. And it's easy to be insensitive you almost have to be".

This change, however, is difficult to judge subjectively. Some visitors may experience a change in attitude yet not recognize it immediately or at all. Therefore, since people may not recognize change, it was not included on the survey.

Survivors' Guilt

Survivors' guilt is another topic that is not directly discussed in the literature and is one that the focus group also felt that was not an overriding factor. This was explained by one participant who stated,

- I've never met a person over here who's talked about it, if they came in here, we certainly didn't notice because you can't see it in their faces, it's just going to be old people. Like you don't know what they did in their past. I don't know if people, like feel guilt for it. And I think that most young people would, not all young people, but most of them would realize that there's, there's no need for a young person to feel guilty because. A young person who's apologizing to a survivor doesn't mean anything because they weren't here.

Although neither the literature nor the focus group considered survivors' guilt a motivator, it was included on the survey due to the potential of high survivor visitation. Due to the recency of the events, a high number of survivors are still alive and able to visit the museum. Furthermore, survivors' guilt is a personal issue that may not be easily expressed by individuals nor recognized by staff or volunteers.

People may therefore be experiencing guilt despite the lack of evidence. However, one respondent did envision some instances where visitors might express guilt in regards to the Holocaust. "I do think there are some religious groups that come in that will tell you they're in here because their religion didn't step up to the plate and try to prevent what went on

3

Dark Tourism: Towards a New Post-disciplinary Research Agenda

Dark tourism – that is, the act of travel to sites of death, disaster or the seemingly macabre – has attracted growing academic interest and global media attention over the past decade or so. Indeed, the term *dark tourism* as a codified research area was brought to mainstream academic consideration in an editorial by Malcolm Foley and John Lennon for the *International Journal of Heritage Studies* in 1996, and subsequently popularised in 2000 by their inspiring yet theoretically tentative book, *Dark Tourism: The Attraction of Death and Disaster*. Moreover, the increasing weight of coverage with regard to dark tourism over the past few years from the press and broadcast media, as well as the internet has been striking.

Consequently, Seaton and Lennon propose dark tourism as a contemporary leisure activity has been aggrandised by the popular press from the status of myth to meta-myth, allowing the media to "depict it, not just as a genre of travel motivation and attraction, but as a social pathology sufficiently new and threatening to create moral panic".

However, the point to be emphasised here is that, prior to the mid-1990s, dark tourism, as a *generic* term for travel associated with death, atrocity or disaster, had not previously featured in the academic literature as a specific element of consumption in periodic typologies of tourism. Of course, the study of the commodification of death has pedigree in broader sociology, anthropology and museology studies. Most notably, Rojeck introduced the concept of 'black spot' tourist sites by highlighting relationships between death sites and commercialism, whilst earlier; Walter suggested that death at a distance was a kind of voyeuristic pornography for a society in which there is no easy language for discussing death.

However, despite some early works on the study of tourist sites associated with death, an encyclopaedia entry by Seaton and a subsequent call by Stone for dark tourism research to be located within social and cultural responses to death and disaster, have controversially elaborated the range and type of sites that may be included as dark tourism. Therefore, the rapid acceptance of the subject as an academic field of study and a distinct area to scrutinise a complex array of meanings and meaning-making within tourism is, according to Seaton and Lennon, "rather akin to astronomers agreeing to recognise the existence of a new planet in a solar system, thought to have been pretty comprehensively mapped and delineated".

Meanwhile, Ryan suggests a significant level of research interest has been expressed in dark tourism, whilst Pre-ece and Price observe that "dark tourism is a relatively new area of research and many aspects still require further investigation to reveal the intricacies of the phenomenon". Sharpley and Stone also recognise the complexity and multifaceted nature of 'the darker side of travel'.

They argue that dark tourism research within a broader socio-cultural and political framework has remained limited; hence, the literature continues to be eclectic, theoretically fragile and thus inconclusive. Similarly, Seaton and Lennon note there are more questions than answers in relation to dark tourism, and "its extent and motivations, and above all the identities of its pursuants, have yet to be revealed". They go on to suggest that there is clearly a need for a much fuller exploration of the consequences of dark tourism in both general and micropopulations.

Likewise, Reader, while noting the distinction between dark tourism and the processes of pilgrimage, suggests "the dynamics through which people are drawn to sites redolent with images of death... and the manner in which they are induced to behave there... that the topic calls out for discussion". Increasingly, therefore, scholars have used dark tourism as an academic lens in which to peer at various socio-cultural practices, political and economic imperatives, as well as moral quandaries. By way of rudimentarily illustrating this increased academic endeavour, at the time of writing, I conducted a Google Scholar search using the generic term 'dark tourism', which, subsequently, generated approximately 63,900 entries, while a similar online search in March 2001 returned under 2,000 entries. However, although this academic attention is welcomed and, indeed, necessary if we are to understand this diverse phenomenon, I suggest some scholars have utilise dark tourism with undertheorised conjectures or empirically fragile frameworks to prop up phenomenological studies.

Indeed, some dark tourism research, to date at least, lacks legitimate synthesis within and beyond disciplinary boundaries. Whilst there has been much valid and important research output over the past decade or so with respect to dark tourism, some scholars have been guilty, perhaps, of lacking conviction in disciplinary positions or failing to offer genuine syntheses between disciplinary perspectives. Thus, future dark tourism research requires much firmer ontological and epistemological foundations. Consequently, I suggest that the dark tourism literature should now be purposefully grounded in broader disciplinary frameworks that attempt to explore and explain the phenomenon in a coherent and systematic manner, rather than creating tourism knowledge for creating tourism knowledge's sake.

Hence, if a fresh approach to the study of dark tourism is adopted, then so too is the ability to increase substantively to the development of a broader range of social theories and concepts, whereby a deeper understanding of dark tourism and its consequences will be provided. Therefore, the purpose of my essay is to outline a call for future dark tourism research to go beyond the usual conventions of disciplinary borders.

Adopting a post-disciplinary stance, and in order to establish a theoretically rigorous and empirically tested literature base, I argue that dark tourism research should be characterised by increased reasonableness, flexibility, integration, and freedom from established and orthodox disciplinary boundaries, constraints, and dogmas.

This emancipated research approach to the study of dark tourism production and consumption may include, but should not be limited to, a variety of socio-cultural, geopolitical, economic and historical contexts. Ultimately, dark tourism research that goes beyond disciplinary borders will allow a critical synthesis of the dynamics and practices of the phenomenon and, in turn, has potential to augment knowledge that will inform broader social theory and cultural practice. Firstly, however, an overview of dark tourism provides a context for my essay.

DARK TOURISM AND DISCIPLINARITY: TOWARDS A NEW RESEARCH STRATEGY

At its most rudimentary level, tourism may be defined simply as the *movement of people*. The study of this movement of people has emerged over the past thirty years or so as an academic success story with a knowledge base that has dramatically expanded in both depth and breadth. However, the diverse intellectual influences that are brought to bear in the study of tourism means that difficulty remains in locating tourism on the established disciplinary map. As a result, Coles et al. suggest that the debate about how tourism knowledge is produced is focussed upon whether there is a coherent and identifiable academic discipline centred on, and defined by its interest in tourism; or, alternatively, is knowledge about tourism as an academic field generated by scholars within and across established disciplines.

Of course, the arguments are too complex to discuss here, but the point I want to make is that dark tourism research – as a sub-theme of tourism studies – will not be advanced by protracted philosophical debates about whether or not the study of tourism is an academic discipline. Rather, within the context of dark tourism, "no single discipline alone can accommodate, treat or understand tourism; it can be studied only if disciplinary boundaries are crossed". Hence, as I noted earlier, because of the diverse and fundamental interrelationships that dark tourism production and consumption has with the cultural condition of society, dark tourism research now demand approaches that provide genuine academic syntheses and 'truths'. This synthesis may occur, as Jamal and Kim point out, if we differentiate between the potentials and opportunities associated with multi and interdisciplinary approaches. Notably, a multi-disciplinary research approach incorporates information that originates in specific disciplinary realms, but without the scholar stepping beyond their own disciplinary boundaries and protocols.

Conversely, an interdisciplinary approach requires scholarly incursions into specific disciplines, where inter-disciplinarity is viewed as "working *between* disciplines, *blending* various philosophies and techniques so that particular disciplines do not stand apart but are brought together intentionally and explicitly to seek a synthesis". Therefore, scholarly endeavours in tourism, generally, may be thriving through blending insights that emerge from a diverse array of multi and interdisciplinary knowledge production processes. Yet, contemporary and relevance-driven research agendas, such as dark tourism, are widening the sphere for legitimate academic scrutiny, thereby providing a rationale to reduce any insularity that tourism research may possess.

Thus, as Coles et al. note, many current themes within tourism studies are inherently transdisciplinary in nature and call for more knowledge production that is elaborated in the context of application through extended peer communities of practice, which challenge and destabilise received understandings of disciplinarity. In other words, Sayer describes the approach as *post-disciplinary* where "scholars forget about disciplines and whether ideas can be identified with any particular one; they identify with learning rather than with disciplines".

Thus, I argue it is this idea of post-disciplinarity that should drive future dark tourism studies forward, where scholars are liberated from the intellectual manacles enforced by ostensible disciplinary gatekeepers. This emancipation will encourage the valorisation of dark tourism knowledge produced in other disciplinary realms, and will "allow ideas and connections to be followed to their logical conclusions, not to some contrived or preordained end point determined by artificial disciplinary strictures". In short, dark tourism scholars adopting a post-disciplinary mode of enquiry will be able to contribute to a broader variety of contexts, and will be able to reject the regulatory measures imposed by artificial paradigm parochialism.

Therefore, postdisciplinarity dark tourism studies will encourage a new hybrid of research directions, each more flexible and integrated in terms of knowledge production – a point I discuss in more detail shortly. However, my call for new flexibility and integration within dark tourism research is not intended to be an intellectual carté blanche. Rather, as Coles et al. argue, whilst post-disciplinarity may reject the requirement for disciplines, the approach is not an academic 'free-for-all' and, thus, demands a degree of auto-regulation. Particularly, Coles et al. suggest a number of principles should guide post-disciplinary approaches, namely: they are framed by reference to what preceded them and by four components of interests, competencies, world-views. Certainly, with regard to the latter, post-disciplinary dark tourism research should be viewed as possessing flexible terms of reference to academic collaborations and dialogues. Hence, these modifiable terms of reference and subsequent topic areas for potential dark tourism investigations are now the focus for the remainder of my essay.

POST-DISCIPLINARITY AND DARK TOURISM: NEW RESEARCH DIRECTIONS

In some subject areas, most notably the study of political economy and its fundamental interrelationship with globalisation, an attempt has been made to establish flexible approaches to scholarly enquiry. Specifically, Hay and Marsh provocatively suggest three new orientations to the study of the global political economy, which, in turn, have interesting possibilities to the social scientific study of tourism generally and, to dark tourism in particular.

Briefly, and within a political economy context, these new flexible research orientations suggest:

- *'Old problems, new approaches'* – there has not been a substantive shift in the nature of the political and the economic, yet a fresh perspective is required to improve analyses of past and present transformational processes within politics and economics.
- *'New problems, old approaches'* – there has been a substantive shift in the contemporary condition of political economies, but old modes of enquiry remain methodologically valid though challenges remain in how they are appropriated to explain contemporary conditions.
- *'New times, new political economy'* – there has been a substantive shift in the contemporary condition of political economies and cannot be readily explained by existing modes of analysis and bodies of theory.

Of course, these modifiable research orientations suggest that where limitations exist within the old political economy, scholars are required to go beyond current and established disciplinary boundaries in order to exploit new modes of knowledge production. Thus, in effect, the first and third approaches imply that formally trained political economists, with an exclusiveness and orthodoxy that such training entails, should not solely advance research in political economy.

Importantly, however, Coles et al. apply this line of thinking to tourism studies and, in particular, they argue that tourism should be re-orientated with the concept of modern mobility as a central unifying construct. Notwithstanding, if we follow similar lines of thought for dark tourism studies, I argue it is possible to identify instances whereby each of the three approaches has significant analytical potential for dark tourism and, subsequently, can contribute to a post-disciplinary research agenda. Firstly, with respect to dark tourism, I contend that new approaches are required to an established and enduringly old research issue, although I suggest the principal issue here is the requirement to inject fresh analytical impetus. For example, sites of death have long been a feature of the tourism landscape.

Indeed, historically, early dark tourism may be identified as places of pilgrimage, with bygone tourists/pilgrims visiting sites associated with religious figures. However, sites of contemporary death and of the 'significant other dead' have often become places of secular pilgrimage – the consequences of which have yet to be fully revealed. So, without embracing insights from religious studies, history, anthropology, sociology or geography, for instance, we may not be able to understand fully dark tourism and its fundamental interrelationships with broader issues of secularisation, spirituality, or memorialisation. Secondly, in the area of the alleged growth of dark tourism, whether through increased supply or demand, old approaches are still relevant to solving new research problems.

For example, is dark tourism simply a result of neo-liberal market forces or, alternatively, is there an increased demand evident to visit media inspired death sites? Whilst the touristification of death may be seen as a current issue, transgressing into subject disciplines that have a longer and richer heritage of exploring capitalism, economics and marketing can broaden and strengthen our understanding of dark tourism within a contemporary visitor economy. Finally, it is often difficult to ascribe a particular subject to a specific categorisation. Indeed, as dark tourism is characterised by a diverse range of global visitor sites and relative tourist experiences and, despite increased academic endeavours, the question remains as to whether dark tourism is an established research theme.

In short, is dark tourism a long-term academic project still in progress? Alternatively, is dark tourism substantively different to previous times – that is, is there is a significant disjuncture between past and present forms of dark tourism – and hence, in requirement of fresh and altogether new analytical approaches? Moreover, it is perhaps in the third approach that the greatest need for flexibility in knowledge production is required. Indeed, contemporary dark tourism does *not* present death *per se*, but rather represents *certain kinds* of death.

Thus, within secular societies that are often labelled death denying – a term rooted in life-prolonging medicinal techniques and pharmacopoeia, as well as disposal of the dead management – death and dying has largely been relocated from the public realm to a private world of medical and funerary professions. However, popular cultural representations of 'significant other death', such as those found within dark tourism, are bringing to the fore issues of how contemporary societies both represent and deal with mortality and the ethics of doing so. Consequently, moral criticism from commentators such as Pagliari lament that whilst society has been *death-denying* due to attitudes towards medicine and mortality, we have subtly transgressed to an era of *death-defying*, where the emphasis on health education carry promises of corporeal extension. Furthermore, Pagliari argues that we are now entering a *death-deriding* age, where death is mocked, commercialised and sold for the sake of art and entertainment.

Therefore, adopting Hay and Marsh's third approach, and the flexibility it entails, the crucial research issue of how dark tourism is influencing and influenced by contemporary perspectives of morality and mortality needs to draw upon discipline areas such as thanatology, deontology, and teleology. Ultimately, a 'new times, new dark tourism studies' perspective will witness a new body of knowledge emerge that can explore fundamental interrelationships between dark tourism and the cultural condition of society, as well as dark tourism as a contemporary institution that mediates mortality and morality. Of course, none of the three approaches outlined should be privileged at the expense of the others but, rather, each of the three research orientations is complementary within a post-disciplinarity research philosophy.

As Coles et al. point out, there should not be "a misguided search for the next 'meta-approach' as past precedents with paradigms may have otherwise suggested". Additionally, the specific issues I have raised are not the only concerns affecting dark tourism at present. Indeed, there are gaps in our knowledge of how dark tourism places are contested, memorialised and politicised, as well as commercialised. There are also omissions in the dark tourism literature that scrutinise the 'dark tourist' experience in a variety of socio-cultural contexts, as well as a lack of empirical data on motivations to visit such sites, and the consequences and implications thereof. Hence, I suggest the embracement of postdisciplinary research frameworks and adoption of new research orientations, such as the three approaches outlined earlier, can begin to address these issues.

More specifically, the nature of many dark sites and the conflicts, tragedies or disasters they represent, point to a number of interrelated issues that demand investigation and understanding. Particularly, these general research directions should include:

- *Ethical/moral issues:* A key question relating to many dark sites and attractions often focuses upon whether is it ethical to develop, promote or offer them for touristic consumption. Significant debate, for example, surrounded the construction of the viewing platform at Ground Zero, enabling casual or even voyeuristic visitors to stand alongside those mourning the loss of loved ones, whilst the proposed construction of a large Tsunami Memorial in the Khao Lak Lamu National Park in Thailand has been highly controversial. More generally, the human rights of those whose death/grief is commoditised or commercialised through dark tourism also represents an important moral dimension deserving consideration.
- *Media/promotional issues:* Many dark tourism sites and attractions are, in a sense, 'accidental'. That is, they have not been purposefully created or developed as tourist attractions but have become so for a variety of reasons, such as the fame of people concerned, the events that once occurred there or, perhaps, even the notoriety of a building. Frequently, the popularity of such sites may be enhanced by the marketing and promotional activity of businesses or organisations anxious to profit through tourism; equally, the media frequently plays a role in 'promoting' dark sites. Whatever the case, greater understanding of the relationship between the site and the media and/or promotion is required.
- *Interpretation/political issues:* The interpretation of tourist sites and attractions, in terms of both the manner in which they are presented and the information they convey, has long been the focus of academic attention. However, interpretative issues that relate to dark sites and attractions and their inherent emotive and provocative representations of death and tragedy take on extra dimensions and, indeed, possibly greater importance. Inevitably, perhaps, greatest attention has been paid to the development and interpretation of Holocaust sites and the dissonance of their (re)presented history. However, other dark tourism sites offer the opportunity to write or re-write the history of

people's lives and deaths, or to provide particular interpretations of past events. For example, Cooper explores the way in which Japan's imperial past is (re)interpreted in the context of Japanese battlefield tourism sites. Hence, the political dimensions of commemoration, and how tragedy influences the collective conscience is an integral component of dark site design and, thus, deserves consideration.

- *Management/governance issues:* Many dark sites and attractions are, by definition, places where individuals or numbers of people met their death, by whatever means. There is, therefore, a need to manage such places appropriately based upon an understanding of, and respect for, the manner of the victim(s) death, the integrity of the site and, where relevant, the rights of the local community. Additionally, appropriate consideration should be given to the meaning or significance of the individual(s) concerned and the place of their death to those wishing to visit. It may be necessary, for example, to control or restrict access to a site. For example, the public are allowed to visit the house and grounds of Althorp, where Princess Diana was born and raised; however, access to her burial place on an island on the estate is not permitted. In the extreme, action that is more drastic may be required, such as in the case of 25 Cromwell Street, Gloucester, England, the home of Frederick and Rosemary West and site of multiple murders by the couple. In 1996, following their trial and imprisonment, the house was demolished and the site transformed into a pathway to prevent it becoming a ghoulish shrine.
- *Socio-cultural/thanatological issues:* Many dark sites and attractions, which exist within a plethora of geopolitical and socio-cultural contexts, have implications and meanings for the broader cultural condition of society. Specifically, questions need to be asked of the role dark tourism plays within the broader secularisation of society, especially in relation to how people, both individually and collectively, confront grief and trauma and, subsequently, contemplate death and dying.

CONCLUSIONS

The social scientific study of places and of people visiting sites of death, disaster or the seemingly macabre has witnessed an academic eruption over recent years. Much of this increased research, as noted in my earlier overview of dark tourism, has a profundity that can and, undoubtedly, will contribute to broader social theories and to our understanding of cultural dynamics. However, I have also suggested that some dark tourism research has been characterised by a banality that either illustrates deficient conceptual underpinning or provides for limited disciplinary synthesis. Thus, in order to assuage any structural deficiencies in dark tourism as a coherent body of knowledge, I have argued for the adoption of post-disciplinary research perspectives within a variety of dark tourism research issues and contexts. That said, however, academic disciplines are enduring and entrenched features within intellectual landscapes and institutions. In many instances, scholars researching 'new' subjects attempt to elevate their field of academic study to disciplinary status, particularly as a means of demonstrating academic eminence.

Quite simply, this should *not* be the case for dark tourism. Rather, I suggest it is time – as with tourism studies in general – to consider dark tourism knowledge production to go beyond the restrictive dogma and parochialism of disciplinarity. In other words, dark tourism because of contemporary conditions of society, requires scholars to transgress traditional disciplinary borders, and to adopt approaches characterised by increased reasonableness, flexibility and inclusivity. As I have argued, and drawing upon the work of Coles et al. and Hay and Marsh, post-disciplinarity dark tourism research does not entitle an intellectual 'free-for all'; rather it accentuates the need for dark tourism issues to be rigorously researched to logical conclusions rather than being dictated to by disciplinary policing. The past decade has witnessed a burgeoning of the dark tourism literature. Much of this output is extremely useful in the sense it has commenced an examination of the contemporary commodification of death, as well as the much broader and, arguably, more important issues that affect society and culture.

In order for this to continue into the next decade, I have suggested that a crucial dark tourism research agenda needs to be post-disciplinary in nature and flexible in research orientation. As such, I have proposed important, though not necessarily exclusive, components of a potential dark tourism research agenda that are critical to building a post-disciplinary approach. Ultimately, however, I offer this essay as a preliminary conversation and invitation to scholars to take up this significant task.

4

Dark Tourism—Evaluation of Visitors Experience

The phenomenon of "dark tourism" Stone has been present since ancient times when numerous spectators filled antique arenas and watched gladiator battles, as well as squares from the Middle Ages filled with spectators of mass executions. Also, according to Stone, famous battlegrounds have attracted many visitors, motivated by what seem to be the same factors as visitors today consider when visiting and inspecting sites of suffering, mass executions, war horros, public figure executions, dungeons, torture musems etc. Mac-Cannell mentions the morgue, as a typical Parisienne tourist attraction of middle class citizens at the turn of the nineteenth to the twentieth century. Also, another popular Paris-ienne attraction was an animal slaughterhouse.

Stone and Sharpley state that members of the western society facing death and suffering at a certain distance were conditioned by the very state of that society. Further-more, Stone and Sharpley claim the motivation and experiences of visitors of thana-tological tourist attractions are conditioned by socio-cultural environments in which the vis-itors find themselves in their everyday lives. Rieger considers tourists constantly looking for new experiences, out of fear of internal "emptiness"; how that emptiness is filled observing suffering and how the experience affect the visitors will be shown through the research.

Every thanatological tourist attraction is thematically predetermined by an event from history and on its own, attracts visitors with vari-ous profiles. Kušen believes that tourist attractions are a magnet that runs the touris-tic system and determines the development of tourism in a destination. According to Jadrešiæ, a touristic experience belongs in the socio-cultural need of the modern man and rep-resents a long-term investment in the sense of acquiring knowledge of other cultures, expe-riences and other elements permanently imprinted in the memory of an individual.

Hughes states that the lack of classic curator practice in destinations where thanatologically themed attractions can be found, brings the modern visitor to unexpected experiential paths. It is recommended to research and evaluate the experineces of Croatian visitors of thana-tological tourist attractions at certain parts of the world, that have been dealing with motiva-tions and experiences of visitors of thanatological tourist attractions, most of which are from Anglo-Saxon countries.

Also, it is interesting to look over the economic potential of such tourist attractions, in order to preserve the existing or form new ones, primarily on the for-mer Yugoslavian territory.

A qualitative research through semistructured interviews of Cro-atian visitors of thanatologic tourist attractions, in order to come to the realization what the experiences while visiting a thanatologically themed tourist attraction are, also whether that experience creates a need for another visit to the same or similarily themed attraction. Using research, it shall be attempted to show at which rate thanatological themes are incorporat-ed in tourist attractions as well as being considered part of the cultural or historical heritage.

CLASSIFICATION AND CATEGORIZATION OF THANATOLOGICAL TOURIST ATTRACTIONS

According to Kušen and his primary classification of tourist attractions, protected cultural-historic heritage, the culture of life and work as well as famous people and histor-ic events are specially extricated. A detailed tourist classification of culturo-historic tour-ist attractions, according to Kušen classifies cemeteries, cemetery parks, memorial areas and structures, in the class of immovable monuments, charateristically independent of the theme of the event that initiated the making of a certain attraction. As opposed to Kušen, Dann additionally characterizes tourist attractions and para attractions through the sub-ject of "dark tourism" into several areas as: danger-ous places, haunted houses, fields of death, tours of torture and exhibits with thanatological themes. Thanatological tourist attractions are also possible to characterize considering their content and distance from the event itself that represents the tourist attraction's basis.

Miles states how the area of Auschwitz-Birkenau concen-tration camp was *darker* as opposed to the Holocaust Memorial Museum in Washington, in itself giving the tourist experience such a marker. This means that thanatologically themed tourist attractions can be differentiated through the intensity of the tourist experience after visiting such a tourist attraction itself.

DARK TOURISM – IN RELEVANT LITERATURE

Thurnell-Read analyses experiences of young visitors of thanatological tourist attrac-tions linked to the Holocaust. He chooses, as a geographical research area, the concentration camp Auschwitz-Birkenau, near Krakow in Poland. The key questions to which the research tries to find answers are various motivational factors that initiated the visit to such a tourist attraction, descriptions of conduct in a place of mass executions as well as experiences after the visit. In order to receive answers to the questions, the research uses a qualitative method.

The data is collected by method of semistructured interviews on a sample of eight respond-ents, male and female, between the ages of 18 and 24. The respondents are natives of Ameri-ca, Australia and Canada; all the interviews have been conducted in Krakow *in situ*. The con-clusion to the research is that the visit to the tourist attraction was not a first, but secondary intention, a friend's or acquaintance's recommendation.

Hughes discusses facing the subject of genocide through tourist activities. The geographical research area is the ominous Tuol Sleng prison in Phnom Penh, Cambodia. The starting point of the research is that the existing theory of dark tourism is not adequate in understanding the motivation, conduct and experiences of the visitors of such tourist attrac-tions. The author believes that it is not enough to suggest that modern tourist are attracted to unconvetional tourist attractions, merely for their nature differentiating them from social-ly acceptable ones. Hughes uses the qualitative method in the research. The data is collect-ed through interviews on a sample of visitors of the Tuol Sleng museum.

The size of the sam-ple is not mentioned, but it is discernible that there are male and female visitors between the ages of twenty seven and fifty two years. Interestingly, some respondents have experienced a more prominent motivation to actively participate in non-government organizations, to help the injured, after visiting the museum. Also, some of the respondents have taken concrete humanitarian steps by donating clothes they have taken on the trip or voluntarily donated blood in a local Cambodian hospital. Based on those results, it is possible to conclude how a visit to a thanatological tourist attraction of that kind significantly magnifies the feeling of empathy in a visitor. Hughes has, like Thurnell-Read limited herself to one thanatol-ogoically themed tourist attraction as well as a population sample with a tourist experience based solely on the visit to the above mentioned tourist attraction. Although the size of the sample is not precisely defined, we can assume that it is too small a sample of respondents, considering the number of quotes taken from the interview transcripts.

Stone discusses the concepts of touristic offers in the field of dark tourism. It is thought that thanatological tourist attraction can be differentiated according to the experi-ence intensity, during and after the visit to such a tourist attraction.

The starting point of such a research represents a concrete and all encompassing classification of tourist attractions,that will contribute to a better understanding of tourist offer and demand in the sphere of dark tourism. Also, it will give pointers for future research of tourist motivation and experi-ence on this type of tourism. External sources of secondary data are a key basis for achiev-ing results and the author is counting mainly on published studies on dark tourism etc. The assumption on differ-entiation of intensity of a tourist experience stems from Miles' study, in which the author discusses on the big difference between associating death and suffering with a certain location and the location of the actual event.

As an example, he uses comparison between the concentration camp Auschwitz-Birkenau near Krakow and the Holocaust – a memori-al musem in Washington, and claims how the touristic experience in Auschwitz is far more intense than the one in Washington. Considering that, Stone classifies the touristic offer of dark tourism, taking into account the main characteristics of such a tourist product. Using the above mentioned parameters, Stone makes an additional differentiation of the touristic offer in a way that differs seven possible categories of touristic offers associated with dark tourism, and these are: fun factories, exhibits, dungeons, laying ground, sacrals, conflict areas and camps. Also, the author points out the possibility of different rates of intensity and motivation in visiting such tourist attractions.

Stone and Sharpley consider the deficit in scientific literature on offers themati-cally based on dark tourism. Even though in recent years the interest for such a theme is ris-ing, the authors believe that the focus of the study is primarily the offer on thanatological-ly themed content, while paying demand little or no attention, using anthropological studies as a reference, as well as studies on the area of dark tour-ism etc. In order to gather as precise references as they can for future research, Stone and Sharpley explore ties between views on death from a socio-cultural standpoint of mod-ern society and that same society's facing death, through a tourist activity in a thanatolog-ical surrounding. In order to achieve results, Stone and Sharpley use internal and external sources of secondary data, *i.e.* already published studies on the subject of dark tourism and anthropological tourism.

Stone and Sharpley in the end believe how a visit to thanatological tourist attractions awakens in visitors a consciousness of value for one's own life, disregard-ing the fact that such attractions are primarily about death and dying, which in itself is an answer to a complex question of motivation, and pointers for researching touristic demand, as well.

The exhibit of plasticised body parts and cadavers named "Body Worlds" is the subject of Stone's research, in which he analyses experiences from visitors of the mentioned exhibit in April 2009, in the O2 Arena, Greenwich, London. Stone bases the research on the fact that there is not enough published studies on the subject of society's perception on death through a leisure activity, like exhibits facing them with their own mortality.

The author conducts a qualitative research using the semistructured interview method and addi-tionally uses the method of covertly observing the visitors of the exhibit. The sample con-sisted of seventeen adult respondents, eight male and nine female, from America, France, Poland and the United Kingdom. The study was conducted in London, *in situ*, from April 20 until April 22, 2009. The conclusion of the study was the mediation of exhibit offers relat-ed to thanatology with the facing of one's mortality at such exhibits or similar tourist attrac-tions.

As a control group in this study, the author mentions a small sample of respondents. Additionally, the study is designed in a way that does not encompass the whole area of dark tourism, only the experiences of visitors of a certain exhibit, in this case "Body Worlds", London. As a recommendation for future studies, Stone mentions the perception of mortal-ity in secular societies. For the purpose of her Master's degree paper, Yuill explores the motivation of visitors of tourist attractions thematically linked to death and accidents. The study was con-ducted in the Holocaust musem in Houston, Texas, USA. The purpose of the study was sep-arated into three parts, depending on type and achievement.

Taking into account literature on psychoanalysis, Yuill delves into a discussion on the survivors' guilt, which surfaces with participants as well as *post festum* viewers. Considering the limitations of today's studies on the subject, Yuill uses two methods of gathering primary data, using a focus group and a questionnaire, on a systematic sample of visitors of the Holocaust muse-um in Houston. The focus group was questioned in the Holocaust museum in situ, while the questionnaire was conducted via e-mail.

The results of the study show that the main motiva-tion of the visit to the musem was education and memories of historic events, as well as a con-firmation of one's national identity. As for future studies, Yuill recommends a more in-depth analysis of motivation of visitors of thanatologically themed tourist attractions connected to the Holocaust, before these are compared to motivations to thanatologically themed tour-ist attractions connected to some other subject. The limitation of the study is the short time period in which it was conducted as well as the sample.

PURPOSE OF THIS CHAPTER AND RESEARCH METHODS

The main purpose of this study is to test and see what the experiences are of tourists after a visit to thanatological tourist attractions, *i.e.* attractions associated with death, suffering and pain.

The starting hypothesis of the study is that the experience of the visit is a cultur-al act; the experience of the visit to a thanatological tourist attraction adds to a better under-standing of the general subject and generates a need for a repeated visit to the destination, as well as the notion that a visit to a thanatologically themed tourist attraction is determined by theme, not by the character of the attraction.

The answers resulted from semistructured interviews are one of the attempts of using a qualitative method of research to come to a conclusion whether visits to a thanatologi-cal tourist attraction contribute to a better understanding of the broader subject to which a certain thanatologically themed tourist attraction is connected and whether thanatological tourist attractions are part of the socio-cultural heritage. Also, the study will attempt to gain a structured view on a visit to a destination with thanatological attractions, especially to test whether such a visit generates the need for another visit where there is an attraction of such characteristics.

In addition to that, it will be attempted to show a possibility of generating the need for a visit to a tourist attraction connected to a certain theme, like the Holocaust in its basic and broader sense, wars and conflicts, various accidents with mass suffering and so on. An additional goal of the study is to come to a conclusion on the profitableness of a thanato-logical tourist attraction at a certain location.

In order to ensure as reliable results and conclusions as possible as well as thorough hypotheses, a qualitative study, with elements of primary and secondary research was used. Also, the method of semistructured interviews on an appropriate sample was used for the needs of collecting data in the primary study.

All respondents are experienced travelers, with a rich touristic background, that have visited some thanatologically themed tourist attractions in certain parts of the world.

The semistructured interview is similar to a conversation, and more flexible, allowing us to skip subjects and control the conversation, pointing it in the right direction, with some prepa-ration aforehand, apart from the non-structured interview that does not require prepara-tion and where there is the possibility of the respondent steering the course of the conversa-tion away from the subject at hand. The structured interview consists of asking closed questions and thereby limiting the possibility of adapting to the situation. In this study, the method of strucutred interviewing is not appropriate for getting qualitative data.

The semistructured interview consisted of nine questions. All the respondents were asked the same questions, and the avarage duration time of the interview was six minutes. The study was conducted in Zagreb, in Croatia. The conversations were taped with a digi-tal voice recorder and lated transcribed. The respondents are an appropriate sample, N=10, *i.e.* five male and five female respondents that have visited some thanatologically themed tourist attractions in certain parts of the world.

Limitations in the primary study are foremost the geographic heritage of the respondents, the number of available respondents, the time needed to conduct the interviews and the lim-ited budget for research. An additional limitation of the study, which surfaced during the process of interviewing, was the question on again visiting a thanatologically themed tourist attraction. That particular question was not precise enough, because the terms tourist destination and tourist attraction are, to most respondents, the same. This is the main reason why some of the answers were pointed towards tourist attractions and others to tourist desti-nations, disregarding the course of the conversation. Even though the interviews were con-ducted in an informal setting, a part of the respondents, *i.e.* the thirty-seven and below age group admitted to feeling uncomfortable with the conversation being taped, even though they were forewarned about the taping as well as methods and goals of the interview. The result of the above mentioned are short answers and avarage duration of around six minutes per respondent, which also represents a certain limitation to the study of the subject. The main limitation in the secondary study was the insufficient number of published studies on the subject of experiences of tourist who have visited thanatologically themed tourist attrac-tions.

Using the method of semistructured interviews on an appropriate sample, ten visitors of thanatological attractions have been interviewed, who have visited the aforementioned on certain parts of the world. The interviews were conducted during December 2010 and Jan-uary 2011 in Zagreb, *in situ*. The semistructured interview consisted of nine questions, *i.e.* three questions for every hypothesis. All ten respondents answered the same questions.

According to most respondents, the visit to a thanatological tourist attraction was moti-vated by cultural need. Several respondents have mentioned the fact how historic events like wars, mass executions and so on, severely influence the very culture of a nation, which means that the visits, thematically connected to such an event, were very much motivated by cultural needs.

The question whether the thanatological attraction was part of the touristic offer, all respondents have answered positively.

Visiting a musem is, in my opinion, the highest form of culturally educating oneself. Of course, there is a moment of pure interest, depending on the theme

– you're interested, but in my opinion, this is about cultural education. Apart from the fact that it's about the Holocaust, it's a vital part of histo-ry!

Briefly, the study shows how thanatological themes are indeed part of tourist attractions and considered a vital part of the cultural or historic heritage. Kušen discusses a very broad theoretical approach in keeping track of cultural monuments. The existing classifica-tion by Kušen on the cultural-historic heritage includes memorial sites and build-ings, like cemeteries, necropoli, historic sites and locations, buildings connected to histor-ic figures and events etc. Seeing this, the question presents itself: are thanatological tourist attractions monuments of culture at the same time? This question was answered positively by most participants.

If a monument of culture is a monument to history and victims and making sure it never happens again, then yes, because it represents the culture of a certain people, for it happened in their history and influenced them. The visit to a thanatological tourist attraction can most definitely be considered an extraordinary touristic experience.

Disregarding the motivation and previous knowledge on the subject that initated the existence of such a tourist attraction, it can be considered that the visitors will better understand the events thematically connected to that attraction. Also, one of the elements of the study is the need to return to a broader destination from where

the certain attraction is situated. Taking this into account, the respondents were asked three questions that confirm or reject the hypothesis. The question whether the need to visit the tourist attraction stemmed from a search of a more in-depth analysis of the theme that has happened at that destination, was answered positively by all participants.

Yes, it certainly does, I mean, after such a visit you have the need to further investigate what hap-pened in that country, what is connected to that destination directly and altoghether just investigate the history of this country and the cultural development in that state, at that time.

When asked wheter they would return to the destintion, after visiting one, the respondents' answers differ from one another, according to the destination they have visited and their per-sonal interest in it. If the destination is one of the world's metropolises, the return to that des-tination is imminent, disregarding the visited thanatological tourist attraction. Also, if the sub-ject is closely related to a personal interest for further research or recommendations to others, the respondents would return to the same destination, *i.e.* same thanatological tourism attraction.

Yes, I have the need to share it with someone and would love to go with someone and show someone all of that, and when you go for the second time – you have a chance to see things you may not have seen before, maybe because of the schedule, fatigue or something else. I think a second visit is a must, which I'm sure is not the case every musem, but this one is worth a second visit.

A destination whose allure is simply the thanatological tourist attraction does not repre-sent a targeted tourist destination that visitors would visit again. The reasons for this are the existence of other tourist attractions in the world (unrelated to the thanatological theme) and an unsufficient offer of other touristic content in the vicinity of the destination. The relation-ship towards the subject, which is the basis for the making of a certain thanatological tour-ist attraction, is one of the key factors of intensity of the experience towards a certain tourist attraction.

The question how their visit has affected their relationship towards the subject after the visit, as opposed to before, respondents have answered differently, depending on the type of attraction they have visited and the level of knowledge they had before the visit.

In any case, I have more information now, and a more complete picture, I mean, it's one thing to read about it, and another to see or hear a million pieces of information from a tour guide. I would say I have a more complete picure now, as opposed to before.

It is interesting to point out the experience of a female visitor to two attactions from recent history, where much more attention was given to informing about the attraction with the more distant past, then the one whose creation witnessed in the last ten years.

For Auschwitz, you get a much heavier feeling, because it wasn't "in our time", it's a different time and you get a lot of information, and all of your previous knowledge comes togehter. Ground Zero we all watched "live", so you get more of an "inside story", but you know what happened and how it hap-pened.

In order to proove that the visit to the thanatological tourist attractions was based on the theme and not the character of the attraction, the respondents were asked three questions related to coming to a decision on visiting and future leisure plans in the field of thanatour-ism. The question on what their reasons for visiting certain attractions were, most partici-pants answered connecting the chance to visit the site while traveling somewhere else.

Well, more or less coincidentally: the idea was to travel across Eastern Europe, for financial reasons, because it is considered to be cheaper than Western Europe. Once we got there, there were some things that were historically important, Chernobil and Auschwitz, who were realtively near.

By mere coincidence, while passing through. We found out that Dachau was there, just a few miles away, so we went to see it; we were traveling from Stuttgart.

The participants would return to the destination or tourist attraction if the subject of that attraction was of personal interest, or if the subject had an abundent tourist offer of other content, non-related to thanatological themes. The respondents who have not yet visited Auschwitz-Birkenau, and have the intention of visiting such an attraction, put this destina-tion above all others.

When it comes to the price the participants are willing to pay for a visit to a certain tourist attraction, the answers were from zero do fifty Euros, or on average, fif-teen Euros. One participant said that if he were to decide to travel and visit an attraction that was far away from this current residence, the price would be irrelevant.

CONCLUSION AND RECOMMENDATION FOR FURTHER RESEARCH

Thanatological tourist attractions encompass attractions associated with death and suffering *i.e.* places of mass executions or war horror, executions of public figures, dungeons, muse-ums of torture, cemeteries, grave sites of famous people etc.

A primary and secondary study have been conducted in trying to find out whether the experience of visiting a thanatologi-cally themed tourist attraction produces the need for another visit to the same or similar site. Also, the study shows in what measure the thanatological themes are considered a tourist attraction and whether they are considered a part of the cultural or historic heritage.

The answers received using the method of semi-structured interviews show in what measure the experiences of visiting a thanatological tourist attraction contribute to a better under-standing of the broader subject and to which a certain tourist attraction is connected, as well as whether thanatological attractions are part of the cultural or historic heritage. Also, the study through interviewing show the existence of the possibility that the thanatologi-cal theme of the destination generates the need to visit a destination geographically locat-ed in another area, with a tourist attraction of the same character. Furthermore, through interviews, we gain answers connected to the possibility of developing a need for visiting a tourist attraction that is of a unique theme, such as the Holocaust, in its basic and broader sense, wars and conflicts, various accidents with consequences of mass suffering and so on.

As for the repeated visits, an additional goal of the study has an economic component, *i.e.* the information of disbursement of the thanatological tourist attraction at a certain destina-tion. According to most particiants, a visit to a thanatological tourist attraction was moti-vated by cultural need. Several respondents have said that historic events like wars, mass executions and such, significantly contribute to the culture of a certain people.

The ques-tions whether a thanatological attraction is part of the tourist destination and whether those attractions were also monuments of culture, most participants answered positively. Also, all participants consider that a visit to a thanatological attraction develops a need for a more in-depth analysis of the subject that occured at the destination.

The research has shown that the visitors would return to the destination or attraction if the thanatologic theme that initi-ated the inital visit was a subject of personal interest. Also, the participants would return to the same destination if it has an abundant tourist offer of content unrelated to thanatological themes.

If, however, the thanatological content were the only one at the destination, such a destination would not represent a targeted destination for the next several tourist travels.

The effects of the experiences during the visit in effect to knowledge before and after dif-fer, related to the type of attraction and the amount of data that one participant had received prior to the visit. The events the participants have not witnessed spark more attention dur-ing the informative period of the visit, as opposed to those in recent history.

Like Thurnel- Read's, this study shows how the visit to thanatologically themed tourist attractions was more "passer-by", because such attractions are in offer with other tourist attractions of the area. This suggests a conclusion that the offer between thanatological tourist attrac-tion doesn't represent a key factor in selecting a destination.

The participants that have the intention of visiting a thanatological tourist attraction they have not visited before mostly consider visiting places of mass executions. The price Croatian participants would pay for a visit to a certain tourist attraction amounts to an average of fifteen Euros. It is important to point out one participant's answer, who stated that the price of the entrance ticket was not important if he were able to visit a certain thanatological attraction that was of person-al interest at some time.

The participants from the study that Hughes mentioned believe how the experi-ence of visiting an area in more recent history is much more intense than those from World War II, even though they have not personally participated in them. Some of the participants, after visiting Toul Sleng Musem in Cambodia have become moti-vated to activcly participate in non-goverment organizations, while others have taken con-crete measures on site, like donating clothes or gifts.

Taking these results into considera-tion, it is possible to come to the conclusion that a visit to such a thanatological attraction raises the level of empathy within the visitor. Yuill, in her Master's paper, presents this feeling of survivors' guilt as a motivational factor that awakens the value of one's life in the visitors, disregarding the fact that the attraction is, in fact, related to death and dying, which in itself is a complex question of motivation and thus give pointers for tourist offers.

Futhermore, Stone concludes that the offer of exhibits related to thanatology mediates between facing one's own mortality and gives way for further research on the subject of per-ception of mortality in secular societies.

A significant number of thanatological tourist attractions have emerged as a result of eth-nic conflicts. According to Giddens, ethnic diversity gives way to social abundance and animosity between certain ethnic groups. The results of animosity are ethnic conflicts and genocide, like the Nazi Holocaust or Armenian genocide. After some time, in places of massive deaths, there emerge manumental areas that, with time, become tourist attractions and where, for pleasing a certain touristic need, members of historically conflicted ethnic groups gather.

Taking the above into consideration, as a recommendation for future research it is possible to suggest a qualitative research of ethnic groups who visit a certain thanato-logical tourist attraction, taking into account the ethnicity of one or the other. For example, the ratio between Bosnian and Serbian visitors of the Tunnel of Salvation in Sarajevo or the experiences of visitors of concentration camps and museums with a Holocaust theme, and considering ethnicity.

In his analysis of touristic observations, Urry states how a number of tourist pro-fessionals systematically undertake development measures to develop new objects for touris-tic observations. Taking into consideration recent history, several thanatological tourist attrac-tions have emerged on the territory of former Yugoslavia, as well as a predisposition for certain object to become such attractions.

This mainly refers to locations in Bosnia and Herzegovina, Croatia and Kosovo, where there have been many ethnic conflicts during the nineties. Foley and Lennon list several locations in Sarajavo, like the massacre of twelve civilians near the Cathedral, or Sniper Avenue, that create a business opportunity out of the tragedy of war in former Yugoslavia.

The greater area of Bosnia and Herzegovina and Kosovo also represent a targeted market for visitors whose leisure motives are researching the life and work of some public figures. The results of this study show the willingless of visitors to giving an average amount of fifteen Euros per visit to a thanatological tourist attraction.

According to Marušiæ and Prebe•ac, the very development of tourism influences the economic advancement, especially in underdeveloped and developing countries, and as a recommendation for further reseach, it is possible to single out economic research of cost and revenue of existing thanato-logical tourist attractions in countries on the territory of former Yugoslavia.

5

Significance of Dark Tourism in the Process of Tourism Development

Dark tourism is a relatively new area of tourism research. It is defined by Foley and Lennon as.the phenomenon which encompasses the presentation and consumption of real and commodified death and disaster sites.. The phenomenon has drawn substantial attention from academic research in recent years, for instance and is becoming widely recognised as a tourism niche for both tourism academia and practitioners. The definitions of the phenomenon and its components are somewhat vague and have emerged as being unnecessarily comprehensive.

Academic research focuses on a certain aspect of the phenomenon. Tarlow defines it as having the dimension of the interaction between supply and demand as.visitation to places where tragedies or historically noteworthy death has occurred and that continue to impact our lives..

Although research continues to flourish concerning the supply-side of the phenomenon, the area which concerns the social component, for instance local communities where the site is located, has been largely neglected within the current literature. Recent studies of dark tourism are concerned with depicting its concept.

Stone defines dark tourism as depending on the intensity of the interest and the actual motive to travel to see the site. His concept presents the difference between the actual sites of dark tourism and the sites which are associated with dark tourism. An instance for the former is Auschwitz and an instance of latter is the Holocaust Museum in Washington DC. He notes that places which are the sites of dark tourism are.darker.

Than the places which are associated with an actual phenomenon. Hardly any research related to the dark tourism phenomenon takes into account recent conflict and the views of those communities involved in the conflict. The relationship between the local community, the visiting of the site and the conflict is not clearly explained. Additionally, current research does not elaborate the time dimension, i. e. What is the meaning of the word recent in this context? Here it is defined as the status that still impacts on the lives of the people who live within the area and is still influenced by legislation and regulations which are the consequence of the conflict. Sites associated with relatively recent conflict and their openness to tourism has an impact on a community within the area where the site is located.

The early work of Smith and Liesle acknowledges the impact conflict has on a society. Their research illustrates a strong link between war and tourism. They depict conflict as heritage. Weaver presents the influence which war has on a tourism area life cycle, explaining that some phenomena related to war are relatively popular with the tourists and therefore influence the tourism area life cycle. Inherently, the consequence of a long-term conflict is conceptualised as a dark tourism phenomenon.

Therefore, this paper sets the discussion in the context of local communities directly involved in conflict. After the conflict they deal with tourists who come to see the sites. The aim of this research is to understand local communities and their role in the whole process of tourism development related to dark tourism.

This learning explores the process of tourism development in Belfast, the capitol of Northern Ireland, where severe troubles and political violence escalated in the period from 1967 to 1995 between loyalists as a protestant and republicans as a catholic community. The violence ended in August 1995 with the Good Friday Agreement.

According to the Agreement tourism emerged as one of six.matters for co-operation for the North-South Ministerial Council. It resulted in a creation of Tourism Ireland (TI), an organisation charged with the promotion of the tourism of both the Republic of Ireland (ROI) and Northern Ireland (NI) as one destination in a joint tourism promotion.

METHODOLOGY

The fieldwork follows a qualitative methodological approach. This is required in order to gather complex information concerning an issue of this type of tourism in a post-conflict society.

The main research method involved thematic analysis of in-depth interviews, which were previously conducted with tourism decision-makers and tour providers.

As an auxiliary method, the research employed a participant observation technique, which included political tours of Belfast. The next section presents the process of data collection and introduces the interview sample. Semi structured in-depth interviews with ten respondents were conducted over a two 2- week period in May 2006 in Belfast, Northern Ireland. Sampling criteria were as follows:

- Represent a wide range of decision-makers within the tourism industry in NI
- In NI during the trouble; Most of the interviewees worked within the tourism industry during the troubles. I2, I6, I7 started to work in the tourism industry in the period since the Good Friday Agreement. I8 joined tourism in NI in 2000.
- Recognized as key players within the industry. Their position allows them to represent the opinion of the employers in the organization
- Experience of managing tourism in the post conflict society

The most important selection criterion was that the interviewee was a decision- maker with the experience of the issues which emerged during the process. The learning aim was achieved by understanding how people involved in tourism development in the area after a political conflict perceived the whole process. In that sense, the interview sample is important to the validity of the learning.

As an auxiliary method, the researcher employed participant observation. The researcher observed three political tours in Northern Ireland and one general city tour of Belfast. The researcher found this important as it provided the learning with the details which enabled understanding of the phenomenon as a whole and linked the issues. A phenomenological research was employed in this research.

This methodological approach consists of the subject of the learning, the researcher who interprets the meanings interviewees are giving to the learning and the process of phenomenological reflection, which links the researcher to the meanings given to the phenomena. The first step in phenomenological reflection lies in conducting a thematic analysis. It gives a degree of order and systematizes the task. Ultimately, the interpretive purpose of theme is to determine the experiential structures that constitute the understanding. It is the essence of phenomenological research. Through the process of reflection on essential themes, the research resulted in phoenix tourism as a part of a wider conceptual framework which defines tourism development in the context of reconciliation after a long term political conflict and includes visitation to the sites of a political significance.

Another dimension to the dark tourism discourse is added; exploring the interaction between this type of tourism, urban regeneration and social reconciliation after the war or long-term political conflict. Therefore, this research redefines the term dark tourism as phoenix tourism. The term phoenix tourism the researcher defines as the process of social reconciliation and urban regeneration of the people and areas which were directly involved in a political conflict, having tourism development through the visiting of these sites as the main factor within the process. In analyzing the data, four major features were identified:

- Networks and partnerships
- Delivery and interpretation
- Market segmentation
- Terminology

NETWORKS AND PARTNERSHIPS

According to Selin and Chavez, crises present a significant catalyst for the partnership. As a part of a development framework of the City of Belfast, there emerged a Local Strategic Partnership (LSP) which defined its role as.promotion of reconciliation and regeneration.. It consists of the bodies which represented communities within the city of Belfast beyond ethnic space. Five boards exist; North, South, East, West and Greater Shankill.

Under LSP umbrella, there emerged a partnership between the organisations related to the West Belfast area inhabited mostly by Nationalists and the Greater Shankill area inhabited mostly by Loyalists, who were directly involved in sectarian troubles between 1967 and 1995. Partnerships are formed if there is a common vision to share. The partnership between the communities who were previously in conflict was established through tourism development. There were two main reasons for developing this partnership. Firstly, it was customers' demand. Niche markets, mainly motivated by education purposes, wanted to understand both communities' points of view on the recent political conflict. West Belfast and Great Shankill formed a partnership. In essence this was a relationship formed between former political prisoner's organisations in both areas.

- We are a community- based organization, we joined together to deliver this product, it is a market, a niche who wants it. We both share a great interest in facilitating and providing those tours. They want to hear both sides and, of course, that we will join together to deliver that. We understand each other well; both communities are having the same problem, we are from the same world
- There is a huge demand from the universities, various peace studies and conflict resolution studies. Republicans were more proactive in that project. But they cannot do it alone as those university groups want to hear both sides. Then republicans contacted us and we started thinking about tourism and political tours as well. We saw the opportunity in that as well

- There are the whole university classes. We are not just facilitating republican viewpoints, but we are also facilitating unionist viewpoints, different issues, victims, ex prisoners, a wide range, all sorts of examples

Secondly, both communities were deprived areas with common social problems. Interviewees identified the issues of unemployment, social exclusion and former political prisoners. The issues were common to both communities and they related to each other easily in that sense. According to a Belfast City Council Report, both boroughs are included in the worst 10 per cent in the UK. Tourism is, according to Szivas and Riley an attractive and accessible employment for people with various set of skills and labour intensive activity is therefore positively correlated with job provision. Those findings were important for the area which was overwhelmed with the problems of social exclusion and unemployment. Political prisoners have been experiencing legal barriers in finding jobs. Tourism presents an employment opportunity. Provision of training helps in a process of gaining collective self-esteem and confidence which is a prerequisite for any further development.

- It is very worth, I have to admit. I think more people have training, they have a better background, confidence, and their product will be stronger
- So.political ex prisoners is really discriminated in a way. It is a huge percentage of the population in West Belfast, 15 000 of them went through the jails in the past 30 years. 6 000 of them now live in West Belfast... If it wouldn't have been a conflict here, they would not have been in prison. We see it as a sizable section of our community that was discriminated against in everyday life
- They are by majority normal people, political prisoners, not criminals. The toughest remits are to secure employment for them and it was what motivated us to start with tourism jobs

It emerged that economic and social exclusion put political issues and conflict in the background. Although those two communities were in a direct violent conflict for more then thirty-five years, they managed to develop a working relationship and formalize it into a partnership. Tourism was perceived as a neutral in this case as it brought neutral people, a third party, on the scene.

DELIVERY AND INTERPRETATION

There are two distinct providers of political tours. The distinction is based on whether they are based within the local community or they are based outside. The main difference between them is related to issues of delivery and interpretation. The next section will illustrate the main characteristics of both providers. Providers based outside of the communities deliver *a sanitized version* of the conflict, a tour appealing to the generic markets. The community lacks tourism infrastructure which is necessary for generic markets. Therefore, social and economic benefits from this type of tour do not stay within the community. Tourists come in large numbers, but due to the lack of tourism facilities appealing to generic markets; they do not stay within the area. In the community there are no hotels or tourism amenities.

Furthermore, local communities are not in favour of tours provided in that way. They feel thus being stared at and in extreme cases are even hostile as it was perceived that people from the outside are exploiting the legacy of conflict. Local communities are concerned with verbal communication and mannerisms tour guides employ when interpreting the issues of the recent troubles. The verbal communication employed by tour guides when delivering the tour is important for the community. Tour guides from outside the community use language and expressions, which the community perceives as insensitive and wrong.

- They are using language which is not very appropriate and of course when local people hear it, they do not like it. These guys starved themselves to death, they committed suicide in jail, and this is not the language. People who pass by, they would stop and say, excuse me!!! They would not be so happy.

On the other hand, tour providers from the community deliver tours which are more acceptable by local community and which offer evidence of a real reconciliation between those two communities made on tourism. Tour groups organised by providers from the outside of the community tended to be large. Their size was considered as being in disproportion to the community ability to cope with their feelings.

The researcher named tourism providers from outside the community Red bus providers and referred to the whole phenomena as the.Red bus syndrome.. During the interviews red buses were often used as an example. They were easily noticed on the streets. They present the official voice, disproportionably big and different. It was a phenomenon which emerged from this analysis. The company which runs red buses is a franchise of a company that runs tours all over Europe.

In a community, the red bus was seen as a symbol of middle- class intrusion; it was brought in from the outside in order to capitalize on their struggle; it can be seen as a certain form of the history commodification. The researcher saw it as a phenomenon when tourist numbers in certain areas were growing, but the benefits derived from tourism were not staying within the area and people there were not included in delivering a tourism product and making decisions about it. The following quotes illustrate a lack of understanding between the communities on one side and official tourism bodies on the other. The official tourism authority has a positive view on the issue, i. e;

- People began to see people coming here more. For people in Belfast, one of the things people tends to notice most are city bus tours, the open top bus tours. Those small things which make people realize that the situation nowadays is becoming much more normal if you see tourism around. I always say, tourism is almost like a parameter for normality. If you see tourists here, you are becoming much more normal society

The opposed to the community based view on the issue;

- Its better that we bring people into the communities than having those big buses going around and having somebody talking about the community who is maybe even from outside the city. They don't realize, they don't know what it's like. People may have the feeling that they have been stared at, whereas if we bring people in the community, we say: Come on board, interact, you tell what your opinion is and that gives people a chance to tell the story.

The interpretation given to the issue depends on the context. To I8, *red buses* had the meaning of normalization. They symbolized a positive change. I1 perceive *red buses* as exploitation of the legacy of conflict.

MARKET SEGMENTS

Excluding a small niche segment, this learning finds that tourism associated with the recent conflict is not a motivator for visiting. However, once tourists are there, most would visit the sites. On the other side, developed tourism infrastructure, which would encourage visitors to spend more time within the area, was scarce in the community. Tourists go there to see the sites and go back to the regenerated area.

In order to develop tourism infrastructure, more understanding between local communities and local government is needed. There are two distinct types of tourists which visit these sites. Niche markets with a particular interest in exploring the conflict were young people as individual travelers, young people as a part of a university group with an educational interest in peace studies, conflict resolution or some other socio-political process, solidarity groups (Basque, Palestine, Kurds, Catalan, etc.) who shared similar political ideology and visiting friends and relatives (VFR) segment.

Another market segment is generic market. They are not motivated by political tours, but once in Belfast, they join political tours. They include leisure travelers who come to Belfast for a short break visit, congress and conferences markets, and partly VFR segment. To date, local communities have benefited only from the small niche tourism segment, particularly motivated by exploring the legacy of conflict.

They employed local tour guides and local tour providers as they were perceived to have a better understanding of the conflict. These were university and education groups and political solidarity groups, who pre-arranged the tours. Another market segment was political solidarity groups. They share some similar political issues with their own surroundings (prisoners. issues with Basque County, etc) or they share a similar political philosophy. They are interested to see a community similar to their own.

They are particularly interested in the well-being of the community and usually prefer to utilize the services provided by the communities themselves. Both niche groups are a small fraction of all the tourists coming to Belfast.

- Because constantly people come to our office from all around the world, also students, people doing their PhDs, there is a big demand for knowledge of the conflict. So we needed to create this product. There are whole classes, university classes.
- A lot of our tourists come from the Basque county, but those are the pre arranged ones and mostly from North America. More and more English are *coming over and that's very good for us. Americans, Europeans, but I probably could not put a finger and say which one is the biggest maybe the Basque.*

Parallel is drawn between Cohen's tourist typology and this classification of tourists regarding their interest in political tours. Different markets require different ways of interpretation. For generic markets, the curiosity factor is the most important motivator to take part in a political or war tour or visit a site.

During tours, most questions that tourists asked were related to the conflict.

- I think there is a factor of intrigue which ultimately links them to it. We do not have hard and fast numbers, but I think with most of the people, there is an awareness of it what has happened, this is what Belfast is known for. It ranges from just passing through to real I must come, I must see it, I want to discover every bit, and whether an ex- prisoner is here or there...

Local communities benefit by providing services to the niche markets. Generic markets took a political tour, but it was not managed by the local community. Generic markets were also the biggest proportion of the markets that visit the city. They came, saw the sites, took a few photos and went back.

This was a usual pattern here as the generic market was motivated by a real tourism experience and therefore they needed a proper tourism infrastructure.

- One more project we are working on it is about creating a proper infrastructure, creating proper restaurants, making sure people can come in, shops, as well as hotels, we are also encouraging people to set up B&BS. That's exactly what we are all about.

TERMINOLOGY

Dark tourism is evidently a concept which emerges from a developed western society perspective and associated academic discourse. Although evidence shows that in 2001, 43 per cent of the visitors came to Belfast out of curiosity, linked with the dark tourism sites, this type of tourism ascription rarely enjoys support from the governing bodies, official tourism associations and local communities, in the specific society. It may endanger the efforts to change the image of Northern Ireland.

NI is trying to put itself away from the image of troubles and in that way NI is promoting itself internationally together with ROI. Cross-border cooperation is based on the similarity between tourism products in ROI and NI.

Therefore, dark tourism was not a part of the official promotion strategy as those sites were related exclusively to Northern Ireland. People knew that the troubles happened in NI through other media sources. Tourism promotion of the sites was not a necessity in that sense. For all the reasons stated above, this type of tourism activity is not included in any official promotional activities related to tourism development and is not an integral part of the process of image formation.

However, the tourists who came to Belfast visit the sites. This research found it an opportunity towards the process of community regeneration and revitalization.

It was not regarded as a reason to visit Belfast. It was a secondary attraction, not a motivator. Tourists knew that those sites were there and if they wanted to explore them, they could, but this type of tourism would not be promoted. Visitors and tourists were coming to see the sites, but the tourism infrastructure there was not of the required level. Tourists came, saw the site and left without making a positive impact.

This learning suggests reviewing the whole concept. Dark tourism as a label and as defined in previous studies cannot resemble the true meaning of the phenomenon. It does not conceptualize community revitalization and the regeneration process. The learning found phoenix tourism a more appropriate label.

A phoenix is a mythological bird which rises from the ashes. The areas which were in the conflict were rising literally from the ashes. There were three ways tourism could assist the process of urban regeneration and social reconciliation.

Firstly, tourism infrastructure which would comply with the command of a generic market was not provided. Tourism may assist building the infrastructure and in that way directly influence urban regeneration.

- Because there was a need to create a proper infrastructure for tourism because even in West Belfast, there are no hotels in West Belfast

Secondly, the communities were deprived, with a lack of pride and self-esteem. Although they were coming to the area to see the sites of previous conflict, tourists were showing interest in the community and their way of life and in that sense bringing pride and self-esteem back to the community. Thirdly, if there was a tourism infrastructure developed, tourism may boost small businesses.

Those three outcomes could not be conceptualised under the phenomenon of dark tourism and they are not framed by any of its definitions. Tourists do not know the meaning of dark tourism. They relate their understanding to a single product, calling it a political tour or a war tour. The findings from the official tourism institutions suggest that the promotion of dark tourism will ruin the process of re-imaging.

Being labeled as *dark* resembles a pejorative nuance towards the process. On the other side, it is possible to look upon it from the other angle and give another meaning to the whole concept; there is a possibility for community regeneration, which may solve some of the already noted community problems.

- I know, but the ordinary public would not call it that name. When you call it dark tourism, the ordinary public would not know what it means. That is what you academic people call it like that. There was somebody from your university; she came to speak to me about. When she came over, she was using the terminology dark tourism as well.

CONCLUSIONS AND RECOMMENDATIONS

Dark tourism is evidently a concept which emerged from a developed western society perspective and associated academic discourse. This type of tourism ascription rarely enjoys support from the governing bodies, official tourism associations and local communities. In fact, a dark tourism concept does not resemble the real role it has in the process of tourism development and community reconciliation.

The local community areas lacked tourism infrastructure, which would encourage visitors to spend more time within the area. At the time of writing, tourists went to the sites and then go back to the city centre. This learning recommends that tours be delivered through the partnerships. This would create more understanding between local communities and authorities and assure that the benefits stay in the local area.

Local communities benefited only from a small niche particularly motivated to explore the legacy of conflict. These were university and education groups and political solidarity groups.

They were a small fraction of all the tourists who were coming to Belfast and who were visiting the area. If official tourism institutions supported local communities in delivering political tours, then it may be possible to say that tourism could help revitalize the communities. In 2006, tourism development was concentrated around the areas which were already privileged with urban regeneration.

With tourism development focused only on the privileged areas, the gap between privileged and deprived become even wider. This research shows that it was primarily because a strong partnership between suppliers within the area and local authorities which would support tourism development was not established. Secondly, there was a lack of trust in the communities and their ability to deliver the product.

Thirdly, as this type of tourism was not planned to be promoted internationally, its existence was officially not recognized. This research suggests employing local tour guides to deliver the tour, coming in smaller groups and paying a respect through using a politically correct language and manners with a possibility for interaction with locals during the tour.

If the tour was delivered by the provider from the outside of the community, there was a certain levy to be implemented. With its pejorative understanding by locals, dark tourism would not be a part of the process of image formation and recovery.

The learning concludes that official tourism bodies need to recognize the existence of the demand for knowledge of the conflict, fully integrate the local community in decision making and provide the area with appropriate tourism infrastructure, resulting in community revitalization and regeneration. Tourist interest suggests that this type of tourism is a chance for local communities to directly participate in tourism development.

With respect to the academic discourse, the learning finds the concept of *phoenix tourism* to be more appropriate in the process of destination development after the conflict. This research defines phoenix tourism as a process of destination regeneration, rehabilitation, reemerging and revitalization after a long-term political conflict. Associated terms with phoenix tourism are phoenix destinations, phoenix sites and phoenix tourists.

It is a part of history; it is what made those places what they are. As the main characteristic of phoenix tourism is social reconciliation and urban regeneration, it does not fit in Stone's dark tourism spectrum which is made exclusively upon tourists and their perceptions. The places are rising from the ashes literally. Just like the mythological bird the phoenix.

6

Consuming Dark Tourism

Travel to and experience of places associated with death is not a new phenomenon. People have long been drawn, purposefully or otherwise, towards sites, attractions or events linked in one way or another with death, suffering, violence or disaster. The Roman gladiatorial games, pilgrimages or attendance at medieval public executions were, for example, early forms of such death-related tourism whilst, as Boorstin alleges, the first guided tour in England was a train trip to witness the hanging of two murderers.

Similarly, MacCannell notes visits to the morgue were a regular feature of nineteenth century tours of Paris, perhaps a forerunner to the 'Bodyworlds' exhibitions in London, Tokyo and elsewhere that, since the late 1990s, have attracted visitors in their tens of thousands. It is also a phenomenon that, over the last century, has become both widespread and diverse. Smith, for example, suggests that sites or destinations associated with war probably constitute 'the largest single category of tourist attractions in the world', yet war-related attractions, though diverse, are a subset of the totality of tourist sites associated with death and suffering.

Reference is frequently made either to specific destinations, such as the Sixth Floor in Dallas, Texas or to forms of tourism, such as graveyards, the holocaust, atrocities, prisons, or slavery-heritage tourism. However, such is the diversity of death-related attractions from the 'Dracula Experience' in Whitby, UK or Vienna's Funeral Museum to the sites of 'famous' deaths, or major disasters, that a full categorization is extremely complex. Despite the long history and increasing contemporary evidence of travel to sites or attractions associated with death, it is only relatively recently that academic attention has been focused upon what has been collectively referred to as 'dark tourism'.

In particular, a number of attempts have been made to define or label death-related tourist activity, such as 'thanatourism', 'morbid', 'black-spot' or, as Dann alliterates, 'milking the macabre'. Additionally, attempts have been made to analyse specific manifestations of dark tourism, from war museums adopting both traditional and contemporary museology methods of (re)presentation, to genocide commemoration visitor sites and the political ideology attached to such remembrance. Attention has also been focused, though to a lesser extent, on visitor motivations to seek out such sites or experiences,, including proposed 'drivers' which vary from morbid curiosity, through schadenfreude, to a collective sense of identity or survival 'in the face of violent disruptions of collective life routines'.

Nevertheless, the literature remains eclectic and theoretically fragile. That is, a number of fundamental issues remain, not least whether it is actually possible or justifiable to categorize collectively the experience of sites or attractions that are associated with death or suffering as 'dark tourism'. More specifically, it remains unclear whether dark tourism is demand or supply driven or, more generally, the manifestation of what has been referred to as a modern propensity for 'mourning sickness' or what has been termed 'grief tourism'. Other questions are also raised, but go unanswered.

For example, has there indeed been a measurable growth in 'tourist interest in recent death, disaster and atrocity... in the late twentieth and early twenty-first centuries' or is there simply an ever-increasing supply of dark sites and attractions? Are there degrees or 'shades of darkness' that can be related to either the nature of the attraction or the intensity of interest in death or the macabre on the part of tourists? And, does the popularity of dark sites result from a basic fascination with death, or are there more powerful motivating factors and, if so, what ethical issues surround the exploitation of tragic history ? In order to address many of these questions it is necessary to possess some understanding of tourist behaviour with respect to dark sites and attractions.

In other words, the analysis of dark tourism cannot be complete without a consideration of why tourists may be drawn towards sites or experiences associated with death and suffering. As noted above, a variety of motives are proposed in the literature, most comprehensively by Dann who identifies eight influences, including: the fear of phantoms; the search for novelty; nostalgia; the celebration of crime or deviance; basic bloodlust; and, at a more practical level, 'dicing with death'—that is, undertaking journeys, or 'holidays in hell', that challenge tourists or heighten their sense of mortality. However, as Dann accepts, these categorizations are largely descriptive and may be related more to specific attractions, destinations or activities rather than individuals' motivations.

Conversely, Krakover's study of the attitudes of tourists at the Yad Vashem Holocaust commemoration site in Israel considers, to a limited extent, visitor motives. Nevertheless, much of the literature remains supply-side focused whilst the motivation(s) for dark tourism has yet to be revealed and systematically interrogated. The purpose of this paper, therefore, is to address this gap in the literature.

Drawing upon contemporary sociological theory related to death and grief in modern societies, it seeks to establish a theoretical foundation for exploring the consumption of dark tourism experiences. More specifically, it proposes a thanatological paradigm of the relationship between contemporary socio-cultural perspectives on death and mortality, consequential responses to the inevitability of human mortality, and the potential role of dark tourism consumption in confronting death and dying.

In so doing, it establishes a basis for subsequent theoretical and empirical research into dark tourism in particular, whilst contributing to the contemporary sociology of death more generally. First, however, it is necessary to review briefly the extant literature as a framework for the subsequent discussion.

DEATH AND CONTEMPORARY SOCIETY

Sociology has been traditionally concerned almost exclusively with the problems of life, rather than with the subject of death. However, Berger's seminal text suggested death is an essential feature of the human condition, requiring individuals to develop mechanisms to cope with their ultimate demise. According to Berger, to neglect death is to ignore one of the few universal parameters in which both the collective and individual self is constructed.

Hence, although death and the discussion of death within the public realm was once considered taboo or at least proclaimed to be taboo, commentators are now challenging death taboos, exploring contexts where the dead share the world with the living. In particular, Harrision examines how the dead are absorbed into the living world by graves, images, literature, architecture and monuments. Similarly, Lee reviews the disenchantment of death in modernity and, suggesting that death is making its way back into social consciousness, concludes that the time has come to dissect death without prejudice.

He goes on to advocate that death is 'coming out of the closet to redefine our assumptions of life', thus breaking the modern silence on death. Therefore, although the inevitability of death continues to be disavowed, particularly in contemporary society, it can never be completely denied. Indeed, contemporary society increasingly consumes, willingly or unwillingly, both real and commodified death and suffering through audio-visual representations, popular culture and the media.

Of course, 'contemporary society', or the cultural framework within which individuals construct coping mechanisms to deal with human finitude, is itself a contested term, particularly within sociological discourse relating to modernity and post-modernity. According to Giddens, however, it is misleading to interpret contemporary societies as evidence of a radically new type of social world, whereby the characteristics of modernity have been left behind.

He suggests that social life is still being forged by essentially modern concerns, even though it is only now that the implications of these are becoming apparent. Moreover, a Giddensian perspective points in particular to a significant characteristic of contemporary society that can be correlated with death and mortality: namely, an individual's perceived erosion of personal meaningfulness and rational order which, in turn, is often propelled by the privatization of meaning and sequestration of death within public space.

At the same time, when discussing mortality and its contemplation, a critical feature of Western society may be seen in the extensive desacralisation of social life which has failed to replace religious certainties with scientific certainties.

Whilst the negation of religion and an increased belief in science may have provided people the possibility of exerting a perceived sense of control over their lives (though, crucially, it has not conquered death), it fails to provide values to guide lives, leaving individuals vulnerable to feelings of isolation, especially when contemplating death and an end to life projects. Hence, that the 'secularization of life should be accompanied by the secularization of death should come as no surprise: to live in the modern is to die in it also'. Further to this, Giddens suggests a privatization of meaning in contemporary society, where both experience and meaning have been relocated from public space to the privatized realms of an individual's life.

Consequently, this has served both to both reduce massively the scope of the sacred and to leave increasing numbers of individuals alone with the task of establishing and maintaining values to guide them and make sense of their daily lives. Ultimately, therefore, people require a sense of order and continuity in relation to their daily social lives, to which Giddens refers to as 'ontological security'.

ONTOLOGICAL SECURITY: MEANING AND MORTALITY

A distinctive feature of contemporary society, Giddens argues, is the 'purchasing of ontological security' through various institutions and experiences that protect the individual from direct contact with madness, criminality, sexuality, nature and death. Giddens, who associates contemporary society with an 'exclusion of social life from fundamental existential issues which raise central moral dilemmas for human beings', suggests that ontological security is anchored, both emotionally and cognitively, in a 'practical consciousness of the meaningfulness' of our day-to-day actions.

However, this sense of meaningfulness is consistently threatened by the angst of disorder or chaos. As Mellor notes, 'this chaos signals the irreality of everyday conventions, since a person's sense of what is real is intimately associated with their sense of what is meaningful'. Giddens, drawing upon Kierkegaard's concept of dread, argues that individuals are faced with a seemingly ubiquitous danger of being besieged by anxieties concerning the ultimate reality and meaningfulness of daily life.

Hence, contemporary society strives to address this sense of dread by 'bracketing out of everyday life those questions which might be raised about the social frameworks which contain human existence'. Death is clearly one such issue that raises uncertainties and anxieties and, hence, becomes a major issue to bracket out of everyday consciousness. This bracketing out may have resulted in the contemplation of death becoming taboo, as noted above. Nevertheless, as Mellor notes, the bracketing process is not always successful. Indeed, it is contingent upon societies to be able to control factors which offer pertinent threats to ontological security.

This level of control will, naturally, vary from society to society but, regardless of the cultural condition of society, death is a potent challenge to the bracketing process in all societies. Therefore, the existential confrontation of death has the potential to expose the individual to dread, the inevitability of death causing the individual to question the social frameworks in which they live and participate. As Giddens notes:

- 'Death remains the great extrinsic factor of human existence; it cannot as such be brought within the internally referential systems of modernity... death becomes the point zero: it is nothing more or less than the moment at which human control over human existence finds an outer limit'.

Therefore, death becomes a psychological and problematic issue for both the collective and individual self. People must face up to their inevitable demise, yet the social systems in which they reside must allow them to live day-to-day with some sort of commitment and, thus, to a certain extent deny death. Consequently, modern ideology espouses a celebration of life and living, amplified by a post-modern focus on youth, beauty and the body.

As a result, thoughts of death as an inevitable event are repressed. It is, perhaps, for this reason that both Giddens and, previously, Berger associate death with those 'fateful moments' and 'marginal situations', whereby individuals have to confront problems which society has attempted to conceal from public consciousness.

As Berger suggests, 'death is the most significant factor individuals can encounter in marginal situations'.

This is because death has the potential to radically undermine an individual's sense of meaningfulness and reality of social life, thus calling into question ontological security and even the most fundamental assumptions upon which social life is constructed. Indeed, for Berger, death is an unavoidable characteristic of the human condition, and one which all societies, contemporary or otherwise, inevitably have to address. Hence, if death and mortality is not dealt with by adequate confrontation mechanisms, not only will the individual have to face up to challenges of personal meaningfulness and a significant loss of ontological security, but the social framework as a whole becomes vulnerable to collapse into chaos.

However, in a contemporary age defined by rapid technological, economic and scientific progress, a cultural milieu remains that challenges the maintenance of ontological security. In this context, death is difficult to deal with, especially when values and meanings are constantly reappraised and reflected upon, thus aiding a sequestration of death from the public realm.

THE SEQUESTRATION OF DEATH: AN ABSENT-PRESENT PARADOX

One of the fundamental discontinuist impulses of the contemporary age is expressed by Giddens in the pervasiveness of 'reflexivity' - that is, the systematic and critical examination, monitoring and revision of all beliefs, values and practices in the light of changing circumstances. This continual process of systematic and potentially radical reappraisal of contemporary life can sentence the individual to a pervasive 'radical doubt' and a perceived reduction of ontological security. Although the constant re-evaluation of social life may be profound and liberating for some, it is unclear how reflexivity can ultimately help individuals deal with the phenomenon of death.

More specifically, death 'is a universal parameter within which reflexivity occurs, rather than an object to which reflexivity can be convincingly applied'. Nonetheless, it can be argued that contemporary societies are sufficiently culturally diverse and flexible to permit individuals to draw and reflect upon a variety of cultural resources to deal with death, thus creating multiple mechanisms to confront mortality. Even so, this diversity may compound the difficulties that individuals may experience when death and dying is encountered.

As Mellor argues, 'reflexivity may be increasingly applied to death in a multitude of ways, but this multiplicity of particular approaches to death accentuates the reality-threatening potential of death in general'. In other words, the more diverse the approaches to death in contemporary societies, the more difficult it becomes to contain death within social frameworks and, thus, limit existential anxiety and the level of ontological security it potentially offers to the individual. This apparent cultural diversity, reflexivity and flexibility, Mellor argues, in contemporary approaches to death 'can therefore be explained as being consistent with the sequestration of death from public space into the realm of the personal'.

Further to this, Mellor and Shilling conclude that public legitimisations of death are becoming increasingly absent, thus ensuring the challenge of death to an individuals' sense of reality, personal meaningfulness and, ultimately, ontological security.

This ostensible absence of death from the public realm may help explain the 'intense confusion, anxiety, and even terror which are frequently experienced by individuals before signs of their own mortality'. Thus, reviews of contributions to the sociology of death and dying have drawn attention to the sequestration of death in contemporary society. Most notably, these contributions concentrate on the privatisation and medicalization of death whereby death, rather than being an open, communal event, is now a relatively private experience marked by an 'increased uneasiness over the boundaries between the corporeal bodies of the living and dead'.

A full analysis of death sequestration from public space is beyond the scope of this paper. Nevertheless, it is important to note fundamental transformations within contemporary society towards mortality. As Mellor and Shilling point out:

- '...these changes have themselves been affected by a gradual privatisation of the organisation of death (or a decrease in the public space afforded to death); a shrinkage in the scope of the sacred in terms of the experience of death; and a fundamental shift in the corporeal boundaries, symbolic and actual, associated with the dead and living'.

Hence, the absent death thesis is most notably manifested in the loss of communal and social events which, combined into a series of ritual actions, contained death by ensuring it was open or public, yet subject to religious and social control. The omnipresent religious order that encompassed human finiteness in pre-contemporary societies offered a 'good death', thus contributing to a sense of ontological security for the bereaved who would inevitably evolve into the deceased.

However, it is suggested that death and the prospect of dying is now unprecedently alarming because contemporary society has deprived increasing numbers of people with an overarching, existentially meaningful, ritual structure. Indeed, in relation to mortality, it can be argued that contemporary society has 'not just emptied the sky of angels, but has emptied tradition, ritual and, increasingly, virtually all overarching normative meaning structures of much of their content'. Thus, the reflexive deconstruction of religious orders, that promised post-corporeal life after death, and the lack of stable replacement meaning systems, has tended to leave contemporary individuals isolated and vulnerable in the face of their inevitable end.

Augmenting this perceived sense of individualization and privatization of death is the increased medicalization of the dying process. In other words, the medical professional and the hospice movement have helped relocate death away from the community and into a closed private world of doctors, nurses and specialists.

As Elias notes, 'never before have people died as noiselessly and hygienically as today, and never in social conditions fostering so much solitude'. Moreover, death is often represented in terms of its medical causes,, so that people are no longer 'dying of mortality'. Combined with the professionalization of the death industry, the management of disposal is largely relocated away from a front region of the community gaze and safely into a back region of death-industry professionals. However, this cumulative effect of the institutional sequestration of death is not to resolve the problem of death by neutralising its implicit threat and sense of dread but, ironically, to leave many people uncertain and socially unsupported when it comes to dealing with mortality, as a transpersonal, existential phenomenon. For this reason, Walter suggests that the meaning of mortality in contemporary societies 'points to death being highly problematic for the modern individual, but not at all problematic for modern society—hence the lack of ritual surrounding it today'.

Nevertheless, to suggest death is totally absent from the contemporary public domain is to deny the pervasiveness of death within popular culture and media output. Indeed, death has long been recognised as present within wider popular culture and the media. Gorer, for example, asserted that the demise of social and religious rituals surrounding death and dying resulted in mortality resurfacing in society through the seemingly obsessive 'pornographic' media coverage of death, whereby 'death became removed, abstracted, intellectualised, and depersonalised'. Similarly, Tercier notes that 'the televised pornography of death, with its slippages of reality and representation, is no more likely to replace the experience of the deathbed than the dirty movie is likely to replace sex'.

Nevertheless, as Bryant and Shoemaker observe, 'thanatological themed entertainment has been and remains a traditional pervasive cultural pattern, and has become very much a prominent and integral part of contemporary popular culture'. This is no more so than within the realms of dark tourism, but thanatological themes are also evident in television news and programming; cinema production; music; print media; the arts: and through jokes often referred to as 'gallows humour'. Indeed, death can be traced back through popular culture to folklore, in which folklorists have maintained an interest in the cultural aspects of death for many years.

It is here where the apparent paradox of death sequestration lies. On the one hand, absent death through privatization of meaning, the medicalization of dying and the professionalization of the death process is evident yet, on the other hand, death is very much present within popular culture and, of course, very present since death is the single most common factor of life. It is, perhaps, because of this paradoxical position that death appears institutionally hidden rather than forbidden, invisible rather than denied.

Durkin offers two salient explanations of this absent-present paradox. Firstly, he suggests that whilst contemporary society brackets out and insulates the individual from death, it is this very insulation that leads us to crave some degree of information and insight concerning death. Secondly, he suggests that the presence of death themes in popular culture and the treatment of mortality as an entertainment commodity is simply a way of bringing death back into the social consciousness. As Durkin notes, 'by rendering death into humour and entertainment, we effectively neutralize it; it becomes innocuous, and thus less threatening, through its conversion and ephemerality' in popular culture and the media. It is this social neutralization of death and the potential role of dark tourism that the paper now evaluates.

MAKING ABSENT DEATH PRESENT: DARK TOURISM, NEUTRALIZATION AND DE-SEQUESTRATION

The social neutralization of death, which may be considered a means of bracketing dread and boosting ontological security, can help to assuage the disruptive impact of death for the individual. At the same time, dark tourism, as reviewed above, is an increasingly pervasive feature in the popular cultural landscape.

Indeed, depending upon the social, cultural and political context it may be considered fascinating, educational or even humorous. However, whilst the consumption of death appears to be in inverse ratio to our declining direct experience of death itself, dark tourism, within a thanatological framework, may help explain contemporary approaches to mortality and its contemplation and vice versa.

More specifically, dark tourism allows the re-conceptualization of death and mortality into forms that stimulate something other than primordial terror and dread. Despite modern society's diminishing experience with death as a result of institutional sequestration, Tercier suggests that, whilst people are now spectators to more deaths than in any prior generation, driven by both real and represented images, 'we see death, but we do not 'touch' it'. With this in mind, it is argued that individuals are left isolated in the face of death and, thus, have to call upon their own resources when searching for meanings to cope with the limits of individual existence.

Therefore, dark tourism, in its various guises and with its camouflaged and repackaged 'Other' death, allows individuals to indulge their curiosity and fascination with thanatological concerns in a socially acceptable and, indeed, often sanctioned environment, thus providing them with an opportunity to construct their own contemplations of mortality. With a degree of infrastructure and normality that surrounds the supply of dark tourism, albeit on varying scales, the increasingly socially acceptable gaze upon death and its re-conceptualization for entertainment, education or memorial purposes offers both the individual and collective self a pragmatic confrontational mechanism to begin the process of neutralizing the impact of mortality.

Consequently, this can help minimize the intrinsic threat that the inevitability of death brings. This neutralizing effect is aided by dark touristic exposures to death, where the process of continued sensitization of dying ultimately results in a sanitization of the subject area. This creates a perceived immunity from death, in addition to a growing acceptance that death will ultimately arrive. Thus, both sensitizing and sanitizing death allows individuals to view their own death as distant, unrelated to the dark tourism product which they consume, and with a hope that their own death will be a 'good' death. Furthermore, it can be argued that dark tourism further individualizes and, thus, fragments the meaning of death.

Indeed, whilst consuming the dark tourism product, people are generally exposed to the causes of death and suffering of individual people in individual circumstances, thus perhaps encouraging the view of death as avoidable and contingent. As Bauman points out, these kind of deaths are 'therefore reassuring rather than threatening, since they orient people towards strategies of survival rather than making them aware of the futility of all strategies in the face of mortality'. Of course, given the enormous diversity both of dark tourism places and of the needs, experience and expectations of visitors, in addition to various socio-cultural circumstances of individuals, the potential effectiveness of dark tourism consumption as a mechanism for confronting, understanding and accepting death will vary almost infinitely.

It may be argued, for example, that war cemeteries, sites of mass disasters, memorials to individual or multiple deaths/acts of personal sacrifice and so on may be more powerful and positive means of confronting death than more 'playful' attractions, such as 'houses of horror'. Certainly, a visit to Gallipoli, where the mass graves of the fallen (including that of a young British soldier who died before reaching his 17th birthday) lie above the beaches and cliffs, is an inevitably emotive and meaningful experience, verifying, perhaps, the cultural and popularised representations (both visual— the Mel Gibson movie Gallipoli—and musical) of that tragic event. Similarly, the proposed Tsunami 'Mountains of Remembrance' memorial in Khao Lak-Lam Ru National Park in Thailand may provide a focus for contemplation, mourning, hope and survival.

Conversely, contemporary visitors to places such as Auschwitz and other Nazi death camps, perhaps the epitome of a dark tourism destination, may come simply 'out of curiosity or because it is the thing to do' rather than for more meaningful purposes. Importantly, this latter point may result in any potential meaning of mortality within contemporary society as consequential to the visit. In other words, tourists may implicitly take away meanings of mortality from their visit, rather than explicitly seek to contemplate death and dying as a primary motivation to visit any dark site.

Additionally, the level of mortality meaning to the individual will undoubtedly depend upon their socio-cultural background, and of course, to the varying 'intensities of darkness' perceived in any given dark product and/or experience.

Nevertheless, as this paper has already suggested, the present cultural condition of contemporary Western society calls for a revaluation of meaning systems which, in general, permit individuals to confront mortality. Hence, the re-conceptualization of death through dark tourism allows for the reconstruction of a replacement meaning system, whereby the reflexive deconstruction of religious orders are being relocated and reconstructed by the consumption of image and the pseudo. Accordingly, dark tourism may offer a revival of death within the public domain, thereby de-sequestering mortality and ensuring absent death is made present, transforming death into public discourse and a communal commodity upon which to gaze.

For this reason, dark tourism may offer a new social institution whereby the functional value of death and mortality is acknowledged, its precariousness is appreciated, and efforts to assure ontological well-being and security become a source of not only playfulness, humour and entertainment but also education and memorial. Indeed, its consumption may allow the individual a sense of meaning and understanding of past disasters and macabre events that have perturbed life projects.

This new understanding may, in turn, help shore up the fragility of the self's survival strategy. Thus, dark tourism can potentially transform the seemingly meaningless into the meaningful through the commodification, explanations and representations of darkness that have impacted upon the collective self.

This, in turn, may allow the individual to confront and contemplate their own mortality by gazing upon macabre illusions and images. Subsequently, the confrontation of death and contemplation of mortality, within a socially acceptable dark tourism environment, may potentially bracket out some of the sense of dread death inevitably brings, by insulating the individual with information and potential understanding and meaning. Of course, it may be also the case that particular dark sites do not provide the sense of 'meaning' that a particular visitor may be seeking, thus negating the effectiveness of the overall bracketing process and the ability to keep any 'dread threats' at bay. Nonetheless, within dark tourism, death becomes real for the individual.

Consequently, the real is represented so that the represented might become real. In other words, real actual death is (represented and commodified within dark tourism sites in order for it to become existentially valid and therefore inevitable for the individual who wishes to gaze upon this 'Other' death.

CONCLUSION

Despite increasing academic attention paid to the subject, the analysis of dark tourism has, to date, adopted a largely descriptive, parochial perspective whilst questions surrounding the consumption of dark touristic experiences have, for the most part, been avoided. This paper, therefore, set out to enhance the theoretical foundations of the phenomenon by considering it within a broader thanatological perspective, exploring in particular the relationship between dark tourism consumption and contemporary social responses to death and mortality. In linking the concept of dark tourism with the sociology of death, the paper has not only developed a model that provides a conceptual basis for the further empirical study of its consumption, but has also contributed to wider social scientific understanding of mechanisms for confronting death in contemporary societies. A number of key points have emerged from the preceding discussion.

Firstly, dark tourism allows death to be brought back into the public realm and discourse, thus acting as a de-sequester that allows absent death to be made present. Secondly, the consumption of dark tourism may aid the social neutralisation of death for the individual, either implicitly or explicitly, thereby reducing the potential sense of dread that death inevitably brings and permitting a search for, and a purchase of, ontological security through a new social institution. Finally, this new social institution facilitates the reconstruction of a meaning system for individuals in the face of reflexivity, desacralisation and institutional sequestration, thus creating an opportunity to confront and contemplate 'mortality moments' from a perceived safe distance and environment.

This, in turn, allows for some immunity and reassurance from the actual death or macabre event which has been (reproduced through dark tourism. In conclusion, however, it would be naive to suggest that the consumption of dark tourism rests solely upon a theoretical notion of providing individuals an opportunity to contemplate death and mortality.

Whilst the concepts outlined in this paper require operationalization and testing through empirical research, both within a variety of social and cultural environments and relating to varying dark 'products', other conceptual issues undoubtedly deserve consideration. In particular, dark tourism production is multi-faceted, multi-tiered and exists in a variety of social, cultural, geographical, and political contexts, Thus, the demand for such products will no doubt be equally as diverse and fragmented, pointing to the need for further targeted empirical and theoretical analysis.

In addition, dark tourists' motives will certainly vary according to intensities of meanings for various individuals within different social networks. Indeed, an awareness of mortality and the anticipation of death will differ amongst various social and cultural groups. It is also highly likely that dark tourism consumption will rest on numerous disparate factors, including, but not limited to, the contemplational aspects of death and dying. In particular, other aspects of the 'consumption jigsaw' may lie within grief and therapeutic discourse; conspicuous compassion and narcissism; media induced emotional invigilation; and schadenfreude.

Additionally, the notion of discourse ethics and metamorality and its impact upon dark tourism supply and demand is also suggested for future consideration, as some Western societies are propelled from a 'conventional' to a 'post-conventional' stage, and where potential moral lessons are sought and provided from sites of death. In short, the consumption of dark tourism, largely justified on the basis of untested assumptions in the extant literature, is a complex process.

Nevertheless, this paper has commenced the interrogation of dark tourism consumption and located it within a thanatological framework for further study. In so doing, it has suggested that consuming dark tourism can help individuals, within a social structure, to address issues of personal meaningfulness—a key to reality, thus to life and sustaining social order, and ultimately to the maintenance and continuity of ontological security and overall well-being. It is with this latter point in mind that dark tourism may have more to do with life and living, rather than the dead and dying.

7

Understanding Dark Tourism Planning

Dark tourism is one of many activities in a community or region that requires planning and coordination. Here we provide a simple structure and basic guidelines for comprehensive dark tourism planning at a community or regional level.

Planning is the process of identifying objectives and defining and evaluating methods of achieving them. By comprehensive planning we mean planning which considers all of the dark tourism resources, organizations, markets, and programme within a region. Comprehensive planning also considers economic, environmental, social, and institutional aspects of dark tourism development.

TWO SIDES OF DARK TOURISM PLANNING

Dark tourism planning has evolved from two related but distinct sets of planning philosophies and methods. On the one hand, dark tourism is one of many activities in an area that must be considered as part of physical, environmental, social, and economic planning. Therefore, it is common to find dark tourism addressed, at least partially, in a regional land use, transportation, recreation, economic development, or comprehensive plan. The degree to which dark tourism is addressed in such plans depends upon the relative importance of dark tourism to the community or region and how sensitive the planning authority is to dark tourism activities.

Dark tourism may also be viewed as a business in which a community or region chooses to engage. Individual dark tourism businesses conduct a variety of planning activities including feasibility, marketing, product development, promotion, forecasting, and strategic planning. If dark tourism is a significant component of an area's economy or development plans, regional or community-wide marketing plans are needed to coordinate the development and marketing activities of different dark tourism interests in the community.

A comprehensive approach integrates a strategic marketing plan with more traditional public planning activities. This ensures a balance between serving the needs and wants of the tourists versus the needs and wants of local residents. A formal dark tourism plan provides a vehicle for the various interests within a community to coordinate their activities and work towards common goals. It also is a means of coordinating dark tourism with other community activities.

STEPS IN THE PLANNING PROCESS

Like any planning, dark tourism planning is goal-oriented, striving to achieve certain objectives by matching available resources and programmes with the needs and wants of people. Comprehensive planning requires a systematic approach, usually involving a series of steps. The process is best viewed as an iterative and on-going one, with each step subject to modification and refinement at any stage of the planning process.

There are six steps in the planning process:

1. Define goals and objectives.
2. Identify the dark tourism system.
    a. Resources
    b. Organizations
    c. Markets
3. Generate alternatives.
4. Evaluate alternatives.
5. Select and implement.
6. Monitor and evaluate.

STEP ONE

Obtaining clear statements of goals and objectives is difficult, but important. Ideally, dark tourism development goals should flow from more general community goals and objectives. It is important to understand how a dark tourism plan serves these broader purposes. Is the community seeking a broader tax base, increased employment opportunities, expanded recreation facilities, better educational programmes, a higher quality of life? How can dark tourism contribute to these objectives?

If dark tourism is identified as a means of serving broader community goals, it makes sense to develop plans with more specific dark tourism development objectives. These are generally defined through a continuing process in which various groups and organizations in a community work together towards common goals. A local planning authority, chamber of commerce, visitors bureau, or similar group should assume a leadership role to develop an initial plan and obtain broad involvement of dark tourism interests in the community. Public support for the planning process and plan is also important.

Having a good understanding of dark tourism and the dark tourism system in your community is the first step towards defining goals and objectives for dark tourism development. The types of goals that are appropriate and the precision with which you are able to define them will depend upon how long your community has been involved in dark tourism and dark tourism planning. In the early stages of dark tourism development, goals may involve establishing organizational structures and collecting information to better identify the dark tourism system in the community. Later, more precise objectives can be formulated and more specific development and marketing strategies evaluated.

STEP TWO

Identifying Your Dark tourism System When planning for any type of activity, it is important to first define its scope and characteristics. Be clear about exactly what your plan encompasses. A good initial question is, "What do you mean by dark tourism ?"

Dark tourism is defined in many ways. Generally, dark tourism involves people traveling outside of their community for pleasure. Definitions differ on the specifics of how far people must travel, whether or not they must stay overnight, for how long, and what exactly is included under traveling for "pleasure". Do you want your dark tourism plan to include day visitors, conventioneers, business travellers, people visiting friends and relatives, people passing through, or seasonal residents?

Which community resources and organizations serve tourists or could serve tourists? Generally, tourists share community resources with local residents and businesses. Many organizations serve both tourists and locals. This complicates dark tourism planning and argues for a clear idea of what your dark tourism plan entails.

You can begin to clarify the dark tourism system by breaking it down into three subsystems:

1. Dark tourism resources,
2. Dark tourism organizations, and
3. Dark tourism markets.

An initial task in developing a dark tourism plan is to identify, inventory, and classify the objects within each of these subsystems.

Dark tourism Resources are any:

1. Natural,
2. Cultural,
3. Human, or
4. Capital resources that either are used or can be used to attract or serve tourists.

A dark tourism resource inventory identifies and classifies the resources available that provide opportunities for dark tourism development. Conduct an objective and realistic assessment of the quality and quantity of resources you have to work with. Some data suggested classification to help obtain a broad and organized picture of your dark tourism resources.

Dark tourism Organizations combine resources in various proportions to provide products and services for the tourist. Given below is a partial list and classification of organizations that manage or coordinate dark tourism -related activities. It is important to recognize the diverse array of public and private organizations involved with dark tourism.

The most difficult part of dark tourism planning is to get these groups to work towards common goals. You should develop a list of these organizations within your own community and obtain their input and cooperation in your dark tourism planning efforts. Setting up appropriate communication systems and institutional arrangements is a key part of community dark tourism planning.

DARK TOURISM RESOURCES

Natural Resources:

- Climate-seasons
- Water resources-lakes, streams, waterfalls
- Flora-forests, flowers, shrubs, wild edibles
- Fauna-fish and wildlife
- Geological resources-topography, soils, sand dunes, beaches, caves, rocks and minerals, fossils
- Scenery-combinations of all of the above

Cultural Resources:

- Historic buildings, sites
- Monuments, shrines
- Cuisine
- Ethnic cultures
- Industry, government, religion, etc.
- Anthropological resources
- Local celebrities

Human Resources:

- Hospitality skills
- Management skills
- Seasonal labour force
- Performing artists-music, drama, art, storytellers, etc.
- Craftsman and artisans

- Other labour skills from chefs to lawyers to researchers
- Local populations

CAPITAL

- Availability of capital, financing
- Infrastructure-transportation roads, airports, railroads, harbors and marinas, trails and walkways
- Infrastructure: utilities water, power, waste treatment, communications.

DARK TOURISM MANAGEMENT ORGANIZATIONS AND SERVICES

Off-Site:

Coordination, planning, technical assistance, research, regulation:

- Federal and state departments of commerce, transportation, and natural resources
- Federal, state, regional, and local dark tourism associations
- Educational organizations and consultants, *e.g.*, Travel and Dark tourism Research Association; U.S. Travel Data Centre; Travel Reference Centre, Univ. of Colorado, Boulder; Travel, Dark tourism, and Recreation Resource Centre, Michigan State University.
- Travel information and reservation services

On-Site:

Development, promotion and management, of dark tourism resources:

- Federal agencies, NB. departments of commerce, transportation, and land management agencies.
- State agencies, NB. departments of commerce, transportation, and land/facility management agencies
- Local government organizations, *e.g.*, visitor information, chamber of commerce, convention and visitor's bureaus, parks.

Businesses:

- *Accommodations*: Hotels, motels, Lodges, resorts, bed and breakfast cabins and cottages, Condominiums, second homes, Campgrounds
- *Food and Beverage*: Restaurants, Grocery, Bars, nightclubs, Fast food, Catering services
- *Transportation*: Air, rail, bus; Local transportation: taxi, limo, Auto, bicycle, boat rental; Local tour services
- *Information*: Travel agencies, Information and reservation services, Automobile clubs

Recreation Facilities and Services

Winter sports: Ski, skating, snowmobile areas; Golf courses, miniature golf; Swimming pools, water slides, beaches; tennis, handball, racquetball courts, bowling alleys; Athletic clubs, health spas; Marinas, boat rentals and charters; hunting and fishing guides; Horseback enterprises; Sporting goods sales and rentals

Entertainment

Nightclubs, amusement parks, spectator sport facilities; Gambling facilities: casinos, horse racing, bingo; video arcades; art galleries and studios, craft shops, studios, demonstrations; performing arts: theater, dance, music, film; historic and prehistoric sites; museums: art, history, science, technology; arboreta, zoos, nature centres,

Support Services

Auto repair, gasoline service stations; boat and recreation vehicle dealers and service; retail shops: sporting goods, specialties, souvenirs, clothing; health services: hospitals, clinics, pharmacies; laundry and dry cleaning; beauty and barber shops; babysitting services; pet care; communications: newspaper, telephone; banking and financial services dark tourism markets.

Tourists makeup the third, and perhaps most important subsystem. Successful dark tourism programmes require a strong market orientation. The needs and wants of the tourists you choose to attract and serve must be the focus of much of your marketing and development activity. Therefore, it is important to clearly understand which dark tourism market segments you wish to attract and serve. Tourists fall into a very diverse set of categories with quite distinct needs and wants. You should identify the different types of tourists, or market segments that you presently serve or would like to serve. This may involve one or more dark tourism market surveys.

A visitor survey identifies the size and nature of the existing market and asks the following questions:

- What are the primary market segments you presently attract?
- Where do they come from?
- What local businesses and facilities do they use?
- What attracted them to the community?
- How did they find out about your community?
- How satisfied are they with your offerings?

A market survey (usually a telephone survey) also can be conducted among households in regions from which you wish to attract tourists. This type of study helps identify potential markets, and means of attracting tourists to your area.

DARK TOURISM MARKET SEGMENTS

In a general dark tourism plan, some clear target dark tourism market segments should be identified. You might begin by defining the market area from which you will draw most of your visitors. The size of your market area depends upon the uniqueness and quality of your "product", transportation systems, tastes and preferences of surrounding populations, and your competition. Identifying the market area will help target information and promotion and define transportation routes and modes, competition, and characteristics of your market.

Next, divide your travel market into the following trip length categories:

- Day trips from a 50 mile radius,
- Day trips from 50 to 200 miles away,
- Pass-through travellers,
- Overnight trips of 1 or 2 nights (most likely weekends), and
- Extended overnight vacation trips.

After you have an idea of your market area and kinds of trips you will be serving, begin defining more specific market segments like vehicle campers, downhill skiers, sightseers, family vacationers, single weekenders, and the like. These segments can be more clearly tied to particular resources, businesses, and facilities in your community.

What kinds of products and services are likely to attract each of these groups? Tourist needs as well as their impact on the local community are quite different for day tourists versus overnight tourists. Areas catering primarily to weekend traffic will experience large fluctuations in use. In deciding the relative importance of these different segments, communities need to assess both their ability to provide required services (do you have enough rooms?), as well as the demand for different types of trips relative to the supply and your competition.

THE ENVIRONMENT

A dark tourism plan is significantly affected by many factors in the broader environment. Indeed, one of the complexities of dark tourism planning is the number of variables that are outside of the control of an individual dark tourism business or community. These include such things as dark tourism offerings and prices at competing destinations, federal and state policy and legislation, currency exchange rates, the state of the economy, and weather. These factors are discussed more fully in Extension bulletin E-1959 as part of the market environment analysis.

Local populations also must be considered in dark tourism planning. As they compete with tourists for resources, they can be significantly affected by dark tourism activity, and they are an important source of support in getting dark tourism plans implemented.

A survey of local residents can be conducted to assess community attitudes towards dark tourism development, identify impacts of dark tourism on the community, and obtain local input into dark tourism plans.

Public hearings, workshops, and advisory boards are other ways to obtain public involvement in dark tourism planning. Local support and cooperation is important to the success of dark tourism programmes and should not be overlooked.

STEP THREE

Generating alternative development and marketing options to meet your goals requires some creative thinking and brainstorming. The errors made at this stage are usually thinking too narrowly or screening out alternatives prematurely.

It is wise to solicit a wide range of options from a diverse group of people. If dark tourism expertise is lacking in your community, seek help and advice outside the community.

Dark tourism planning involves a wide range of interrelated development and marketing decisions.

The following development questions will get you started:

- How much importance should be assigned to dark tourism within a community or region?
- Which general community goals is dark tourism development designed to serve?
- Which organization(s) will provide the leadership and coordination necessary for community dark tourism planning?
- What are the relative roles of public and private sectors?

Dark tourism marketing decision questions include:

- *Segments*: Which market segments should be pursued; geographic markets, trip types, activity or demographic subgroups?
- *Product*: What kinds of dark tourism products and services should be provided? Who should provide what?
- *Place*: Where should dark tourism facilities be located?
- *Promotion*: What kinds of promotion should be used, by whom, in which media, how much, when? What community dark tourism theme or image should be established?
- *Price*: What prices should be charged for which products and services. Who should capture the revenue?

STEP FOUR

Dark tourism development and marketing options are evaluated by assessing the degree to which each option will be able to meet the stated goals and objectives.

There are usually two parts to a systematic evaluation of dark tourism development and marketing alternatives:

1. Feasibility analysis, and
2. Impact assessment.

These two tasks are interrelated, but think of them as trying to answer two basic questions:

1. Can it be done?, and
2. What are the consequences?

A decision to take a specific action must be based both on feasibility and desirability.

Feasibility Analysis: First, screen alternatives and eliminate those that are not feasible due to economic, environmental, political, legal, or other factors. Evaluate the remaining set of alternatives in more detail, paying particular attention to the market potential and financial plan. Make a realistic assessment of your community's ability to attract and serve a market segment or segments. This requires a clear understanding of the dark tourism market in your area and how this market is changing. Also carefully identify your competition and evaluate your advantages and disadvantages compared to the competition. Plan towards the future because it takes time to implement decisions and for your actions to take effect. Therefore, look at the likely market and competition for several years to come. Review forecasts for the travel market in your area, if available. Careful tracking of dark tourism trends in your own community can help identify changes in the market that you will have to adapt to.

IMPACT ASSESSMENT

When evaluating alternative development and marketing strategies it is important to understand the impacts, both positive and negative, of proposed actions. A classification of economic, environmental, and social impacts associated with dark tourism development. The types of impacts and their importance vary across different communities and proposed actions.

Generally, the size, extent, and nature of dark tourism impacts depend upon:

- Volume of tourist activity relative to local activity
- Length and nature of tourist contacts with the community
- Degree of concentration/dispersal of tourist activity in the area
- Similarities or differences between local populations and tourists
- Stability/sensitivity of local economy, environment, and social structure
- How well dark tourism is planned, controlled, and managed.

Look at both the benefits and costs of any proposed actions. While dark tourism development can increase income, revenues, and employment, it also involves costs. Evaluate benefits and costs of dark tourism development from the perspectives of local government, businesses, and residents.

IMPACTS OF DARK TOURISM

Economic Impacts:

- Sales, revenue, and income
- Employment
- Fiscal impact-taxes, infrastructure costs
- Prices
- Economic base and structure

Environmental Impacts:

- Lands
- Waters
- Air
- Infrastructure
- Flora and fauna

Social Impacts:

- Population structure and distribution
- Values and attitudes
- Education
- Occupations
- Safety and security
- Congestion and crowding
- Community spirit and cohesion
- Quality of life

Impacts on Local Government

Local government provides most of the infrastructure and many of the services essential to dark tourism development, including highways, public parks, law enforcement, water and sewer, garbage collection and disposal.

Evaluate dark tourism decisions with a clear understanding of the capacity of the local infrastructure and services relative to anticipated needs, and take into account both the needs of local populations and tourists. A fiscal impact analysis evaluates the impact of dark tourism on the community's tax base and local government costs.

It entails predicting the additional infrastructure and service requirements of dark tourism development, estimating their costs, deciding who will pay for/ provide them, and how. Will dark tourism generate increased local government revenue through fees and charges, local sales or use taxes, increased property values or property tax rates, or larger local shares of federal and state tax revenues?

Impacts on Business and Industry

Businesses that are directly serving tourists benefit from sales to tourists. Through secondary impacts, dark tourism activity also benefits a wide range of businesses in a community.

For example, a local textile industry may sell to a linen supply firm that serves hotels and motels catering primarily to tourists.

A local forest products industry sells to a lumberyard where local woodcarvers or furniture makers buy their supplies. They in turn sell to tourists through various retail outlets. All of these businesses benefit from dark tourism.

If most products and services for tourists are bought outside of the local area, much of the tourist spending "leaks" out of the local economy. The more a community is "self-sufficient" in serving tourists, the larger the local impact.

Impacts on Residents

Local residents may experience a broad range of both positive and negative impacts from dark tourism development. Dark tourism development may provide increased employment and income for the community. Although dark tourism jobs are primarily in the service sectors and are often seasonal, part time, and low-paying, these characteristics, are neither universal nor always undesirable. Residents may value opportunities for part time and seasonal work. In particular, employment opportunities and work experiences for students or retirees may be desired.

Residents may also benefit from local services that otherwise would not be available. Dark tourism development may mean a wider variety of retailers and restaurants, or a better community library. It may also mean more traffic, higher prices, and increases in property values and local taxes. The general quality of the environment and life in the community may go up or down due to dark tourism development. This depends on the nature of dark tourism development, the preferences and desires of local residents, and how well dark tourism is planned and managed.

STEPS FIVE AND SIX

We will not attempt a complete discussion of decision making, plan implementation, and monitoring, but these are critical steps in the success of a dark tourism plan. A set of specific actions should be prescribed with clearly defined responsibilities and timetables. Monitor progress in implementing the plan and evaluate the success of the plan in meeting its goals and objectives on a regular basis. Plans generally need to be adjusted over time due to changing goals, changing market conditions, and unanticipated impacts. It is a good idea to build monitoring and evaluation systems into your planning efforts.

NATIONAL AND REGIONAL DARK TOURISM PLANNING

The importance of effective dark tourism planning in ensuring economic benefit and sustainability is now widely recognized. Here we introduce concepts of national and regional dark tourism planning and look at the basic approaches, techniques and principles applied at this level.

It is now recognized that dark tourism must be developed and managed in a controlled, integrated and sustainable manner, based on sound planning. With this approach, dark tourism can generate substantial economic benefits to an area, without creating any serious environmental or social problems. Dark tourism 's resources will be conserved for continuous use in the future. There are numerous examples in the world where dark tourism has not been well planned and managed.

These uncontrolled developments may have brought some short-term economic benefits. Over the longer term, however, they have resulted in environmental and social problems and poor quality tourist destinations. This has been detrimental to the area's residents, and tourist markets have been lost to better planned destinations elsewhere. Many of these places are now undergoing redevelopment. It is obviously better to plan for controlled development initially, and prevent problems from arising in the first place.

Dark tourism planning is carried out at all levels of development - international, national, regional and for specific areas and sites. National and regional planning lays the foundation for dark tourism development of a country and its regions. It establishes the policies, physical and institutional structures and standards for development to proceed in a logical manner. It also provides the basis for the continuous and effective management of dark tourism which is so essential for the long-term success of dark tourism.

This publication is divided into two parts. The first part briefly explains planning concepts and describes planning and marketing methodologies. Emphasis is placed on the integrated approach, balancing economic, environmental and socio-cultural factors, and achieving sustainable development. Importance is also given to techniques that need to be used in implementing plans. Without adopting and applying these techniques, dark tourism plans cannot be realised.

The second part presents case studies of dark tourism policies and plans which have actually been prepared and, for the most part, are being implemented. The case studies have been selected to represent the several different elements of plans that must be considered in integrated development. Most of the case studies are ones that have been prepared by the WTO for several countries and regions during the past decade.

One of the important functions of the WTO is its technical cooperation activities. The organization has assisted many countries throughout the world in preparing planning, marketing, economic and other types of dark tourism studies, advising on all aspects of dark tourism development, and training local dark tourism -related personnel. Both Parts I and II of this publication reflect the WTO's basic approach to planning for the integrated and sustainable development of dark tourism in its global technical cooperation activities. The WTO hopes that this publication will provide dark tourism officials, planners and others involved in dark tourism with an understanding of national and regional dark tourism planning. Their application of sound planning practice can then provide the basis for their countries to achieve successful dark tourism development.

THE IMPORTANCE OF PLANNING DARK TOURISM

Planning dark tourism at all levels is essential for achieving successful dark tourism development and management. The experience of many dark tourism areas in the world has demonstrated that, on a long-term basis, the planned approach to developing dark tourism can bring benefits without significant problems, and maintain satisfied tourist markets. Places that have allowed dark tourism to develop without the benefit of planning are often suffering from environmental and social problems. These are detrimental to residents and unpleasant for many tourists, resulting in marketing difficulties and decreasing economic benefits. These uncontrolled dark tourism areas cannot effectively compete with planned tourist destinations elsewhere. They usually can be redeveloped, based on a planned approach, but that requires much time and financial investment.

Dark tourism is a rather complicated activity that overlaps several different sectors of the society and economy. Without planning, it may create unexpected and unwanted impacts. Dark tourism is also still a relatively new type of activity in many countries. Some governments and often the private sector have little or no experience in how to develop dark tourism properly. For countries that do not yet have much dark tourism, planning can provide the necessary guidance for its development. For those places that already have some dark tourism, planning is often needed to revitalize this sector and maintain its future viability.

First, dark tourism should be planned at the national and regional levels. At these levels, planning is concerned with dark tourism development policies, structure plans, facility standards, institutional factors and all the other elements necessary to develop and manage dark tourism. Then, within the framework of national and regional planning, more detailed plans for tourist attractions, resorts, urban, rural and other forms of dark tourism development can be prepared. There are several important specific benefits of undertaking national and regional dark tourism planning.

These advantages include:

- Establishing the overall dark tourism development objectives and policies -what is dark tourism aiming to accomplish and how can these aims be achieved.
- Developing dark tourism so that its natural and cultural resources are indefinitely maintained and conserved for future, as well as present, use.
- Integrating dark tourism into the overall development policies and patterns of the country or region, and establishing dose linkages between dark tourism and other economic sectors.
- Providing a rational basis for decision-making by both the public and private sectors on dark tourism development.
- Making possible the coordinated development of all the many elements of the dark tourism sector. This includes inter-relating the tourist attractions, activities, facilities and services and the various and increasingly fragmented tourist markets.
- Optimizing and balancing the economic, environmental and social benefits of dark tourism, with equitable distribution of these benefits to the society, while minimizing possible problems of dark tourism.
- Providing a physical structure which guides the location, types and extent of dark tourism development of attractions, facilities, services and infrastructure.
- Establishing the guidelines and standards for preparing detailed plans of specific dark tourism development areas that are consistent with, and reinforce, one another, and for the appropriate design of tourist facilities.
- Laying the foundation for effective implementation of the dark tourism development policy and plan and continuous management of the dark tourism sector, by providing the necessary organizational and other institutional framework.
- Providing the framework for effective coordination of the public and private sector efforts and investment in developing dark tourism.
- Offering a baseline for the continuous monitoring of the progress of dark tourism development and keeping it on track.

The planned approach to developing dark tourism at the national and regional levels is now widely adopted as a principle, although implementation of the policies and plans is still weak in some places. Many countries and regions of countries have had dark tourism plans prepared. Other places do not yet have plans, but should consider undertaking planning in the near future.

In some countries, plans had previously been prepared but these are now outdated. They need to be revised based on present day circumstances and likely future trends. Founded on accumulated experience, the approaches and techniques of dark tourism planning are now reasonably well understood. There is considerable assurance that, if implemented, planning will bring substantial benefits to an area.

APPROACHES TO DARK TOURISM PLANNING

It is important to understand the basic approaches to planning and managing dark tourism development. These are described in the following sections.

PLANNING DARK TOURISM AS AN INTEGRATED SYSTEM

An underlying concept in planning dark tourism is that dark tourism should be viewed as an inter-related system of demand and supply factors. The demand factors are international and domestic tourist markets and local 'residents who use the tourist attractions, facilities and services. The supply factors comprise tourist attractions and activities, accommodation and other tourist facilities and services.

Attractions include natural, cultural and special types of features - such as theme parks, zoos, botanic gardens and aquariums - and the activities related to these attractions. Accommodation includes hotels, motels, guest houses and other types of places where tourists stay overnight. The category of other tourist facilities and services includes tour and travel operations, restaurants, shopping, banking and money exchange, and medical and postal facilities and services. These supply factors are called the dark tourism product. Other elements also relate to supply factors. In order to make the facilities and services usable, infrastructure is required. Dark tourism infrastructure particularly includes transportation (air, road, rail, water, etc.), water supply, electric power, sewage and solid waste disposal, and telecommunications.

Demand Factors:

- International tourist markets
- Domestic tourist markets
- Residents' use of tourist attractions, facilities and services

Supply Factors:

- Attractions and activities Ïper cent Accommodation

- Other tourist facilities and services Ïper cent Transportation
- Other infrastructure
- Institutional elements

Provision of adequate infrastructure is also important to protect the environment. It helps maintain a high level of environmental quality that is so necessary for successful dark tourism and desirable for residents.

The effective development, operation and management of dark tourism requires certain institutional elements.

These elements include:

- Organizational structures, especially government dark tourism offices and private sector dark tourism associations such as hotel associations.
- Dark tourism -related legislation and regulations, such as standards and licensing requirements for hotels and tour and travel agencies.
- Education and training programmes, and training institutions to prepare persons to work effectively in dark tourism.
- Availability of financial capital to develop tourist attractions, facilities, services and infrastructure, and mechanisms to attract capital investment.
- Marketing strategies and promotion programmes to inform tourists about the country or region, and induce them to visit it, and tourist information facilities and services in the destination areas.
- Travel facilitation of immigration (including visa arrangements), customs and other facilities and services at the entry and exit points of tourists.

The institutional elements also include consideration of how to enhance and distribute the economic benefits of dark tourism, environmental protection measures, reducing adverse social impacts, and conservation of the cultural heritage of people living in the dark tourism areas.

As an inter-related system, it is important that dark tourism planning aim for integrated development of all these parts of the system, both the demand and supply factors and the physical and institutional elements. The system will function much more effectively and bring the desired benefits if it is planned in an integrated manner, with coordinated development of all the components of the system. Sometimes, this integrated system approach is also called the comprehensive approach to dark tourism planning because all the elements of dark tourism are considered in the planning and development process.

Just as important as planning for integration within the dark tourism system is planning for integration of dark tourism into the overall development policies, plans and patterns of a country or region. Planning for this overall integration will, for example, resolve any potential conflicts over use of certain resources or locations for various types of development. It also provides for the multi-use of expensive infrastructure to serve general community needs as well as dark tourism.

Emphasis is given to formulating and adopting dark tourism development policies and plans for an area in order to guide decision-making on development actions. The planning of dark tourism, however, should also be recognized as a continuous and flexible process. Within the framework of the policy and plan recommendations, there must be flexibility to allow for adapting to changing circumstances. Planning that is too rigid may not allow development to be responsive to changes. There may be advancements in transportation technology, evolution of new forms of dark tourism and changes in market trends. Even though allowed to be flexible, the basic objectives of the plan should not be abrogated although the specific development patterns may be changed. Sustainable development must still be maintained.

Planning for dark tourism development should make recommendations that are imaginative and innovative, but they must also be feasible to implement. The various techniques of implementation should be considered throughout the planning process. This approach ensures that the recommendations can be accomplished, and provides the basis for specifying the implementation techniques that should be applied. Implementation techniques can also be imaginative and not only rely on established approaches. It is common practice for a dark tourism plan to include specification of implementation techniques, and sometimes a separate manual on how to achieve the plan recommendations.

PLANNING FOR SUSTAINABLE DEVELOPMENT

The underlying approach now applied to dark tourism planning, as well as to other types of development, is that of achieving sustainable development. The sustainable development approach implies that the natural, cultural and other resources of dark tourism are conserved for continuous use in the future, while still bringing benefits to the present society The concept of sustainable development has received much emphasis internationally since the early 1980s, although dark tourism plans prepared even before that period often were concerned with conservation of dark tourism resources.

The sustainable development approach to planning dark tourism is acutely important because most dark tourism development depends on attractions and activities related to the natural environment, historic heritage and cultural patterns of areas. If these resources are degraded or destroyed, then the dark tourism areas cannot attract tourists and dark tourism will not be successful. More generally, most tourists seek destinations that have a high level of environmental quality - they like to visit places that are attractive, clean and neither polluted nor congested. It is also essential that residents of the dark tourism area should not have to suffer from a deteriorated environment and social problems.

One of the important benefits of dark tourism is that, if it is properly developed based on the concept of sustainability, dark tourism can greatly help justify and pay for conservation of an area's natural and cultural resources. Thus, dark tourism can be an important means of achieving conservation in areas that otherwise have limited capability to accomplish environmental protection and conservation objectives.

A basic technique in achieving sustainable development is the environmental planning approach. Environmental planning requires that all elements of the environment be carefully surveyed, analysed and considered in determining the most appropriate type and location of development. This approach would not allow, for example, intensive development in flood plain and steep hillside areas.

An important aspect of sustainable development is emphasizing community-based dark tourism. This approach to dark tourism focuses on community involvement in the planning and development process, and developing the types of dark tourism which generate benefits to local communities. It applies techniques to ensure that most of the benefits of dark tourism development accrue to local residents and not to outsiders. Maximizing benefits to local residents typically results in dark tourism being better accepted by them and their actively supporting conservation of local dark tourism resources.

The communitybased dark tourism approach is applied at the local or more detailed levels of planning, but it can be set forth as a policy approach at the national and regional levels. The benefits accruing to local communities are also beneficial to the country, through the income and foreign exchange earned, employment generated and support that local communities give to national dark tourism development and conservation policies.

Also related to sustainable development is the concept of quality dark tourism. This approach is being increasingly adopted for two fundamental reasons - it can achieve successful dark tourism from the marketing standpoint and it brings benefits to local residents and their environment. Quality dark tourism does not necessarily mean expensive dark tourism. Rather, it refers to tourist attractions, facilities and services that offer 'good value for money', protect dark tourism resources, and attract the kinds of tourists who will respect the local environment and society. Quality dark tourism development can compete more effectively in attracting discriminating tourists. It is also more environmentally and socially self-sustaining. Achieving quality dark tourism is the responsibility of both the public and private sectors. This concept should be built into the dark tourism planning, development and management process.

LONG-RANGE AND STRATEGIC PLANNING

Long-range comprehensive planning is concerned with specifying goals and objectives and determining preferred future development patterns. Dark tourism development policies and plans should be prepared for relatively long-term periods - usually for 10 to 15 and sometimes 20 years - depending on the predictability of future events in the country or region. These may seem to be long planning periods, but it commonly requires this length of time to implement basic policy and structure plans. Even development of specific projects, such as major resorts or national park-based dark tourism, can require a long time.

A planning approach which has received considerable attention in recent years, and is applicable to some dark tourism areas, is strategic planning. While the outcomes of strategic and long-range comprehensive planning may be very similar, strategic planning is somewhat different. It focuses more on identification and resolution of immediate issues. Strategic planning typically is more oriented to rapidly changing future situations and how to cope with changes organizationally. It is more action oriented and concerned with handling unexpected events.

Applied only by itself, strategic planning can be less comprehensive in its approach. By focusing on immediate issues, it may deviate from achieving such long-term objectives as sustainable development. But if used within the framework of integrated long-range policy and planning, the strategic planning approach can be very appropriate.

PUBLIC INVOLVEMENT IN PLANNING

Planning is for the benefit of people, and they should be involved in the planning and development of dark tourism in their areas. Through this involvement, dark tourism development will reflect a consensus of what the people want. Also, if residents are involved in planning and development decisions - and if they understand the benefits the dark tourism can bring - they will more likely support it. At the national and regional levels of preparing dark tourism plans, the common approach to obtaining public involvement is to appoint a steering committee. This committee offers guidance to the planning team and reviews its work, especially the draft reports and policy and planning recommendations that are made.

A planning study steering committee is typically composed of representatives of the relevant government agencies involved in dark tourism, the private sector, and community, religious and other relevant organizations. Also, open public hearings can be held on the plan. These hearings provide the opportunity for anybody to learn about the plan and express their opinions. Another common approach, when the plan is completed, is to organize a national or regional dark tourism seminar. This meeting informs participants and the general public about the importance of controlled dark tourism development and the recommendations of the plan. Such seminars often receive wide publicity in the communications media.

In a large country or region, the usual procedure is for the dark tourism plan to be prepared by the central authority with public involvement. This can be termed the 'top-down' approach. Another procedure sometimes used is the 'bottom-up' approach. This involves holding meetings with local districts or communities to determine what type of development they would like to have. These local objectives and ideas are then fitted together into a national or regional plan.

This approach achieves greater local public involvement in the planning process. But it is more time consuming and may lead to conflicting objectives, policies and development recommendations among the local areas. These conflicts need to be reconciled at the national and regional levels in order to form a consistent plan.

It is important that the development patterns of the local areas complement and reinforce one another, but also reflect the needs and desires of local communities. Often a combination of the 'top-down' and 'bottom-up' approaches achieves the best results.

THE DARK TOURISM PLANNING PROCESS

The first step in the planning process is careful preparation of the study so that it provides the type of development guidance that is needed. Study preparation involves formulating the project terms of reference, selecting the technical team to carry out the study, appointing a steering committee, and organizing the study activities. The terms of reference (TOR) for the planning study should be carefully formulated so that the study achieves its desired results and outputs. The TOR for a national or regional plan indicates the outputs and activities that are necessary to prepare the development policy and plan. The special considerations to be made in planning - such as economic, environmental or social issues and the critical institutional elements - should be specified in the TOR.

Identification of implementation techniques are also specified. The TOR format typically follows the planning process explained here, but it is tailored to the specific characteristics and needs of the planning area. Many places already have some limited dark tourism development, and these existing patterns must be considered in formulating the TOR. Other countries or regions will have considerable existing dark tourism development, but it may be declining or not be in a form that generates optimum benefits. The TOR will therefore emphasize how to rejuvenate and improve existing development, along with how to provide guidance on the future expansion of dark tourism. It is common for a single study include various levels of dark tourism planning, such as national and regional plans along with detailed planning for priority development areas and projects. The planning for all these levels will need to be specified in the TOR.

BUDDHIST CIRCUIT

India is the birthplace of one of the most widely accepted religions in the world - Buddhism. The four holy places associated with Gautam Buddha in India are - Lumbini, his birthplace, which now lies in Nepal; Bodhgaya, where he attained enlightenment; Sarnath, near Varanasi, where he preached his first sermon; Kushinagar, near Gorakhpur, where he achieved Mahanirvana. The other important tourist places associated with Buddhism are: Sanchi, Vaishali, Nalanda, Amravati and Nagargunakonda. All these places together are known as the famous Buddhist circuit in India.

Bodhgaya is the most important Buddhist pilgrimage amongst all these places in India. Apart from being a significant archaeological site, it is renowned for the Mahabodhi Temple, which houses a 50 metre high pyramidal spire and an image of the Buddha. Sarnath near Varanasi is a vital centre of the Buddhist world where he delivered his first sermon and set in motion the wheel of law, the Dharmachakra. Buddhism germinated in Sarnath amidst the deer park.

Nalanda is the famous education centre of Buddhism where the Chinese scholar and traveller Hiuen Tsang stayed in the 7th century to explore the roots of Buddhism. Vaishali is significant to Buddhists as Lord Buddha announced his impending Nirvana here. One of the famous pillars erected by Ashoka to propagate Buddhism also stands here in Nalanda. Sanchi in Madhya Pradesh is known for its numerous stupas, monasteries, temples and pillars dating from the 3rd century B.C. to the 12th century A.D.

Amaravati on the bank of river Krishna in the South India, is famous for its temple, dedicated to Lord Amarewara. The temple is the dilapidated 2000-year-old Buddhist stupa that draws millions of archaeologists and pilgrims every year. Named after the great scholar of Buddhism, Nagarjunakonda, located on the banks of river Krishna rctains its status as the greatest centre of Buddhist learning in the South of Vindhyas. Earlier known as Vijayapuri, Nagarjunakonda was the venue of the massive congregation of monks and scholars during the bygone era. The Buddhist circuit in India thus introduces you with the major townships in India that mark the evolution, development and propagation of Buddhism. After Gautam Buddha, it was Emperor Ashoka followed by his daughter and son Sanghmitra and Mahindra, who took the charge of propagating Buddhism in India as well as the South Asian countries like Burma, Nepal, China, Japan, Malaysia, Sri Lanka etc.

8

Need for Tourism Modelling Need for Tourism Modelling

The TPF model consists of an innovative integration of tourism and travel analysis within a computable general equilibrium (CGE) modelling framework, to assist the formation of government policies relating to tourism and travel. The current research with Tourism Satellite Accounts (TSAs) can be complemented and extended by the use for analysing tourism and travel. These models are formal economic models that extend, rather than replace, tourism satellite accounts (TSAs).

Indeed, the increasing implementation of TSAs is a stimulus to the use of TPF models because they provide data that is ideal for implementing a TPF model.

These models allow the full potential of the detailed data contained within TSAs to be realised and facilitate:

- The assessment of tourism's overall economic impact,
- The analysis of tourism policy,
- Tourism forecasting, predicting long-term trends in tourist numbers and expenditures.

TOURISM SATELLITE ACCOUNTS AND TPF MODELS

Tourism satellite accounts are being formulated by countries across the world, in order to provide accurate measures of the size of tourism sectors, the nature of demand for tourism, the nature of supply in tourism sectors, and the direct contribution of tourism to GDP and employment. This makes an invaluable contribution to our knowledge of the tourism sector. When measuring the economic impact of tourism, input-output (IO) models have often been used in the past. While these models successfully capture some of the economic impact of tourism, they do not capture all of the economic impact, leading to estimates of the economic impact of tourism that are not only unreliable but heavily biased.

Computable general equilibrium (CGE) models have their historical origins in input-output methodology, but were developed to overcome the many shortcomings of IO models. In particular, CGE models allow prices to vary and resources to be reallocated between production sectors. Tourism Policy and Forecasting (TPF) models build upon this framework by including tourism data from TSAs to provide a consistent means of modelling tourism in the entire economy.

Computable general equilibrium modelling is one of the most flexible and innovative economic techniques developed in recent decades. It has been used extensively by such international organisations as the World Bank, the World Trade Organisation and the OECD as well as in academia. It has been used in the fields of international trade, economic development, agricultural economics and environmental economics. Tourism impact models have traditionally relied on input-output (IO) modelling.

More recently, there have been initial applications of CGE models in the tourism field. The use of CGE models uses the latest methodology and gives more accurate predictions than techniques such as IO modelling. CGE models are formulated in a way that is radically different from input-output modelling, macroeconomic modelling, partial equilibrium modelling or, indeed, any other form of numerical simulation. Whereas the other modelling techniques rely on an initial stimulus which is then traced through the economic system in a systematic and deterministic manner, CGE models are formulated by specifying how economic agents react to changes in the economy. A CGE model is then solved simultaneously for all markets, production sectors and economic agents.

This gives CGE models a significant advantage in flexibility over other forms of modelling, because other forms of modelling can only trace the effects of specific initial stimuli, and do so in a one-way deterministic system. In a CGE model, the initial stimulus can originate anywhere in the economy, and can be literally anything that can occur in an economic framework, ranging from changes in taxes and subsidies, to technological change, population growth, shifts in demand and regulatory changes. CGE models are not deterministic in the same way that other simulation approaches are.

The initial stimulus affects markets, production sectors and economic agents who react to the stimulus and provide further changes to the economy. These changes do not work in a one-way direction, so effects can feed back to where the stimulus started. Broadly speaking, the construction of a CGE model is a process of setting up a series of markets (for goods, services and factors of production), production sectors and demand groups (households). Each market, sector and household has its own set of economic rules that determine how it reacts to external changes.

Typically, markets for goods and services are market clearing, so that if demand exceeds supply, the price of the good or service will increase until the market clears. If the price of the good that a production sector produces increases, the output of the sector will increase. Consequently its use of factors of production will increase and the supply of the good will increase. Eventually these demand and supply changes will (due to the demand-supply correcting behaviour of prices in markets) increase the price of factors of production and decrease the price of the output good, until it is no longer profitable to increase output any further.

By setting up the economic conditions whereby each market, sector and household reacts to changes in the economy, a CGE model can then model a variety of possible scenarios. In other forms of numerical simulation, models are set up whereby the simulation follows a direct causal relationship from one effect to the next. CGE models by their very nature allow interactions between markets, and between sectors, that may be very complex. IO models rely on an input-output table for data, and trace the intermediate demands for goods and services that are needed to satisfy final demands by consumers, the government, investment and exports.

Hence, they calculate the indirect effects of final demand. The earnings of income (by private consumers and the government) can also be included to calculate the induced effects, which are similar to Keynesian multipliers. CGE models include other effects through factor markets and foreign currency. In doing so, the CGE models include not only the indirect effects but also the induced effects. Tourism Policy and Forecasting models extend the CGE framework to incorporate tourism and travel, with data on tourism demand and the supply of tourism industries, and frameworks for modelling tourism and travel.

Four basic characteristics differentiate Nottingham TPF models from IO models of tourism and travel:

- A TPF model includes flexible prices and wages. This enables factors of production, such as labour and capital, and foreign exchange markets to be modelled.
- Income-expenditure consistency must be maintained for all private households, the government, firms and any other economic agents that are modelled.
- Consumers' responses to changes in prices and income levels are taken into account by behavioural assumptions.
- Substitution between intermediate inputs and factors of production, as prices and wages change, is taken into account by production assumptions.

A TPF model contains four types of equation:

- Equilibrium conditions for each market ensure that supply is equal to demand for each good, service, factor of production and for foreign exchange.
- Income-expenditure identities ensure that the economic model is a closed system. All earnings must be accounted for through expenditure or savings. These conditions apply to all private house holds, the government, firms and any other economic agents that are modelled.
- Behavioural relationships state how economic agents react to changing prices and income levels. These then determine consumers' demand levels for each good and service.
- Production functions determine how much is produced for any given level of factor employment. With assumptions regarding market structure, these determine what levels of labour employment, capital usage and intermediate input usage are required to satisfy a given level of output for a set of prices.

One of the strengths of the TPF models is their flexibility. As demonstrated in figure 3, the TPF models usually contain certain core components of the model structure, and can be expanded by extending the scope of the model to suit the circumstances of the tourist origin/destination country or region.

Model structure components include:

- Market competition. Various forms of market competition can be included, from perfect competition to monopoly.
- Labour markets can be modelled in various forms, with the possibility of allowing for unemployment.
- Foreign trade can be treated in several different ways, to enable the modelling of small and large countries.
- Dynamics can be incorporated to show how the economy moves through time, with economic agents' expectations about future events incorporated into their decision-making processes.

In addition, extensions to the model scope can be made, such as:

- Income distribution can be modelled by incorporating many household groups. The distributional effects of tourism or tourism policies could then be examined.
- Inter-regional effects could be modelled by modelling distinct regions within a country.
- International effects can show how tourism's effects are spread between countries.
- The environment can be incorporated to show the effects of tourism and tourism policy on environmental issues.

IMPACT MODELLING

TSAs represent a major step forward in the measurement of the economic size of tourism, but do not assess the total impact of tourism. Estimating the impact of tourism has the advantage of showing the desirability of tourism, in addition to measurement of size. It can also show what impact tourism has on different sectors, regions or on income distribution, depending on the specification of the model. One problem with any attempt to measure the size of a sector such as tourism is that it is usually measured from the demand-side and it is difficult to compare results with sectors such as mining, agriculture or manufacturing that are usually measured from the supply- side. The direct impact of tourism is, on the surface, the most comparable with supply-side sectors, but falls into definitional problems. If an aircraft is owned by an airline, for example, a proportion (corresponding to the proportion of airline services consumed by tourists) of the aircraft will be included in the direct measurement of tourism.

If, however, the airline rents the aircraft from another company, the value of the rental service will be attributed as an intermediate input into tourism, and the corresponding returns to investment will not be included in tourism value added. In an attempt to rectify this situation, various countries have included indirect effects through input-output (IO) models as an alternative in their TSAs.

While this solves problems relating to definitions of intermediates, it goes beyond the measurement of the size of tourism in an accounting sense and loses direct comparability with supply-side sectors. IO models include some intermediate purchases (such as food and fuel, for example) that should clearly be thought of as intermediate purchases and not as being within the tourism sector itself. In short, the IO models go some way beyond measuring the size of the sector to measuring its economic impact. IO models do not, however, measure the full impact of tourism.

These models make various assumptions that evidently exclude some of the economic effects that a sector has. Therefore the measurement of indirect impacts through IO models gives only a partial picture of the full impact of tourism.

In fact, the TPF results are more comprehensive and IO results more misleading because they incorporate only some of the impact of tourism.

TOURISM POLICY ANALYSIS

The TPF models can be readily utilised to provide other forms of economic analysis. Policy analysis is an important way in which the potential of TPF models can be further demonstrated.

The TPF models offer the ability to perform "what-if" simulations:

- Examine the economic effects of existing policies on tourism or of proposed alternatives. For example, they can show the net effective taxation of tourism that exists or provide a quantitative assessment of policy alternatives.
- Provide a theoretical viewpoint or an applied quantitative estimate.
- Examine purely taxation issues, or other policy instruments such as investment incentives and planning regulations.
- Examine the effects of tourism policy, or the effects that other policies have on tourism.

These examples demonstrate that the scope for tourism policy analysis with the TPF models is large.

Cases of particular relevance include:

- Examination of the current levels of tourism taxation, *i.e.* whether tourism is taxed at too low or too high rates relative to the rest of the economy.
- Quantitative estimates of tourism policy alternatives, such as planned tax changes or tourism development plans.
- Quantitative estimates of the effects of other policies on tourism, such as trade liberalisation or general taxation changes.

FORECASTING

TPF models can be used to forecast future trends in the tourism industry. Such forecasting models show how changes in the world economy will feed through to tourism.

Three main causes of change are highlighted here:

- Factor accumulation, including capital accumulation through investment, labour growth through population growth, and changes to the skills of labour through education and training.
- Technological change, through technical progress.
- Policy changes, which may be foreseeable.

These factors influence both income growth on the demand side and production costs on the supply side. As each factor may be changing at different rates in different sectors and in different countries, forecasting their total effect requires a TPF model. Relative prices balance the demand and supply side factors to achieve equilibrium in each market. Continuing increases in overall skill and education levels will, for example, lead to high growth rates in sectors that use highly skilled and highly educated labour.

How this affects tourism depends very much on the skill and education levels in tourism characteristic sectors, and on the intermediate relationships between tourism characteristic sectors and the rest of the economy. Differential growth rates between tourist source countries will affect international tourism growth rates in different destination markets. Tourism growth will, in general, be highly responsive to increases in income levels in source countries, and will depend on the relative prices for tourism and other goods and services. The TPF models provide the opportunity to assess the potential long-term growth of tourism in response to changes in the economy (such as population growth and changing education levels) that are highly predictable, as well as the short-term impact of macroeconomic changes such as currency market crises and natural disasters.

TSAS AND A TPF MODEL OF THE USA

Tourism satellite accounts provide detailed data on tourism activities that are not otherwise available in national accounts because national accounts provide data classified according to production activities and commodities, and tourism spans many of these standard classifications. The U.S. TSA used here specifies 18 industries and 23 commodities.

The tables that it provides are:

1. Production Account of Tourism Industries and All Other Industries.
   This table provides a "make" matrix showing the output of each commodity in each industry and a breakdown of costs by industry into three categories: intermediate inputs, compensation of employees, and other value added.
2. Supply and Consumption of Tourism and All Other Commodities.
   This table shows (i)a breakdown of total supply of each commodity into various categories - such as domestic production, imports government sales; and
   (ii) A breakdown of demand into categories - intermediate, personal consumption, investment, exports and government expenditures.
3. Tourism Demand by Type of Visitor.
   This provides expenditures on each category by visitors, broken down into the following categories: business, government, resident and non-resident.
4. Tourism GDP of Tourism Industries and Other Industries.
   Using a tourism industry ratio derived as tourism output divided by industry output, this table provides details of how much GDP is generated by tourism in each industry.
5. Tourism Employment and Compensation of Employees.
   Using the tourism industry ratio, this table derives tourism employment and compensation of employees by industry. The ability

to define different categories of tourism expenditure and trace the effects of this expenditure through the economy is an important and substantial step in tourism research. The data provided by such tables are invaluable for economists when modelling tourism.

The data requirements of tourism policy and forecasting models are that input-output tables and tourism demand data are available for a consistent classification of industries and commodities. Therefore, where published input-output tables adequately classify tourism and travel sectors, only the demand data is required from TSAs.

Where published input-output tables do not adequately define tourism industries, data from the TSAs on the structure of supply may also be necessary. The U.S. TPF model combines the tourism demand data for 1997 with the published 1997 benchmark input-output table containing data for 494 sectors and 37 categories of final demand, in addition to other sources of data. We present illustrative results here of an aggregated version of the Tourism Policy and Forecasting Model for the USA.

It has 18 sectors and commodities that correspond as closely as possible, given the necessary matching of TSA data, IO data and data from other sources, to the published TSA.

THE EFFECT OF A 10 PER CENT INCREASE IN FOREIGN TOURIST EXPENDITURES

In order to measure the impact of foreign tourism, we simulate a 10 per cent increase in foreign tourist expenditures. This 10 per cent increase is $9.6bn. Economic welfare, as measured by equivalent variation rises by $5.8bn, just under 0.1 per cent of GDP. These comparative illustrate that just over half of the expenditure is captured as an increase in welfare, as markets adjust to reallocate resources, imports increase, and other exports are crowded out.

The impact of this expenditure is captured by GDP, in terms of:

(i) Direct expenditure impact,

(ii) Input-output estimates, and

(iii) General equilibrium estimates with the TPF model. While the direct impact of the $9.6bn extra expenditures is $4.5bn and the input-output estimate is $9.4bn, the TPF estimate is $6.0bn. This indicates that:

- A large proportion of the expenditures leads directly to purchases of intermediate inputs, hence the low figure for the direct expenditure impact.
- Almost all of the expenditure leads to increased GDP in the input-output estimate. The IO estimate has no crowding-out, and there is very little import leakage.

- The TPF estimate includes significant levels of crowding-out and resource reallocation.
- Some tourism and travel sectors have significantly higher increases in GDP in the TPF model than the IO model suggests. Here, the initial stimulus of foreign tourism expenditures is reinforced by domestic expenditures as firms benefiting from the initial expenditures increase there own expenditures on business tourism, and private households which have increases in income spend more on domestic tourism.
- Others tourism and travel sectors, such as water and rail transport, have a lower GDP increase than the IO model suggests. These are sectors that sell products that are relatively small proportions of the foreign tourist's expenditures. Resources are reallocated to other sectors that are able to pay higher wages. These reallocation effects outweigh the induced effects that these sectors experience from higher incomes.
- Non-tourism industries (here, 'all other commodities') have a decline in sector GDP that the IO model completely misses, because it does not include price crowding-out effects and resource allocation. Here, there is no direct stimulus from the foreign tourism expenditures. Indirect (intermediate demands, as captured through the IO model) and induced effects are positive, but are outweighed by resource allocation effects.

INDIRECT TAXATION

The overall effect of indirect taxation exposes the levels of effective protection that the structure of taxation gives to industries, and shows how distortions that indirect taxes introduce lead to economic loses. As such, it is an important indicator as to how economically efficient taxes are in each sector. The results therefore remove arguments about the motives for taxation because the total level of taxation is maintained. The changes to the GDP contribution of labour and capital are given in the first column.

Changes to the GDP contribution of taxation are given in the second column. Changes to the total GDP contribution by sector, and in total, are given in the third column, and in the fourth column as a percentage of the 1997 GDP contribution.

Overall, removing all indirect taxes and replacing them with non-distorting direct taxes leads to an improvement to GDP of $528.4bn, which is 2.1 per cent of GDP in 1997. This therefore is the measure of the total distortionary impact of the indirect taxation system.

This improvement to GDP comes about through an increase in the GDP contribution of labour and capital ($1,033.8bn) outweighing the loss in indirect taxation revenue ($-505.4bn). With some exceptions, tourism and travel sectors have a lower GDP increase than the national average of 2.1 per cent. Non-tourism sectors ('all other commodities' is a much larger sector than 'gasoline and oil' or the wholesale sector) have a larger GDP effect than the national average. This implies, since tourism sectors do not expand by the national average when indirect taxation is removed, that the tourism sectors have levels of effective taxation that are higher than the national average. The results of these 17 separate simulations are summarised as the welfare effect of removing the individual taxes.

Taxes in a range of sectors such as auto and truck rental, recreation and entertainment and retail margins, impose distortions on the economy that lead to a higher welfare loss than the tax revenue that they raise. Some sectors, such as water transport, air transport and hotels and lodging places, have much lower distortionary impact when compared to the tax revenue.

There are many reasons why sectors have different distortionary impacts, including:

- The distortionary impact of tax rates are often more than proportional to the tax revenue raised, so that higher tax rates lead to a higher distortion/revenue ratio.
- The distortionary impacts are related to other sectors through intermediate demands, and substitution in final demand. Sectors that have high distortions can effectively pass some of these distortions to related sectors.
- The distortionary impacts are related to how readily supply and demand change in response to price changes, in other words to the elasticities of supply and demand. Sectors with inelastic supply and demand (*i.e.* low levels of supply and demand response to prices) tend to have lower distortionary impacts from taxation. In a general equilibrium framework, the responsiveness of supply and demand depends on many factors, such as who purchases the product (a product mainly purchased by firms will often have a lower demand elasticity than one purchased by households) and the structure of production (an industry that relies heavily on one type of input will tend to have a lower supply elasticity than other industries).

What-if' scenarios can simulate the effects of anything from productivity growth, changes to competition (anti-trust) legislation and environmental controls. The total general equilibrium effects of such diverse issues can be a complex product of many different changes. Here, we show the results of a productivity improvement in air transport. The $20.6bn increase in GDP that results is spread across industries, with air transport itself increasing in size to account for an extra $2bn in GDP, industries that use air transport such as 'all other commodities' also increasing.

Most sectors that have a reduced GDP contribution are other transport industries, which compete with air transport. The Nottingham Tourism, Policy and Forecasting models apply tourism within a general equilibrium setting. They are an innovative and significant means of combining tourism satellite accounts, input-output tables and economic modelling. They expand on the TSA's measurement of tourism's economic size to provide estimates of tourism's economic impact, including many effects that are not captured in input-output models. TPF models also provide an important tool for policy analysis, enabling the complex interactions in the economy that result from policy actions to be traced through a general equilibrium framework and assessed. The ability to have quantitative estimates of the effects of policy is of vital importance to policy makers.

TPF models can also be used as a basis for forecasting the levels and expenditures of tourists, taking relatively stable and predictable long-term trends in tourism source and destination countries to provide a method of robust long-term forecasting. The results presented here for the USA Tourism, Policy and Forecasting model provide an example of the TPF model's capabilities. The impact of tourism when including induced income effects and resource reallocation effects is dramatically different to the standard input-output results. In particular, the IO models overestimate the total GDP effect, underestimate the total effect on tourism sectors and completely miss the negative effects on non-tourism sectors. The results of the policy analysis using the TPF model are that most tourism sectors are effectively taxed at higher than the national average level.

In sectors such as hotels and transport sectors indirect taxation imposes lower welfare losses on the economy than in other sectors. This implies that the most urgent sectors for tax reductions (*i.e.* those where welfare distortions are disproportionately high relative to tax revenues) are auto and truck rental, retail, eating and drinking, recreation and entertainment, participant sports, and parking, automotive repair and highway tolls. We also report the results of a 'what-if' scenario that shows the effect of improved productivity in the air transport sector.

The results show that increases in GDP are spread across the economy in sectors that use air transport. Competing transport sectors may contract as a result. The USA TPF model is intended to give an indication of the potential applications that TPF modelling has.

While the sector classification for this model is small to match the U.S. TSA as closely as possible, a full 494-sector model is also in operation. For the U.S., the model can be extended in various directions: tourism demand data on domestic tourism by state would enable the TPF model to include state effects. Otherwise, the model can be expanded to include different skill categories of labour and different households groups according to geographical location, income category, or other classification. This would be able to show how these different household groups are affected by both an expansion in tourism and by policies. Other possible ways of expanding this model are to incorporate similar data from other countries: a model of North America would, for example, include Canada and Mexico.

This would incorporate cross-border effects, to assess the effects that a tax on a tourism sector in the U.S. has on the economies of Canada and Mexico. As well as these extensions the U.S. TPF model, it is of course possible to build similar models for any country where a TSA and input-output table exist, and these can also incorporate regional differences, household distributions and different types of labour as well as incorporating more than one country. The underlying methodology of TPF models is well suited to developing countries, for which computable general equilibrium modelling has long been used.

COASTAL IMPACT OF TOURISM

Tourism provides an essential lifeline for many coastal communities. Faced with the prospect of increasing financial hardship, more and more coastal communities have turned to tourism as a means of generating income and survival. Tourism's impact on the coastal zone has, therefore, been largely positive. Of course, as in any area, if Tourism is not properly managed and developed, it can be harmful.

Impacts arise from the construction of infrastructure (hotels, marinas, transport, waste treatment facilities, groynes etc.) and from recreation (golf courses, water sports, theme parks etc). Coastal communities are now faced with tourism on a considerable scale, and the host to guest ratio can be very high in such areas. At the same time, coastal communities must try to maintain the resort's attraction as tourist demands change, sometimes quite rapidly.

With coastal regions being primary tourist destinations, sensitive marine and coastal environments can suffer dramatically. For example, as a result of large-scale sea-front tourist development, considerable beach and dune erosion can occur.

Tourism also impacts on environmental quality in the following ways:

- Ribbon development, infrastructure requirements, particularly transport links;

- The treatment and disposal of solid and/or liquid wastes, particularly during peak tourist seasons, may be inadequate or at worst non-existent; and
- Water is often consumed excessively, not only for drinking but for showers, laundry, swimming pools, maintenance of golf courses etc. This can affect the quantity and quality of fresh water available to indigenous coastal populations.

Recreational activities can also have a significant impact on the coastal zone:

- Golf course's impact can be considerable, with those situated directly on coastal habitats(especially sand dunes) in particular;
- Erosion of reefs and coral from divers and swimmers;
- Pollution from boats and jets skis; and
- Noise from motor boats and jet skis, cars and buses, nightlife and other activities.

The development of a sustainable tourism industry in the coastal zone offers numerous opportunities. Opportunities includes, those for nature conservation - which, given the increasing interest in high quality natural and cultural experiences, can help to reverse the decline in market share of many coastal destinations. Tourism also provides important opportunities for strengthening local industries. Where industries are in decline, tourism ventures can help supplement declining income.

The following examples illustrate what can be done to make the most of the opportunities offered by tourism in the coastal zone:

Calvia is a Municipality on the Mediterranean coast that has undertaken an Agenda 21 project to assist the sustainable development of its tourism sector, in order to counter the negative impact of short-term tourism development since the 1960s. The local council has now implemented a transferable policy aimed at modernising, improving and diversifying the local tourist industry, involving all stakeholders, including the local population.

A Project Plan was enacted, and achievements so far include:

- Indigenous development, based on the sustainable use of available resources;
- High quality services and an appropriate bed night capacity;
- A ban on new development on 1,700 acres;
- Active participation of the residents in community life; and
- Environmental management of municipality buildings, waste recycling, reduction in spending on electricity, and use of environmentally friendly materials for office use.

Quicksilver Tours, Queensland, Australia, is owned by one of the largest tourism operators to the Great Barrier Reef. Quicksilver have five large catamarans, which take about 1,000 tourists a day to dive on the reef. They have their own reef site with fixed diving platforms. They employ a team of biologists, both for environmental management and assessment as well as widespread environmental interpretation. Recent assessment of the reef, in the vicinity of the operation, shows that it is being maintained in pristine condition.

Kingfisher Bay Resort is found at Fraser Island, Queensland. It is a large five star "ecotourism" resort built in a beautiful, but fragile environment off the Queensland coast. Its concept, design, construction and management were conceived using the latest ecologically sustainable principles. It is a state-of-the-art "ecotourism" resort, which has won Australia's top tourism awards, and its economic and environmental success has influenced new coastal tourism developments.

Maho Bay's camps and studios in the US Virgin Islands have based their product on a commitment to minimise impact on the environment, conserve natural resources, engage in active and passive environmental education of their guests, and contribute to the local economy. Specific initiatives introduced at Maho Bay include the following: use of new technology; purchasing policies; waste management; environmental education; energy and water conservation; and support for local communities and culture.

These initiatives show an appreciation of the need for alternative solutions to issues such as packaging and waste disposal through landfill. These are issues, which as the industry grows, will be increasingly important for the Travel and Tourism industry as a whole to address.

The agents, partnerships for change and areas for further action in relation to tourism in the coastal zone are similar to the development of broad based sustainable tourism in general. A number of issues do, of course, have particular importance for the coastal zone. Above all, the key to success is better participation at destination level among all the stakeholders concerned. In the case of the coastal zone, there are a number of additional organisations with an interest in coastal policy, marine conservation, shipping etc., which needs to be identified and included in partnerships for the coastal zone.

Successful planning for tourism is very important for the future of the industry in coastal regions, because a significant percentage of tourism occurs within the geographical parameters of the definition of a coastal zone. Concerted support from all countries involved (and the industries within them) is vital to protect the shared natural resources that coastal zones represent.

Historically, the influence most hoteliers have on the environmental impact of their business is limited to working within existing buildings, or after a new site has been completed. In April 1998, the IHEI convened a group of hoteliers, tour operators, architectural firms and sustainable development specialists with the goal of creating a partnership to be called the "Sitting and Design Programme".

The new initiative's mission will be to define responsible planning and design specifications that will cause minimal environmental damage at new sites. Particular attention will be paid to sites located within ecologically sensitive areas and upon waterfronts.

The "Siting and Design Programme" will strive to reach hotel owners, investors and developers to bring these issues to the attention of the entire industry. Linkages with government authorities that uphold responsible development standards would complete the partnership.

Travel and Tourism has a number of advantages over other industry sectors:

- It creates jobs and wealth whilst;
- At the same time, it can contribute to sustainable development;
- It tends to have low start-up costs;
- Is a viable option in a wide range of areas and regions;
- Is likely to continue to grow for the foreseeable future; and
- The industry is, in a large part, aware of the need to protect the resource on which it is based - local culture and built and natural environment - and it is committed to these resources' preservation and enhancement.

The industry is, therefore, making a concerted effort to build up programmes for sustainable development. However, it cannot do this alone. If Travel and Tourism is to continue to flourish and to contribute to sustainable development, it needs help from national Governments. This assistance is needed in two forms: - both positive encouragement for sustainable tourism initiatives and an understanding that policy decisions in other areas can effect Travel and Tourism. In practical terms, what this means is the following:

The first point of action needed from Governments is to incorporate Agenda 21 principles into tourism policies at international and national level, and to promote their inclusion in regional and local tourism strategies. By providing such a lead and establishing a coherent global framework based on Agenda 21, national governments will make a vital contribution to developing a more sustainable tourism industry.

Governments should also recognise that Travel and Tourism is a core service sector which should always be considered when looking at policies to expand trade, increase employment, modernise infrastructure and encourage investment - at both domestic and international level. It should also bc included in national statistics with its economic impact calculated by means of a national tourism satellite account.

Governments should also consider helping Travel and Tourism by seeking to minimise regulatory impediments and by offering appropriate investment incentives. By supporting tourism and allowing it to compete in open and fair markets, tourism's benefits can be more easily secured. Finally, governments can address some of the fundamental barriers to tourism growth by looking at how to expand and modernise infrastructure, to apply taxes fairly and to invest in human resource development. If the programme of action outlined above can be undertaken by national governments in co-operation with continued industry commitments and initiatives for sustainable tourism then we can look to a brighter future.

THE IMPORTANCE OF TOURISM

Tourism can also be one of the most effective drivers for the development of regional economies. These patterns apply to both developed and emerging economies. Travel and Tourism is the world's largest industry and creator of jobs across national and regional economies. WTTC/WEFA research show that in 2000, Travel and Tourism will generate, directly and indirectly, 11.7 per cent of GDP and nearly 200 million jobs in the world-wide economy. These figures are forecasted to total 11.7 per cent and 255 million respectively in 2010. Jobs generated by Travel and Tourism are spread across the economy - in retail, construction, manufacturing and telecommunications, as well as directly in Travel and Tourism companies.

These jobs employ a large proportion of women, minorities and young people; are predominantly in small and medium sized companies; and offer good training and transferability.

CONTRIBUTING TO SUSTAINABLE DEVELOPMENT

The 1992 United Nations Conference on Environment and Development (UNCED), the Rio Earth Summit, identified Travel and Tourism as one of the key sectors of the economy which could make a positive contribution to achieving sustainable development. The Earth Summit lead to the adoption of Agenda 21, a comprehensive programme of action adopted by 182 governments to provide a global blueprint for achieving sustainable development. Travel and Tourism is the first industry sector to have launched an industry-specific action plan based on Agenda 21.

Travel and Tourism is able to contribute to development which is economically, ecologically and socially sustainable, because it:

- Has less impact on natural resources and the environment than most other industries;
- Is based on enjoyment and appreciation of local culture, built heritage,

and natural environment, as such that the industry has a direct and powerful motivation to protect these assets;

- Can play a positive part in increasing consumer commitment to sustainable development principles through its unparalleled consumer distribution channels; and
- Provides an economic incentive to conserve natural environments and habitats which might otherwise be allocated to more environmentally damaging land uses, thereby, helping to maintain bio-diversity.

There are numerous good examples of where Travel and Tourism is acting as a catalyst for conservation and improvement of the environment and maintenance of local diversity and culture. (Some of these are set out in Section B of this paper and a fuller illustration of the range of industry action can be found on the World Travel and Tourism Council's. Of course, there are also examples where development has not been sustainable.

PROVIDING INFRASTRUCTURE

To a greater degree than most activities, Travel and Tourism depends on a wide range of infrastructure services - airports, air navigation, roads, railheads and ports, as well as basic infrastructure services required by hotels, restaurants, shops, and recreation facilities (*e.g.* telecommunications and utilities).

It is the combination of tourism and good infrastructure that underpins the economic, environmental and social benefits. It is important to balance any decision to develop an area for tourism against the need to preserve fragile or threatened environments and cultures. However, once a decision has been taken where an area is appropriate for new tourism development, or that an existing tourist site should be developed further, then good infrastructure will be essential to sustain the quality, economic viability and growth of Travel and Tourism. Good infrastructure will also be a key factor in the industry's ability to manage visitor flows in ways that do not affect the natural or built heritage, nor counteract against local interests.

CHALLENGE FOR THE FUTURE

Travel and Tourism creates jobs and wealth and has tremendous potential to contribute to economically, environmentally and socially sustainable development in both developed countries and emerging nations. It has a comparative advantage in that its start up and running costs can be low compared to many other forms of industry development. It is also often one of the few realistic options for development in many areas. Therefore, there is a strong likelihood that the Travel and Tourism industry will continue to grow globally over the short to medium term.

Of course, if Travel and Tourism is managed badly, it can have a detrimental effect - it can damage fragile environments and destroy local cultures. The challenge is to manage the future growth of the industry so as to minimise its negative impacts on the environment and host communities whilst maximising the benefits it brings in terms of jobs, wealth and support for local culture and industry, and protection of the built and natural environment.

INDUSTRY INITIATIVES

Travel and Tourism takes many different forms - from a trip only a few hours away from home to long distance travel overseas. A common belief is that most Travel and Tourism involves large numbers of visitors from developed countries travelling by air to destinations in emerging countries. In fact, in most countries, the domestic tourism market is larger than the inbound market. Of course, the social and cultural impact of inbound visitors is often greater than that of domestic tourists.

Whether tourism is domestic or international, it involves visiting a destination away from the area in which one lives and using the services available in that destination. Therefore, tourists' requirements are for travel services to reach their destinations and once there, for services such as shelter, water, food, sanitation and entertainment.

What makes tourism special is that, many of these different products and services are often supplied by different operators: usually small or medium sized businesses in local ownership. This makes tourism a highly fragmented and diverse industry and so co-ordinated, industry-wide action is difficult to achieve. The influence of Travel and Tourism's demand also extends far beyond traditional tourism companies, into upstream suppliers like aircraft manufacturers or food producers and into the downstream service providers for travellers, like retail shops.

Despite the difficulties caused by fragmentation and lengthy supply chains, there has been a steady growth in environmental good practice across the industry in recent years. There are examples of airlines and airports reducing pollution and noise impacts; cruise liners practising marine conservation; hotels implementing energy consumption and waste disposal programmes; car rental companies investing in increasingly fuel efficient fleets and railways sound proofing to dampen noise.

The result is that there are a number of excellent initiatives in place designed to improve the environmental management of Travel and Tourism businesses. Of course, more needs to be done.

WTTC with 105 members is the global business leaders' forum for the Travel and Tourism industry. The WTTC have set in place an extensive strategy to promote a culture of sustainable development and have put in place a three-tiered structure for its achievement. This involves:

In 1996 the WTTC, the World Tourism Organization and the Earth Council, joined together to launch an action plan entitled "Agenda 21 for the Travel and Tourism Industry: Towards Environmentally Sustainable Development" - a sectional sustainable development programme based on the results of the Rio Earth Summit in 1992. Since the launch of the document, the three organisations have begun a series of regional seminars to increase awareness of the conclusions, and to adapt the programme for local implementation. The programme has held regional seminars in London and Jakarta in 1997 and Victoria Falls and Dominica in 1998.

WTTC has recently introduced a major addition to the programme - the "Alliance for Sustainable Tourism", which invites public and private sector Travel and Tourism organisations to record their Agenda 21 based activities on a central web site and commit to co-operation with all other partners. In order to develop the programme from global principles to community based action, WTTC is also discussing with the International Council for Local Environment Initiatives (ICLEI) on how the principles of "Agenda 21 for Travel and Tourism" can be built into Local Agenda 21 programmes. Furthermore, WTTC is considering pilot projects in 5 cities around the world to serve as models for other destinations.

In 1994, WTTC initiated the "GREEN GLOBE", an Agenda 21 based industry improvement programme, which provides guidance material and a certification process linked to both ISO standards and Agenda 21 principles. There are now 500 "GREEN GLOBE "members in 100 countries dedicated to improving environmental practice. The first certification has commenced with hotels groups in Jamaica and Manchester (UK). "GREEN GLOBE" has also developed a specific Destination Programme, which provides a methodology for Travel and Tourism destinations to implement sustainable development.

The ultimate aim is that "GREEN GLOBE" will become the primary global standard of environmental commitment by the global Travel and Tourism industry and will be recognised by the public as such. Currently, "GREEN GLOBE" has the support of over 20 international industry organisations representing thousands of businesses world-wide and the support of the World Tourism Organization, the United Nations Environment Programme and the Earth Council.

WTTC have also developed "ECoNETT", a web-site containing advice and data on good practice and sources of help and advice. "ECoNETT" is increasingly recognised as a focal point for environmental information, good practice, new techniques and technologies. The International Hotel and Restaurant Association (IH&RA), based in Paris, represents over 700,000 establishments in more than 150 countries. Its membership comprises some 50 national and international hotel and restaurant chains, over 110 national hotel and restaurant associations, independent hotel operators and restaurateurs, industry suppliers and 130 hotel schools. The IH&RA has offices in Asia-Pacific and Latin America. It is also the voice of the world's hotels and restaurants and plays a global role in representing, protecting, promoting and informing the industry to enable its members to achieve their business objectives.

The IH&RA has:

- Raised environmental awareness and developed programmes through joint workshops with national hotel associations and regularly encourages them to develop their own environmental awareness programmes;
- Established an annual Environmental Award sponsored by American Express and judged by the United Nations Environment Programme (UNEP) that recognises efforts by independent and chain hotels to "green" the industry;
- Published advice including practical publications such as the "Environmental Action Pack for Hotels" with the International Hotel Environment Initiative and UNEP and "Environmental Good Practice in Hotels" with UNEP;
- Supported regional initiatives such as the Caribbean Action for Sustainable Tourism; and
- Joined forces with UNEP and the International Hotel School Directors' Association to develop an "Environmental Teaching Resource Package for Hospitality Educational Institutes".

CORPORATE INITIATIVES

The International Hotel Environment Initiative (IHEI), based in London, England, is a programme of The Prince of Wales Business Leaders Forum. Founded in 1992 by a consortium of chief executives from 10 multinational hotel groups, IHEI is an educational charity designed to encourage continuous improvement in the environmental performance of the global hotel industry.

It does this through:

- Raising environmental awareness in the hotel industry by promoting good practiceinternationally;
- Developing hotel-specific guidance, enabling hotels of all sizes to implement environmentalprogrammes; and

- Multiplying the reach and impact of IHEI by working with partners, including hotelassociations, governments, NGOs, tourism bodies and businesses.

IHEI is a catalyst and conduit for hotels to pool their resources and to share experience via a non- competitive platform. In 5 years it has evolved into an organisation with global impact. IHEI has worked in 111 countries, stimulating and assisting with the establishment of local initiatives such as New Zealand's "Environmental Hotels of Auckland, the Asia Pacific Hotel Environment Initiative" and the Caribbean Action for Sustainable Tourism.

Member hotels now represent over 1 million guest rooms and more than 8,000 hotels on 5 continents.

The Co-operative Research Centre for Sustainable Tourism, based in Australia, was established in 1997 to enhance the strategic knowledge available to the Travel and Tourism industry through:

- Long-term high-quality scientific and technological research which contributes to the development of an internationally competitive tourism industry;
- Strengthening the links between research and its commercial and other applications;
- Promoting co-operative research; and
- Stimulating education and training, particularly in graduate programmes, through active involvement of researchers from outside the higher education system in educational activities, and of graduate students in major research programmes.

COMPANY INITIATIVES

The number of initiatives undertaken by individual companies is large. Just two examples from this are as follows:

The Kandalama hotel in Sri Lanka has been a recipient of the "GREEN GLOBE" award, 3 years in a row, for its commitment to environmental excellence.

The hotel has undertaken measures in the following areas to ensure that its operations are more sustainable:

- Cultural and social - hotel employment, providing community infrastructure and development;
- Natural environment - soil erosion measures and planting forests;
- Pollution - sewage, solid waste and noise pollution reduction programmes; and
- Environmental communication - construction of an Eco Park where all waste is treated within the park, a dry debris sorting centre, a

lecture room to promote environmental awareness and a sustainable development library.

Canadian Pacific Hotels, the largest hotel conglomerate in Canada, has developed an environmental programme, which is recognised as the most comprehensive in the North American hotel industry. Based on the results of a survey, employee suggestions and the recommendations of a professional environmental consultant, Canadian Pacific Hotels developed a list of 16 goals to be attained by all hotels. In addition to individual projects implemented at each of the 26 hotels, the goals set for the chain as a whole were ambitious:

(i) To reduce the amount of waste sent to landfill by 50 per cent across the chain, by launching an extensive recycling programme;

(ii) To redesign purchasing policies to ensure that waste is reduced at source, and supplies used in the hotels are nature friendly.

INTER-REGIONAL LEVEL

The Caribbean Action for Sustainable Tourism (CAST) is an alliance for sustainable growth developed by the Caribbean Hoteliers Association with the support of the WTTC, the IHEI and the Caribbean Tourism Organisation.

CAST has developed workshops, training courses and guidance material for its members on a wide range of environmental issues, including:

- Setting up environmental management systems;
- Energy efficiency;
- Renewable energy; and
- Waste water management.

AGENTS AND PARTNERSHIPS FOR CHANGE

The public sectors, particularly national and local government, have an important role to play by setting the agenda and providing the framework in which action should take place. The regulatory environment also plays an important role in creating the conditions suitable for sustainable tourism. Self-regulation involving the agreement and co-operation of industry is always likely to be the most effective solution. Therefore, the role of trade associations and industry organisations in distributing information among their members and encouraging participation is essential.

The major partnerships to be formed are between:

- Industry and the public sector - to ensure consistency with the framework;
- Industry and the voluntary sector - to tap into the enormous resources of expertise and goodwill that this sector is able to generate; and
- Industry and the public - both travellers themselves and the people

who live in the places they visit to develop more sustainable forms of tourism.

AREAS FOR FURTHER ACTION

The industry is already doing much to improve its performance in terms of sustainable development. The challenge for the new millennium is to move from the existing ad hoc approach to a more systematic one. To do this will involve a partnership between industry and national governments to deliver the following:

(i) Governments:
   - Integration of travel and tourism policy into broader government policies, especially the environment;
   - Incentives for the Travel and Tourism industry, backed up where necessary by effective regulation.

(ii) Public/Private partnership:
   - Infrastructure planned and developed with a long-term view and within a reference framework based on Agenda 21;
   - Indicators and environmental impact assessment tools to enable effective local management and appropriate development.

(iii) International bodies:
   - Co-ordination at an international level of environmental action undertaken by all sectors of the Travel and Tourism industry;
   - Review of existing voluntary initiatives to improve the quality of reporting, their transparency and credibility, and the assessment of their contribution to sustainability.

(iv) Companies:
   - Commitment to place sustainable development issues at the core of the management structure;
   - Innovation of process and application through new technology;
   - Commitment to education and environmental training of staff.

INFLUENCING CONSUMER BEHAVIOUR TO PROMOTE SUSTAINABLE TOURISM

At the 1998 World Travel Market, WTTC hosted, as a part of its Environmental Awareness Day, a seminar entitled "Does the Consumer Care?" At this event, MORI presented the latest findings from their Business and the Environment survey - an annual UK survey devoted to public attitudes to the environment.

The survey is now in its tenth year and illustrates the challenge facing the Travel and Tourism industry in influencing consumer behaviour to promote sustainable tourism. According to this survey, Travel and Tourism is now more associated with environmental damage than it has been in the past.

Despite this decline in perception, the industry's economic success is not dependent on its green record - public sensitivity to environmental problems on holiday/business trips has not increased and is no more of a deterrent to repeat travel than it was previously. There is a downward trend in the public's willingness to pay extra for environmental protection and environmentally friendly products, including "green" Travel and Tourism. Awareness of companies making environmental commitments is only marginally up.

Therefore, the challenge is to persuade the consumer that it is in their interests to adopt and promote a sustainable approach in their activities and purchasing decisions. Education programmes and the development and widespread acceptance of codes of conduct are useful tools in achieving this step. Once this message has been conveyed, it is then important to back this up with the necessary information to enable consumers to make informed choices. It is here that "ecolabels" and award programmes have value.

EDUCATION PROGRAMMES

The Foundation for Environmental Education in Europe (FEEE) seeks to promote environmental education by carrying out campaigns and improving awareness of the importance of environmental education. It is composed of a network of international organisations.

The FEEE (headquarters in Denmark) runs three major campaigns in Europe for providing safe and clean beaches and marinas. The award itself is given annually to beaches and marinas that satisfy a number of essential criteria in three separate areas: water quality; beach management and safety; and environmental information and education.

"GREEN GLOBE"'s Dodo Campaign, is based on a cartoon character, who features in 65 Travel and Tourism videos. Dodo explains and promotes the actions that visitors can take to reduce the impacts of their travels. The videos are aimed at children and are designed to be fun, whilst conveying important messages about sustainable Travel and Tourism. The aim is to have these videos shown on in flight and in-room television channels to raise awareness and influence consumer behaviour.

CODES OF CONDUCT

Codes of conduct are also used to try and influence consumer behaviour. For example, "Guidelines for Responsible Environmental Tourism" are prepared and distributed by the American Society of Travel Agents to all customers who book holidays through their members' branches. The Guidelines aim to "encourage the growth of peaceful tourism and environmentally responsible travel" and include 10 recommendations to encourage tourists to act responsibly and show respect for their hosts and the environment of their destinations.

The Pacific Asia Tourism Association (PATA) is an industrial association, which promotes the Pacific Asia area's Travel and Tourism destinations, products and services. PATA also serves as a central resource of information and research, travel industry education and training, as well as quality product development with sensitivity for culture, heritage and environment. In 1992, PATA introduced its "Code for Environmentally Responsible Tourism" to strengthen the principles of preservation in the region.

Businesses, organisations and individuals wishing to affirm their support for the PATA Code are encouraged to participate in the PATA Green Leaf programme. The Africa Travel Association has produced "Responsible Traveller Guidelines"; the Japanese Association of Travel Agents has produced the "Declaration of Earth Friendly Travellers" and there are many more examples of industry codes aimed at educating and influencing their customers.

ECO LABELLING

There are numerous examples of industry sponsored labelling schemes, whose aim is to recognise good industry practice and influence consumer behaviour into purchasing the labelled products. For example, the "Green Key, Denmark" certificate operated by the Hotel, Restaurant and Leisure Industry Association (HORESTA) has 56 criteria that includes environmental information, water and energy consumption and waste management. Special features also include ecological food products, outdoor areas, non-smoking rooms, and adaptations for access by disabled persons. There are a number of industries that runs and sponsors award programmes to highlight and promote examples of good practice.

For example, British Airways has run the "Tourism for Tomorrow" awards since 1992 to encourage action to protect the environment. The awards are directed at tour operators, hotels, national parks and heritage sites, and other activities associated with tourism. By selecting projects showing best practice in their field as role models, others are encouraged to follow suit and consider the environment in the everyday running of their tourism business. The awards are run annually, with a winner selected from each of five regions and an overall winner.

In addition, two special awards are made for mass tourism destinations. The awards are run in association with the British Tourist Authority, the Association of British Travel Agents, the Pacific Asia Travel Association and the American Society of Travel Agents. Entries to the awards have been increases every year. American Express also sponsors a variety of environmental awards for international tourism organisations.

Agents and Partnerships for Change:

- A broad based approach is called for which requires Travel and Tourism to work with: national governments to raise the profile of environmental and social issues within the education system;
- NGOs to raise awareness of tourism issues in their work and activities and provide feedback to the Travel and Tourism industry;
- Development organisations to communicate with host communities to understand their needs and requirements;
- Local authorities to engage local people through the inclusion of tourism issues in Local Agenda21 plans;
- National and international trade associations, labour representative organisations and training providers to increase awareness and training of staff in environmental and social issues;
- Travel and Tourism publications (such as travel guides);
- Travel and Tourism journalists to raise the profile of reporting environmental and social impacts of tourism among consumers and tourism businesses; and
- The Internet as a source of information for potential travellers.

AREAS FOR FURTHER ACTION

The WTTC/MORI data shows the scale of the task still remaining. The industry has developed a number of initiatives to influence consumer behaviour. However, if consumers do not understand or are not aware of the issues involved and do not demand more sustainable products then, in the long term, it will not be in the industry's interests to move in that direction. The priority for future action, therefore, should be to raise awareness among travellers of the issues associated with tourism and the impact their activities can have on local destinations and cultures.

BROAD-BASED SUSTAINABLE DEVELOPMENT THROUGH TOURISM

The Travel and Tourism industry has a vested interest in protecting the natural and cultural resources that are the core of its business. Travel and Tourism has less impacts on natural resources and the environment than other sectors and it has already done much to address the issues arising from its activities. There are examples, however, from around the world where the impact of Travel and Tourism has been damaging to the local environment and people.

Some of the factors which contributes to the harmful impact of tourism are:

- A lack of awareness on the part of those making decisions about tourism development of the social, economic and environmental balance to be pursued in achieving sustainable development;
- A lack of commitment by tourism operators and travellers to contribute to the maintenance of the local environment and culture of the host destination;
- A weak institutional framework with inadequate controls can lead to tourism development which is both inappropriate and intrusive;
- Unfairly traded tourism, whereby local communities are unable to share in its benefits;
- Large flows of visitors in remote or sensitive locations can place considerable strains on local resources (particularly water) and supply systems. Travellers' expectations of the goods and services, which should be available, can lead to these items or services, being imported from outside or local supply chains, being distorted to meet demands; and
- Tourism can change a destination's cultural make-up and, if poorly developed, can increase crime, prostitution and other social problems.

In order for tourism to realise its potential to achieve broad-based sustainable development, an effective partnership between Government and all sectors of the industry will be required. The following illustrates what is being done:

INTERNATIONAL CO-OPERATION

IH&RA and the United Nations Organisation for Education, Science and Culture (UNESCO) have signed a co-operation agreement to encourage world-wide hotel chains to sponsor UNESCO cultural heritage sites and attract tourism to them via their marketing campaigns.

NATIONAL GOVERNMENTS

In India, the government is pump priming local "eco-tourism" activities, which are primarily driven by local women. In Mexico, the government is kick starting village development for "eco-tourism" lodges in the Chiapas region involving the whole community.

In England, the government has recently held a national consultation on sustainable tourism and, as a result, is developing a new strategy for tourism, which incorporates the principles of sustainable development as a core component. The Caribbean Tourism Organisation has developed a comprehensive strategy to develop "eco-tourism" in the Caribbean region. This strategy is closely integrated with the goals of the Association for Caribbean

States (ACE) for a green Caribbean. "GREEN GLOBE" has developed a specific "Destinations" programme to recognise those tourist destinations where there is a concerted effort by all those involved in the local tourism industry to improve the quality of the environment.

The Destinations process provides a framework to guide tourist locations towards achieving sustainable development based on the principles of Agenda 21. The Destinations programmes are tailor made to reflect local circumstances, such as the level of environmental awareness, action taken to date and available resources. Each programme is based on achieving progressive environmental improvements.

Targets are set within a realistic timetable and are developed by a steering group made up of key partners. The island of Jersey has become the first "GREEN GLOBE" Destination. Vilamoura in Portugal, Dominica in the Caribbean and 3 destinations in the Philippines have also entered the Destination programme.

For example, in 1996 Luso tour SA, a tourism development company, enacted a management plan for Vilamoura whereby employees are given responsibility for individual environmental tasks. The company has invested money into rehabilitating the surrounding natural environment, which includes pine forests and a lake that has significance to local wetland areas. Guests are provided with a copy of the environmental policy and are encouraged to participate in the scheme through specialised brochures.

The campaign includes recycling; treating diseased pine areas; regular cleaning of the beaches and marinas; development of a sewage treatment plant and new buildings in the resort are designed to minimise visual and environmental impacts. For its work in Vilamoura, Lusotour SA is also a winner of the British Airways Tourism for Tomorrow Awards.

The "Africa tourism" brand has been developed by the Open Africa Foundation to encourage products, which embraces sustainable ecological, economic and social development based on Africa's unique cultural, natural and wildlife heritage. "Open Africa" is also developing a continuous network of "Africa tourism" routes from the Cape to Cairo, known as the "African Dream". The Dream helps to create awareness of the many rural and environmental projects, which exist throughout Africa. "Team Africa", a transcontinental alliance of governments, corporations, institutions, professionals and individuals, provides leadership and motivation in the development of the "African Dream".

Host Communities

"Whale Watch Kaikoura" is an initiative of local Maori people from a small town on the East Coast of New Zealand's South Island. Within a kilometre of the Kaikoura shore is an area ideal for whales, where visitors are guaranteed to see them all year round. The Whale Watch began 11 years ago and is now a booming tourist destination, run by indigenous people with a strong sense of heritage and a view of the future based on strong principles of sustainability.

Jordan Tourism Investments, has revitalised the traditional village of Taybeh, in Jordan, into a cultural tourist resort, with the help and agreement of villagers. With many of the younger generation moving to the cities, the village was losing its character. By restoring its 19th·century buildings and reviving old crafts, the village is now thriving again. The village lies 9km south east of the historic city of Petra. Opened in July 1994, the village now accommodates around 60,000 guests each year.

Uluru and Kakadu National Parks are both owned by indigenous Australians, the local Aboriginal communities, and jointly run with the National Parks and Wildlife Service. They are both major tourism destinations and involve indigenous participation in planning, management, and ownership of tourism infrastructure, as well as interpretation for visitors. They bring significant economic, social and cultural benefits to the local indigenous communities. The Conservation Corporation in Africa has established a series of high quality game parks in which local communities are major stakeholders and beneficiaries of tourism. This initiative is also helping to re-invigorate local crafts.

AGENTS AND PARTNERSHIPS

The challenge facing the tourism industry in moving towards a more sustainable future is set out in "Agenda 21 for the Travel and Tourism Industry". To achieve the goals set out in this document will require a partnership between government departments, national tourism authorities, international and national trade organisations and Travel and Tourism companies. Working together in close co-operation such partnerships should aim to deliver the following:

- Close co-operation between the public and private sectors to deliver a regulatory regime, which encourages voluntary action but supplement, where necessary, with regulation in areas such as land-use and waste management.
- Agreed common standards and tools to enable the measurement of progress towards achieving sustainable development.
- Certification criteria developed and more widely applied to industry initiatives.
- A commitment to the controlled expansion, where appropriate, of infrastructure.
- Environmental taxes, where applied, should be fair and non-

discriminatory. They should be carefully thought out to minimise their impact on economic development, and revenues should be allocated to Travel and Tourism associated environment improvement programmes.

- International, national and local funding bodies should include sustainable development as apart of their criteria, so that in time, all funding would be dependent on sound environmental practice.
- Contemporary research into sustainable tourism needs to be funded and developed. Issues requiring attention include design, carrying capacity, tour operator activities, environmental reporting, auditing and environmental impact assessments.
- Environmental education and training should be increased, particularly in schools, for future hotel and tourism staff.
- Greater investment and commitment to the use of new technology.

9

Pathway Business of Dark Tourism

TRACKING TRANSACTION

An advanced computer-based electronic security management system is instrumental in making the Mirage Resort Hotel a progressive facility. Security has assumed an increasingly important role in the hotel business. The larger the facility and the more diverse the features, services, and amenities, the more demanding the need for comprehensive security management. Nowhere is this more evident than at a 100-acre entertainment complex like the Mirage Resort Hotel in Las Vegas, where security concerns are heightened by the cash-intensive casino operation.

The creation of a fully integrated security environment at the Mirage represents an exciting new dimension in security management. Opened in 1989, the desert resort is among the most progressive facilities of its type. The Mirage has three 30-story towers and more than 3,000 rooms, including suites, villas, and bungalows with private pools. Two ballrooms, at 20,000- and 40,000-square feet, are available for special events, and meeting rooms can handle groups up to 5,000 people. The complex includes waterfalls, an erupting volcano, a tropical plant atrium, and an artificial coral reef aquarium with sharks and tropical fish. Also available for the enjoyment of guests and visitors are natural animal habitats: one for a pair of rare Royal White tigers, the other for six Atlantic Bottlenose dolphins.

An array of entertainment, recreational, and shopping opportunities are featured, including a 1,500-seat theater and around-the-clock casino operations. Guests can find restaurants, health and fitness centres, interconnected lagoon-shaped swimming pools, boutiques, and lounges. Special events such as prize fights and boat and auto shows compound the importance of security.

Security control in a gaming resort as large and complex as the Mirage is a demanding and never-ending challenge. Sophisticated security controls are in force in the casino, where millions of dollars are transacted every hour in games, including slot machines, video poker, keno, craps, blackjack, baccarat, and poker. Strict compliance with gaming laws and established casino procedures is controlled by close supervision, surveillance, and carefully monitored audits. An advanced computer-based electronic security management system, the Polaroid ID-2000 Plus, plays a central role in supporting the Mirage's integrated security environment. The system has proven to be a formidable management tool. Designed for expansion, the modular system is a core component in the recording and payroll programme.

The system combines advanced data base, computer, and electronic imaging technologies. It provides, for example, a streamlined ID card and badge production capability and a responsive, economical way to manage employee-related security information. The system also serves as an auditing aid to track activities, such as the number of meals served to employees in the cafeteria each day. Swipe readers at cash registers in the cafeteria make the process fast and efficient.

Specific information about the resort's 7,000 employees is input, stored, and retrieved by the digital electronic security management system. It captures image data, including colour portraits and signatures; generates photo ID cards and management reports; and communicates with other data bases. Report-generating capabilities simplify the tracking of ID cards that have been issued for active and former employees. The system also facilitates the monitoring of staff levels.

The electronic production and data base system is connected to a file server in the computer centre. Several sites are now on-line by means of a local area network using standard Ethernet connections and Novell network software. Additional terminals or systems can be added for expansion. One of the locations integrated by the LAN is the ID card and badge production centre in the human resources department. New employees are processed and badged at this location; other areas on the network use the system to validate employee security information.

Verification terminals are installed in the security and finance departments, casino surveillance, and the casino cash cage. Authorized individuals can validate, on-screen, employee photos, signatures, and related data. Although verification information is easily obtained by entering an employee number, access to the complete data base is limited to supervisory personnel. Information available for access includes the employee's full name, signature sample, colour portrait, ID number, job title, work location, and date of hire or termination. The individual's affiliation as a Mirage employee or corporate employee is shown. Powering the system is a high-speed 386 CPU using special workstation software, which incorporates password authorization and an internal audit trail to prevent system abuse. Using an optional 180 megabyte magnetic disk, the Mirage system can store approximately 14,000 full-colour portraits or 11,500 portraits and signatures. Optional storage modules, including larger capacity magnetic disk drives and optical disk drives, are available.

Active files, including signatures, colour portraits, and related textual information, are safely stored in digital format on the hard disk. Safety backups of the complete system are made on magnetic tape by the computer centre at least three times a week.

If an employee is terminated or quits, the photo and signature files are deleted to save storage space. Text files, however, are stored indefinitely. Information systems helped define the requirements and objectives of the departments involved. The system has improved productivity on several operating levels. Working closely with Polaroid engineers, information systems developed a maintenance strategy with flexible service levels and contingency provisions for priority service in designated areas. If emergency maintenance service is required, downtime in critical operations will be minimized.

Producing more than 6,000 ID CARDS a year could be an expensive, time-consuming operation. For the Mirage's human resources department, however, it is merely routine. Human resources is responsible for processing new employees, issuing new ID cards and badges, replacing damaged or lost badges, and responding to the continuing need for special events badges. To handle the challenges of ID card production the company relies on the production speed and efficiency of the computer-based security management system.

"Compared to the marathon effort involved in producing new ID cards when the Mirage first opened," reflects Monalee Stockner, human resources supervisor, "normal day-to-day activities are calm." ID cards were produced for more than 7,000 employees by the human resources team, with assistance from several temporary employees and a few of the management system devices on loan from Polaroid.

Employee processing and imaging activities were completed during a five-day whirlwind operation involving 10- to 12-hour shifts. Cards were assembled at night. According to Stockner, "Without the speed and automated features of the computerized production system, the job could not have been done as quickly, economically, or efficiently." The electronic production workstation includes an operator console consisting of a colour video camera, electronic flash lighting, portrait and text monitors, keyboard, and a signature capture device. A colour film recorder, film cutter, laminator, and print development timers are included in the output unit.

Information acquisition for an ID card, including text entries and video imaging of the subject's portrait and signature, takes less than five minutes per person. The badge is given to the employee the same day. Temporary special event IDs are produced for employees assigned to such activities as large parties, banquets, conventions, and prize fights. Since the Mirage was opened, more than 50,000 employee ID cards have been produced. An operator can enter employee information and capture, digitally store, and retrieve high-fidelity colour portraits and signatures or access data from existing computer data bases.

A freeze-frame feature allows the operator to preview and freeze the subject's video portrait before the card is made. A built-in signature capture camera stores signatures from a signed signature card. At the touch of a button the system electronically merges the digitized video portrait, signature, text, and multicolour Mirage logo contained in the software package. Information entered is contained on a new-hire document prepared by the employee's department. It includes pertinent information about the employee, his or her job title, and where he or she works.

ID cards can be produced in many of visual formats. More than a dozen variations are used by the Mirage to distinguish between different personnel classifications and affiliations.

These include Mirage employees, corporate staff, and contractors. Special formats have also been developed for restricted areas or for temporary use at special events. Although the electronic security management system can automatically assign sequential employee numbers, human resources prefers to control this function. In this way, blocks of numbers can be reserved for special applications in the system. When the employee number is entered, a bar code representing the number is automatically generated and printed on an adhesive-back label by a printer. Inexpensive, hard-copy, black-and-white thermal reference images can also be produced in seconds by a printer at the production station.

With a single keystroke, electronically assembled images for two separate employee badges are exposed on a sheet of instant colour print film. Development takes about a minute. Prints are then die-cut and inserted into a special laminate sandwich with a printed insert containing card use guidelines and the bar code label. The envelope is then permanently sealed. The finished card is attractive, durable, and virtually tamperproof. After lamination the bar code is verified with a test device, which displays the employee number.

Remotely Located Verication

Terminals integrated through the LAN facilitate employee recognition, signature validation, and confirmation of employment status. In addition to the information verification capabilities of the production workstation, data verification terminals on the network provide valuable information for security and management-related functions.

Security staff. Responsible for the safety of patrons and protection of the Mirage's physical assets, the security staff also plays an active role in maintaining guest relations and providing emergency services. The 275-person security staff, larger than the police departments of many small cities, operates around the clock. Security's responsibilities include controlling access in restricted areas, knowing the location of employees in emergencies, and monitoring property removal.

"The ability to access an employee's security records in seconds, to determine where they can be located, saves valuable time in an emergency," says Jennifer Keeney, security coordinator. "We can locate an employee quickly, for example, should there be an emergency at home, without having to make lots of phone calls and be faced with unnecessary delays. We can see what the person looks like and even get fast thermal prints to help our staff recognize the person. In emergencies, visual recognition is extremely important, especially with a workforce involving thousands of people."

Photo ID badges need not be worn in most areas. Employees can carry the ID card in a wallet or purse. In instances where individuals are not recognized by security personnel at employee entrances or in restricted areas, they will be asked to show their ID card. ID information for new hires or terminated employees is available at all verification terminals on a same-day basis.

In yet another important function, the ability to compare signatures with samples stored in the security management system's digital memory has streamlined the Mirage's property removal procedures. Because signatures of people authorized to approve property passes can be easily validated, it is now easier to control the removal of property. Thermal prints of authorized signatures for property removal forms are kept on file and current at various security stations.

Casino surveillance. Rapid information verification is critical for the casino surveillance group. Operating around the clock, 365 days a year, a team of trained observers keeps a watchful eye on cash transactions, operational procedures, and dealer interactions with patrons. Patricia Cipolla, director of surveillance, is emphatic about the importance of security control. "Our job," she states, "is to protect the Mirage's assets and its patrons. We watch the money and the way the games are run. Any deviation in established procedures signals that something may be wrong."

Ceiling-mounted video cameras can record the activities at any game in the casino. Videotapes of randomly selected games or those being monitored are available for review on video monitors located in the surveillance area. Should a transaction involving markers, redemption slips, bills, and credits, or a dealer's performance deviate from established guidelines, information about the dealer can be accessed instantly. Since the videotape can be seen in normal or close-up modes, surveillance specialists start the process by zooming in on the dealer's name badge. By entering the name at the verification terminal, employee information is instantly displayed, including a colour portrait and signature sample.

If irregularities are observed, other than what appears to be an honest mistake, the surveillance team may continue monitoring the dealer. A random check of a particular table could, for example, reveal a disparity between the dealer's photo and the name shown on the badge. This disparity would be checked out immediately with a casino supervisor. In other instances, the dealer's name may not appear on the casino schedule for the shift. The disparity could be attributed to a last-minute schedule change, which can be easily verified by calling the floor supervisor. Occasionally, casino accounting is advised that an audit of documents pertaining to a particular game may be warranted.

"Instant access to employee information, especially ID pictures, makes our job a lot easier," says Cipolla. "It often took hours or days to scour through computer printouts to pinpoint the person involved in a specific transaction. The task can now be done in minutes. The search process, which also involved phone calls to casino supervisors, wasted valuable time, was cumbersome, and expensive." Casino accounting. Casino accounting operates two shifts a day and is responsible for important audit functions for the Mirage's gaming activities. The department is responsible for maintaining the casino's operational integrity and for strict compliance with established procedures.

Timely information about gaming activities and people who authorize transactions is necessary for effective management. "The most important piece of information available," comments Robert Galvin, casino accounting manager, "is an employee's ID number. For us, it provides the means to access a key piece of data, employee signature samples." The accounting department's data verification terminal provides instant access to information needed for transaction audits. Matching photos to names or comparing signature samples with those appearing on documents is extremely helpful.

Cash cage. Because of the large amounts of money involved, the casino cash cage may require complete ID verification, including signatures and photos of unfamiliar people. In the past, matching signatures on cash disbursement forms or receipts to signature cards took hours or even days to accomplish. It now takes minutes. Performing rapid searches of information with specific parameters, such as name, employee number, title, department, and job description, has resulted in significant productivity improvement. "Immediate access to essential information," says Galvin, "has resulted in better control, increased audit speed, and reduced labour hours. Since we've been linked to the security management system, productivity has improved dramatically." The verification terminal, also used by internal auditing and gaming control board personnel, allows greater audit frequency and improved monitoring of money flow.

An innovative time and attendance system, to be fully implemented by early 1993, is being phased into the Mirage's operations on a controlled schedule. The ambitious undertaking is expected to produce enormous cost savings and efficiency improvements while providing significant benefits for both employees and management. As an integral part of a comprehensive management control system, badges provide the media for time clock entries. According to Ernie Pearce, director of information systems, "The new time and attendance system, now in use by several departments, is one of the most progressive programmes to be introduced at the Mirage. The sophisticated, computerized time-keeping and payroll system improves the interaction between supervisors and the workforce. It also eliminates many of the payroll-related transaction errors that inconvenienced employees and wasted valuable company time.

"The ability to use the benefits of the security management system's large data base, along with the photo ID badge as a clock entry system," continues Pearce, "provides important functional and economic advantages." Using sophisticated computer-based time clocks with bar code readers, the new system integrates employee work-time and payroll information with the security management data base. In this way, a long-standing information gap has been bridged. The new, high-tech computer-based clocks—to be located at every work location—will allow employees to use their ID cards to log in and out in a virtually error-free system.

The "smart" clocks are programmed with all the necessary operating parameters. These include authorized clock locations for different departments, employees' normal start and stop times, and overtime pay scales, including holidays, IRS regulations, and applicable union rules. The new system will improve efficiency and minimize transaction discrepancies, such as illegible manual entries. It will also eliminate time-keeping problems for people working at remote locations or whose work locations vary.

In the past, bar codes have been used only to track the number of meals served in the cafeteria. With the new time-keeping system, however, they will play a more significant role in overall efficiency. An opaque strip covering the bar code prevents tampering and reduces the likelihood that copies could be used to fool the clocks. Appearing opaque to the eye and to copy machines, the protected bar code is scanned without difficulty by bar code readers. Applied to the inside of the laminate envelope, the strip is considered tamperproof.

The Mirage's electronic security management system, which has been in operation for more than two years, has provided cost-effective solutions for a variety of problems. Software-driven and modular, important upgrades can be achieved simply by replacing a disk or a module. The combined data base, management, and electronic imaging system is easy to use, requires minimal training, and is inexpensive to operate. During its first 18 months of operation the system was on-line 24 hours a day, seven days a week, with virtually trouble-free performance.

An international company was preparing to evacuate 15 expatriate employees and dependents from a country that had suffered an earthquake. When it came time to meet at the departure point, 25 people showed up. Those arranging for the evacuation had not known that two technical teams were in the country supporting clients at the time. The additional evacuees, who had heard of the evacuation informally from individuals at the local office, disrupted the company's plan. There were not enough vehicles to get everyone to the airport in one trip, and there were not enough seats on the airplane that had been reserved. The other employees had made their way to the departure point hoping to get a seat because the local office employee did not tell them of the limited transportation or inform them that it would be safer to wait in the hotel until other transportation could be arranged.

The company evacuated the 15 people originally expected at that time, and the additional 10 employees were flown out two days later. This meant that an evacuation that should have been completed in approximately 12 hours—from when the employees and dependents arrived at the rendezvous point until they actually departed—ended up lasting 60 hours. Fortunately, everyone was able to get out safely, but the delay could have been disastrous. As companies seek new business in far-flung markets, their employees increasingly need to travel and work around the globe. Companies must be prepared to help these employees through any contingencies, including earthquakes, civil unrest, and other crises.

While some risks are greater in developing countries, emergency situations requiring evacuation can arise anywhere. For instance, Singapore, a relatively safe and natural-disaster-free city, suffered from severe smog in 1999 as the result of forest fires that were raging in nearby Indonesia. The conditions made the city unbearable and forced many foreign personnel to evacuate. Other examples of such incidents include an earthquake in Taiwan, civil unrest in Indonesia, a coup in Fiji, and the invasion of Kuwait—all of which necessitated the evacuation of international personnel. Most companies with international operations have detailed plans in place for evacuating their expatriate personnel should the local security situation deteriorate or in case of a natural disaster. But as the case highlighted at the beginning of this article illustrates, these plans often fail to address the evacuation of another category of employees; Those who are visiting on a business trip when a disaster strikes.

The evacuation of international travellers often falls between the travel advisory service, which provides employees with information on areas where it might be dangerous to travel, and evacuation planning efforts, which focus on expatriate personnel based in the country. Many companies do not even know how many employees are visiting a particular international location. In the event of an emergency, they might spend hours, if not days, trying to determine which employees are there. This problem especially affects companies that are organized along functional lines rather than geographically. It is not uncommon for an in-country office to report to a certain department, such as marketing. Personnel from other departments might travel in and out of the country without ever contacting the local office.

To avoid confusion, companies must coordinate their travel security and international evacuation programmes. Corporate security should serve as a central point for activity and information related to evacuation planning, coordinating the role of other players in the travel process, such as internal departments, travel service providers, employees, host country offices, and hotels.

How travel information is collected, maintained, and distributed will vary among companies. Generally, however, security should not bother with routine tracking of employee travel plans. Instead, the security department can enlist the help of various internal departments to ensure that it is able to locate employees on travel in an emergency. For example, security should ask human resources or travel service providers to collect the data on employee travel. In an emergency, security will know that it can turn to this resource for the information. Security may want to ask the company's public relations department to communicate the details of the travel and evacuation plan to staff as part of the internal communications programme.

Travel Service Provider

A company's travel service provider, whether a company employee or outside firm, can play an important role in gathering information about employees traveling abroad. Generally, these firms keep detailed records for billing purposes, and those records can help the security department to determine the location of employees when needed. The travel service company could also provide weekly or daily reports of which employees are traveling and to where. In addition to regular reports, the travel service provider should be able to give the company access to its staffs travel records 24 hours a day in case of an emergency.

Many companies have erroneously assumed that they could get the necessary staff location information from travel service providers in an emergency. The provider can also be required to book only designated hotels, perhaps ones where corporate security has verified the safety and security of the facility. In addition, because travel itineraries often change while employees are on the road, if the travel service provider has an office in a host country, employees can contact it to change hotel and flight reservations rather than going directly to the hotel or airline.

This means that the changes will immediately be keyed into the system, and the information can be distributed to the corporate security department or another internal point of contact, such as human resources. In addition, the provider can be asked to include emergency telephone numbers and procedures with each airline ticket issued to employees. The security department should periodically audit the programme for tracking employee travel to make sure that the records are being kept and that the contact telephone numbers and other information are all up to date. It also might be useful to test the programme under simulated conditions.

At the same time, security needs to keep the travel agent advised of any high-risk areas so that he or she can caution current or future travellers or, in serious cases, refer them back to security. In companies where there is an approval system for travel, those responsible for approving travel requests must be brought into the system so that they don't approve travel to "no-go" areas.

Employees

In many cases, employees make their own travel changes by contacting the airline or hotel directly, or they use the hotel concierge or business centre. Employees should be required to advise a designated corporate contact or the travel service provider of these changes. Some companies now require employees to submit weekly movement sheets listing travel destinations and contact details for the week to come.

It is generally advisable to include these schedules with some other form of business report, such as the employees' weekly progress or sales reports, to increase the level of compliance. One multinational telecommunications company, which has employees traveling to more than 20 countries every day of the year, implemented a Web-based itinerary tracking system to allow employees to update their travel schedules online. Employees can use any computer with Internet access to enter the password-protected site and update their information.

Host Country Offices

The company's offices abroad are also important players in the security process. Though it would be difficult for international offices to report all of the internal travel movements of visiting employees, they should at least be required to track which employees are visiting their countries and where they are staying.

This task can be made easier by requiring the traveling employees to check in with the local office or to go there to connect to the computer network or access their corporate e-mail account. If the local offices will be responsible for making in-country travel and accommodation arrangements for visiting employees, they should be required to use only designated hotels and they should be asked to provide contact information for hotels and transportation providers as well as other reservation details to headquarters.

One company with several international offices encouraged travellers to check in with the local offices by setting up workstations specifically for travellers and providing technical support to help them connect to the corporate mail system. This approach worked well, especially in the countries where local communications were unreliable. However, the company neglected to put in place a system for the local office to report to headquarters about the travellers in the country.

When an earthquake struck, the main office did not know how many employees were in the vicinity of the earthquake or how to locate them. The information was available at the local office, but it was unreachable. At a minimum, international offices should be required to monitor the internal travel of visitors if a situation shows signs of deteriorating, even if they do not track which employees are visiting their country during normal times. They should also be able to locate and provide assistance, including evacuation, for visiting employees.

Similarly, headquarters or travel vice providers should notify the host country office when employees plan to travel there, though in practice this depends on the company. For instance, if another division of the company runs the host country office, the traveller's division might not even have the contact details for the host country office. Also intra-office politics plays a role.

Host Country Hotels

The hotels that employees use while traveling play an important part in the security process. A strong business relationship between a company and the hotel can be key. The more nights per year that the company contracts for, the more willing a hotel will be to comply with additional security demands. For instance, contracts with hotels can require them to report to a designated corporate contact when employees are staying there and to provide assistance to the employees in case of an emergency. Also, hotels can be expected to provide basic medical care through a contracted doctor as well as emergency cash.

Larger hotels that employ a full-time security manager are preferable. The hotel security manager can be given procedures to follow for corporate employees if an evacuation is necessary. These procedures should provide detailed instructions on how and to where employees should be evacuated. Any reporting procedures and phone numbers for relevant contacts should also be given to the hotel's security manager. Obviously, there will be costs associated with services such as evacuating employees, and arrangements for payment must be made with the hotel.

Non-resident Situations

An international non-profit organization was holding a conference with 150 delegates in a country where it did not have a representative office. The organization had been meticulous with its evacuation planning for all the countries where it had offices, but it failed to draw up a plan for the conference locale.

As a result, when civil unrest suddenly erupted, the organization struggled to get everyone out of the area safely. All the delegates had come from different parts of the world on many different airlines, and they were staying at hotels scattered around the city. When the company tried to get the delegates out, gathering them together and trying to book 150 people on about 20 different airlines initially proved to be an impossible task. Later, the organization decided to prioritize the flights to four airlines, choosing the most available and reliable and issuing new tickets for the delegates who were not originally scheduled to depart on those flights. The delegates should have been required to travel on certain airlines and they should have been booked into fewer hotels that were closer together. Also, arrangements could have been made with the airlines to assist with an evacuation.

If security had done a risk assessment, the organization would have known that the potential for civil unrest was high. In such a case, even if the group did not change the venue, it could have required that delegates fly into a neighbouring country so that everyone could then take the same charter flight to the conference city, which would have made evacuation much easier. As this case illustrates, special plans are needed for countries where the company does not have a permanent presence but to which company employees travel regularly or in large numbers. When problems occur in such areas, employees will have no support from a local office that, even without prior notice, typically has some vehicles, houses, cash, and local employees who know their way around.

A traveller to a country without a company office would have to rely on the embassy, if there is one, the hotel, and in some cases, the client he or she was visiting. But the company can smooth the way by providing contact information to authorities, such as the embassy, and by making prior arrangements with hotels and other resources. Plan preparation. Though it is nearly impossible to draw up separate plans for every country to which company employees travel, a basic threat assessment will determine which of these countries are a high risk. Plans should be created for these countries first. Then, more generic plans should be written and distributed.

The plans should provide instructions for what to do in case of an emergency, factors to consider when trying to leave the country, and resources where employees can seek assistance. Appropriate actions might include traveling in groups, keeping small denominations of cash to give away at roadblocks for the purpose of extortion, traveling in two vehicles in case one breaks down, getting to the airport early, and repeatedly checking that an airplane seat has not been "mistakenly" given to someone else. In addition, evacuees should carry only limited luggage, keeping documents and valuables in a hand-carried bag in case they lose or have to abandon their luggage. Telephone numbers for the police, embassies, airlines, the travel service provider, and other sources of assistance should also be included.

Local Contacts

Corporate security might consider contracting with local security companies in international locations to provide assistance in an emergency. An agreement can be made with a local security company whereby it will locate, secure, and, if necessary, evacuate the company's employees in the host country for a set fee or agreed upon hourly rate. These companies can also provide assistance to the traveling employee for minor emergencies, such as a lost passport or traffic accident. While this might also he done in locations where the company has a permanent facility, it is especially useful if the company does not maintain an office in the country.

Communications

Some local security companies with strong emergency response capabilities may also have satellite communications, which means they might be among the few groups reachable immediately following a disaster. Being able to speak with someone in the country to get firsthand information about local conditions and the well-being of employees is key. Not being able to reach traveling staff or a local office after receiving news of a disaster can often result in the company activating its crisis management team and spending hours working on numerous scenarios and outcomes, only to find out that employees have escaped unscathed.

Travel Claims

Back at company headquarters or the employee's home office, the department responsible for reimbursing travel expenses is in the position to assist with the enforcement of travel security policies. One obvious option is for the company to refuse to reimburse employees for accommodations other than those approved by security. The department can also ensure that employees use the company's travel service provider and not their own travel agent by paying the travel service provider directly.

One U.S.-based multinational firm was able to increase employee use of designated international hotels by contracting with the hotel chain to pay the employees their per diem allowances. The company did not reimburse general travel expenses for accommodation, meals, and incidentals but instead paid a daily allowance via the hotels. The choice was simple. If employees wanted the money, they would have to use the designated hotel. The system achieved almost 100 per cent compliance. It will often be necessary, however, for traveling employees to pay for a number of expenses themselves. Typically, the best approach is to issue the employee a corporate credit card with sufficient limits to pay for several air tickets, rent vehicles, and so forth. But in countries with deteriorating security situations, cash is king.

After an earthquake or other natural disaster, there may not be electrical power to run ATM machines or the point-of-sales machines required to process credit card transactions. Telephone lines may be down or congested, making telephone authorization for a credit card transaction impossible. During civil unrest, merchants may be reluctant to accept credit cards for fear of not being reimbursed by local banks for the transactions.

Traveling employees should, therefore, be required to carry enough cash with them at all times to pay for meals, taxis, and "exit taxes," which are often collected by groups that set up roadblocks on the roads leading to international airports. The best approach is for the traveller to keep a small "mugger's toll" where it can be quickly accessed and to hide the rest on one's person. Cash should be both in local currency and U.s. dollars and should be in small denominations. Corporate travel is unavoidable. And in a world where both natural and man-made disasters are increasing in number, close encounters with crises are also inevitable. But security can ensure that those situations do not result in loss of life by coordinating the company's travel and emergency response plans and getting all parties to understand the importance of compliance.

In 1998, governments and international organizations continued their active efforts to increase regulatory and criminal enforcement of various laws to stem the tide of transnational crime. These efforts were reflected in the criminalization of various business and financial transactions, the imposition of new due diligence measures on the private sector and the concomitant weakening of privacy and confidentiality laws, strengthened penalties for non-compliance with regulatory efforts, and new law enforcement techniques, such as undercover sting operations, wiretapping, expanded powers to search homes and businesses, and controlled deliveries. So obtrusive are many of the law enforcement techniques and the privatization of law enforcement, whereby governments transfer their responsibilities to the private sector, that many professionals engaged in international transfer of wealth counseling analogized the trends to those in Aldous Huxley's A Brave New World. This discussion outlines the trends in six areas and draws some practice pointers from the trends.

Section II will discuss the activities of international organizations that are driving much of the strategy, framework, and minimum standards for the development of an international anti-money laundering regime. Increasingly, international organizations, both of a universal and a more regional level, are consciously trying to build alliances and networks with each other and the private sector.

In Section III, selective elements of the substantive law of anti-money laundering are considered in the context of recent developments, such as the continued erosion of secrecy and the imposition of increased due diligence requirements. Section IV discusses major case and miscellaneous developments, such as the failure of Russian offshore banks in Antigua.

Section V highlights the growth of international tax enforcement, the increased reporting requirements and unilateral extraterritorial application of the law, the increasing bilateral and multilateral cooperation, and the new traps for the wary due to tax enforcement developments.

In Section VI, international asset forfeiture trends are highlighted. These activities pose a much graver threat to the ability of clients to do business internationally than ten years ago. The goal of immobilizing the assets of transnational criminals has become increasingly the watchword. While the rights of innocent third parties are protected in principle, it sometimes takes a lot of money and professional acumen for such persons to obtain due process. Section VII focuses on criminal cooperation mechanisms. Section VIII discusses the use of international human rights provisions as a shield for defendants, fiduciaries, and intermediaries in the context of international anti-money laundering and financial crime cases. As an introductory matter, the life cycle of money laundering is important to grasp.

It has three cycles:

- Placement, whereby the criminal has enormous amounts of dirty money in the form usually of cash that he needs to place or initiate in a way that neither law enforcement nor the private sector will identify as the proceeds of crime;
- Layering, which involves the creation of many layers between the dirty money and the ultimately cleaned money through the use of offshore vehicles, such as trusts in secrecy jurisdictions, in tandem with multiple, entitles, such as companies, and secrecy mechanisms, such as nominees, stamen, bearer shares, and sophisticated structuring; and
- Integration is achieved when the criminal has transformed the dirty money through enough layers of the laundering cycle that a legitimate banker, lawyer, or fiduciary, even one with cutting edge due diligence, would never suspect the criminal source of the money.

Integration means that, in 1999, the money of the many heirs of Joseph Kennedy, the famous former bootlegger during the prohibition days, now is not questioned. Indeed, the money even finances federal elections. In Colombia, the money of the Cali cartel has been integrated for two or three decades into the leading pharmaceutical companies, soccer teams, and also the financing of political elections.

Much of the emphasis of the politics of international anti-money laundering is to try to deprive criminals—especially transnational criminals—and organized crime of the fruits of the crimes and the means of their committing more crimes. Another goal is to allocate the seized proceeds to governments and law enforcement. Hence, the economics and politics of anti-money laundering are to redistribute economics and power of crime. To help with the fight, governments and international organizations have solicited the collaboration of the private sector to prevent money laundering through know-your-customer and identifying and reporting to law enforcement suspicious transactions.

DEVELOPMENTS OF INTERNATIONAL ORGANIZATIONS

Multilateral organizations have set the framework for anti-money laundering standards, mechanisms, and institutions. The United Nations pioneered the 1988 Vienna Convention Against the Trafficking in Illegal Narcotic and Psychotropic Substances, which contains the requirements to criminalize money laundering and immobilize the assets of persons involved in illegal narcotics trafficking.

In 1989, the G-7 Economic Summit Group established the Financial Action Task Force, which operates out of the Office of Economic Cooperation and Development headquarters in Paris. FATF has issued a set of forty recommendations that concern legal requirements, financial and banking controls, and external affairs. FATF operates through a Caribbean FATF and is in the process of establishing a similar group in Asia. It issues an annual report that provides an overview of progress and problems in international anti-money laundering.

The G-10 Basle Group of Central Banks has actively provided guidelines for central bank supervisors and regulatory controls. As mentioned below, on September 23, 1997, the Basle Group issued guidelines on supervision. Regionally, the Council of Europe's 1991 Convention on Laundering,

Search, Seizure and Confiscation of Assets has become the major international convention that obligates signatory governments to cooperate against anti-money laundering from all serious crimes. The European Union, as a signatory to the 1988 Vienna Drug Convention and due to its own actions to combat financial crimes against the Communities, issued a 1991 Anti-Money Laundering Directive that it is poised to strengthen. As mentioned below, it is now in the process of an initiative against cybercrimes.

An important regional organization in the anti-money laundering has been the Inter-American Drug Abuse Control Commission. At its meeting on November 4-7, 1997, CICAD anti-money laundering experts recommended an ongoing assessment of compliance with standards and the creation of national financial intelligence units.

National governments and international organizations are striving to create mechanisms to monitor regularly compliance with international standards. Because the recent FATF annual reports and topologies provide cutting-edge discussions of the status of money laundering trends, they are discussed next.

FATF 1997 Annual Report

In June 1997, the Financial Action Task Force on Money Laundering issued its annual report for 1996-97. The report highlighted the annual survey of money laundering methods and countermeasures covering a global overview of trends and techniques. These methods included the increased use by money launderers of non-bank financial institutions, especially bureaux de change, remittance businesses and non-financial professionals. Special attention was devoted to the money laundering threats of new payment technologies.

The work of the FATF in 1996-97 focused on three main areas: "reviewing money laundering methods and countermeasures; monitoring the implementation of anti-money laundering measures by its members; and undertaking an external relations programme to promote the widest possible international action against money laundering."

- *Reviewing Money Laundering Methods and Countermeasures:* A significant achievement of FATF during 1996-97 was the annual survey of money laundering methods and countermeasures. The survey provides a global overview of trends and techniques, especially the issue of money laundering through new payment technologies, such as smart cards and banking through the Internet. FATF reviewed the issue of electronic fund transfers and examined ways to improve the appropriate level of feedback that should be provided to reporting financial institutions.
- *Trends in FATF Members:* While drug trafficking remains the single largest source of illegal proceeds, non-drug related crime is increasingly important. The most noticeable trend is the continuing increase in the use by money launderers of non-bank financial institutions and of non-financial businesses relative to banking institutions. The trend reflects the increased level of compliance by banks with anti-money laundering measures. The survey noted, "Outside the banking sector, the use of bureaux de change or money remittance businesses remains the most frequently cited threat."

FATF members have continued to expand their money laundering laws, covering non-drug related predicate offences, improving confiscation laws, and expanding the application of their laws in the financial sector in order to apply preventive measures to non-bank financial institutions and non-financial businesses.

FATF discussed money laundering threats that may be inherent in the new e-money technologies, of which there are three categories: stored value cards, Internet/network based systems, and hybrid systems. Important features of the systems that will affect this threat are: the value limits imposed on accounts and transactions; the extent to which stored value cards become inoperable with Internet-based systems; the possibility that stored value cards can transfer value between individuals; the consistency of intermediaries in the new payment systems; and the detail in which account and transaction records are kept. Future issues include the need to review regulatory regimes, the availability of adequate records, and "the difficulties in detecting and in tracking or identifying unusual patterns of financial transactions." Since the application of new technologies to electronic payment systems is still in its infancy, law enforcement and regulators must continue to cooperate with the private sector. Then authorities may understand the issues that must be considered and addressed as the market and technologies mature.

Olicy Issues: Electronic Fund Transfers. As a result of difficulties in tracing illicit funds routed through the international funds transfer system, the Society for Worldwide Interbank Financial Telecommunications board "issued a broadcast to its members and participating banks encouraging users to include full identifying information for originators and beneficiaries in SWIFT field tags 50 and 59." Many countries have acted to encourage compliance within their financial communities with the SWIFT broadcast message.) To strengthen the body of information on identifying the true originating parties in transfers, SWIFT has devised a new optional format for implementation after November 1997. The message format will have a new optional message field for inputting all data "relating to the identification of the sender and receiver of the telegraphic transfer." Additionally, "SWIFT has issued guidance to users of its current system to describe where such information may appear in the MT 100 format." FATF has helped SWIFT devise the new mechanism and is encouraging the use of the new message format.

Providing Feedback to Financial Institutions. FATF recommends that at least the recipient of a suspicious transactions report should acknowledge receipt thereof. If the report is then subject to a fuller investigation, the institution could be advised of either the agency that is going to investigate the report or the name of a contact officer.

If a case is closed or completed, the sending institution should receive timely information on the decision or result. Further cooperative exchange of information and ideas is required for the partnership between units that receive suspicious transaction reports, general law enforcement, and the financial sector to work more effectively. Estimate of Magnitude of Money Laundering. Because of insufficient data, FATF has created an ad hoc group that "will consider the available statistical information and other information concerning the proceeds of crime and money laundering." This ad hoc group will also "define the parameters of a study on the magnitude of money laundering and agree on a methodology and a timetable for the study."

Monitoring the Implementation of Anti-Money Laundering Measures: As part of FATF's work, its members have pledged to monitor the implementation of its Forty Recommendations through a two-pronged approach consisting of "an annual self-assessment exercise," and "more detailed mutual evaluation process under which each member is subject to an onsite examination."

As a result of Turkey's failure to implement FATF's recommendations, FATF issued a public statement, in accordance with Recommendation 21, that Turkey, a member country, was insufficiently in compliance with the Forty Recommendations. Recommendation 21 states that "[f]inancial institutions should give special attention to business relations and transactions with persons, including companies and financial institutions, from countries that do not or insufficiently apply" the Forty Recommendations. On November 19, 1996, Turkey enacted Law no. 4208 on the Prevention of Money Laundering. As a result, FATF decided to lift the application of Recommendation 21.

In 1995, after completing its first round of mutual evaluations of whether all members had adequately implemented the Forty Recommendations, a second round of mutual evaluations was conducted. The second round focused on the effectiveness of members' anti-money laundering measures in practice. Mutual evaluations of Australia, the United Kingdom, Denmark, the United States, Austria, and Belgium occurred in 1996-97.

Asset Confiscation and Provisional Measures. The FATF Secretariat conducted a study evaluating members' confiscation measures and found that an effective confiscation mechanism should encompass a range of serious offences and should act in appropriate cases to confiscate proceeds of crime where it is held in the name of third parties. Countries should also consider widening confiscation laws to permit confiscation without conviction in certain cases, or the more limited alternative of freezing, and where possible, confiscation action against absconders and fugitives from justice.

For most members, the crucial issue was the burden of proof upon the government and whether it can be eased or reversed. Countries have enacted or considered the following measures: "applying an easier standard of proof than the normal criminal standard; reversing the burden of proof and requiring the defendant to prove that his assets are legitimately acquired; and enabling courts to confiscate the proceeds of criminal activity other than the crimes of which the defendant is immediately convicted." Further options are to provide the court with discretion to confiscate a convicted drug trafficker's assets or to require the court to order the confiscation of all assets that are disproportionate to the person's legitimate income. Mutual legal assistance problems include instances arising from questionable members that have ratified the relevant international conventions or do not have the necessary domestic legislation in effect. Relatively limited mutual assistance experience exists among members in the confiscation field, and asset sharing and coordinating seizure and confiscation proceedings are still emerging.

Customer Identification. Because of the comparatively weaker regimes for customer identification in non-bank financial institutions and bureaux de change, these institutions have become more attractive routes for money launderers. Refinements are required for overseas and nominee accounts. In addition, refinements are required for the structuring of large non-financial business intermediaries and situations in which no face-to-face contact between the customer and the financial institution exists. The issue of customer identification arises in the context of rapid development of electronic transactions and financial services through new technologies.

External Relations: In external relations, FATF encourages countries to adopt and implement the FATF Recommendations and monitors and reinforces this process. FATF also cooperates and coordinates with all the international and regional organizations concerned with counter-money laundering measures. Finally, it pursues a flexible approach, "tailoring external relations activity to the circumstances of the region or countries involved." FATF will embark upon more initiatives to encourage the adoption and implementation of the Forty Recommendations. FATF is working to develop a long-term strategic plan in collaboration with other relevant international organizations.

In 1996, FATF adopted both a policy and rules for "assessing the implementation of anti-money laundering measures in non-member governments." The development of a mutual evaluation procedure should encourage countries and jurisdictions not only to develop anti-money laundering laws, but also to improve countermeasures already in existence. Hence, FATF has worked with other international organizations such as CFATF, the Council of Europe, and the Offshore Group of Banking Supervisors to develop countermeasures. In 1996 and 1997, important counter-money laundering developments included the establishment of the Asia/Pacific Group on Money Laundering and the Southern and Eastern African Money Laundering Conference. FATF has supported existing bodies rather than starting new initiatives. The new global project of the U.N. Drug Control Programme/U.N. Crime Prevention and Criminal Justice Division on money laundering will help implement these measures through training and technical assistance.

In the Caribbean, FATF supported the endorsement of the Memorandum of Understanding at the 1996 Ministerial meeting of the CFATF. CFATF finalized mutual evaluation reports of the Cayman Islands and Trinidad and Tobago, and planned six evaluation visits for 1997. CFATF also started its typologies exercise, whereby it will "develop and share among its members the latest intelligence on money laundering and other financial crime techniques used in the Caribbean region and elsewhere."

In April 1997, the Finance Ministers of the Asia Pacific Economic Cooperation issued a ministerial statement welcoming the establishment of the Asia/Pacific Group on Money Laundering. FATF stated that the endeavor required urgent funding from FATF members and those of the Asia/Pacific Group on Money Laundering. Finally, from October 1-3, 1996, representatives of thirteen African countries attended a conference on anti-money laundering and agreed on a proposal to establish a Southern and Eastern African Financial Action Task Force.

FATF 1998 Annual Report

In June 1998, the Financial Action Task Force on Money Laundering released its annual report for 1997-98. The ninth round of FATF was chaired by Belgium and was marked by the elaboration of a five year plan for 1999-2004, highlighted by a decision to broaden the FATF network and the scope of its work, and to strengthen the review of money laundering trends and countermeasures.

Trends and Future Mission of FATF: The most noticeable trend is the continuing increase in the use by money launderers of non-bank financial institutions and of non-financial businesses relative to banking institutions. The trend reflects the increased level of compliance by banks with anti-money laundering measures. Outside the banking sector, the use of bureaux de change or money remittance businesses remain the most frequently cited.

In 1994, five years after the 1989 G-7 Summit established FATF, its members decided that the Task Force—which is not a permanent international organization—should continue its work for a further five years until 1999. Moreover, it was agreed in 1994 that no final decision on the future of FATF would be taken until 1997-98. By mid-1999, it is expected that every FATF member will have experienced two evaluations of their anti-money laundering systems. While the first round of evaluations dealt with the issue of whether all members had adequately implemented the Forty Recommendations, the second round concerns the effectiveness of the anti-money laundering system in each member country. FATF organized "missions and seminars in non-member countries to promote awareness of the money laundering problem" and encourage countermeasures. Although FATF's Forty Recommendations have gained some international recognition, a large number of countries still have not implemented anti-money laundering systems.

FATF has succeeded in achieving an international consensus on the money laundering countermeasures, in persuading many countries to implement the measures, and in establishing a "network" of money laundering experts in each of the FATF members. FATF has improved the flow of information both at the domestic level and internationally. The first major task in the future that the report outlined is "to establish a world-wide anti-money laundering network and to spread the FATF's message to all continents and regions of the globe."

To accomplish the task, FATF will expand its membership to "strategically important countries which already have certain key anti-money laundering measures in place... and are politically determined to make a full commitment towards the implementation of the Forty Recommendations, and which could play a major role in their regions in the process of combating money laundering." FATF will also develop regional bodies emulating FATF, and will cooperate closely with relevant international organizations such as the U.N. bodies and the International Financial Institutions.

The second major task will be to improve the implementation of the Forty Recommendations in FATF members. The focus will be to "ensure that all members have implemented the revised Forty Recommendations in their entirety and in an effective manner." Hence, the existing monitoring mechanisms will receive a renewed assessment focusing on the 1996 Recommendations. This assessment will involve

An enhanced self-assessment process; and a third round of simplified mutual evaluations for all FATF members starting in 2001, focusing exclusively on compliance with the revised parts of the Recommendations, the areas of significant deficiencies identified in the second round, and generally the effectiveness of the countermeasures.

The third main task will be to strengthen the review of money laundering trends and countermeasures. Because money laundering is an evolving activity, FATF members must follow laundering trends and techniques and assess the effectiveness of the FATF recommendations. The geographical scope of the future typologies exercises must be extended. The close monitoring of trends will enable FATF to anticipate and react to the trends by elaborating countermeasures. 2. Monitoring the Implementation of Anti-Money Laundering Measures. Much of FATF's work consists of monitoring the implementation by its members of the Forty Recommen-dations.

FATF members are committed to the discipline of multilateral surveillance and peer review. Member countries have their implementation of the recommendations monitored through a two-pronged approach comprised of "an annual self-assessment exercise," and a "more mutual evaluation process under which each member is subject to an on-site examination."

The 1997-98 self-assessment process consisted of each member providing information concerning the status of their implementation of the Forty Recommendations. The information is then compiled and analysed, providing the basis for assessing to what extent the Forty Recommendations have been implemented. With respect to legal issues, all members have enacted laws criminalizing drug money laundering. All but three FATF members have criminalized laundering of the proceeds of range of crimes in addition to drug trafficking. The report notes that "the overall level of compliance will improve considerably when Japan, Luxembourg, and Singapore have extended their drug money laundering offences to serious crimes," which all three are in the process of doing. "A number of members still must take measures in relation to confiscation and provisional measures, both domestically and pursuant to mutual legal assistance." In regard to domestic confiscation, nineteen members are in full compliance, and six in partial compliance.

For mutual legal assistance, seventeen members are in full compliance, five in partial compliance, and three are out of compliance. Urgent action by some FATF members is required to bring themselves into compliance with the relevant recommendations.

Slight improvement occurred in the 1997-98 implementation of the FATF recommendations on financial issues. Major improvements occurred in relation to two new recommendations that were introduced in 1996, namely Recommendation 13 dealing with the need to monitor laundering using new technologies, and Recommendation 25 on shell corporations. However, non-bank institutions still are not properly implementing the recommendations at the same level as the banking sector.

While nearly all FATF members "comply fully with customer identification and record-keeping requirements for banks... some persistent gaps in coverage with respect to certain categories of non-bank financial institutions" still exist. Serious concerns exist regarding the anonymous passbooks for residents in Austria that FATF is pursuing through the FATF non-compliance procedures. The requirement for financial institutions to report suspicious transactions and related measures has received "very satisfactory" implementation in relation to banks and almost as good for non-bank financial institutions.

However, improvement is required with respect to non-bank financial institutions, especially in countries such as Canada, Iceland, and the United States. The report also discusses the mutual evaluations of Canada, Switzerland, the Netherlands, Germany, Italy, Norway, Japan, and Greece. A section of the report concerning the application of the FATF policy for non-complying members covers, inter alia, the failure of Austria to abolish anonymous passbooks for Austria residents and a series of concerns on Canadian countermeasures.

The proposed Canadian countermeasures include mandatory suspicious transaction reporting, penalizing failures to file a report and filing a false report, as well as a "tipping-off" offence, the establishment of a new financial intelligence unit, protection from criminal and civil liability for any person or body that makes a report, and establishing a cross border reporting system for currency and monetary instruments.

Reviewing Money Laundering Methods and Countermeasures: FATF performed a further survey of money laundering methods and countermeasures that provides a global overview of trends and techniques. The issues of money laundering through new payments technologies—smart cards, banking through the Internet—and of the non-financial businesses and remittance companies were discussed. The survey also considered the issues of how to "improve the appropriate level of feedback which should be provided to reporting financial institutions, and the continuation of work on estimating the magnitude of money laundering." Moreover, FATF convened a second meeting with representatives of the world's financial sector trade institutions. With respect to new technology—for example, e-cash—the report concluded that much work remains before all the related money laundering dangers can be clearly identified and before any possible specific countermeasures can be considered. FATF has also directed its attention towards money laundering in sectors such as insurance or money changing. In connection with the latter, consideration is given to the consequences of the conversion of European currencies into the Euro.

With respect to providing feedback to financial institutions, the FATF guidelines are not mandatory because they recognize "that ongoing law enforcement investigations should not be put at risk that secrecy laws in some countries may prevent their financial intelligence unit from disclosing significant feedback, and that general privacy laws can also limit feedback." Hence, the guidelines are designed to assist financial intelligence units, law enforcement and other government bodies involved in the receipt, analysis, and investigation of suspicious transaction reports, and in the provision of feedback to reporting institutions on those reports.

The guidelines suggest that at least regulatory authorities make available sanitized cases to reporting institutions, and "each case could include a description of the fact, a summary of the result, a description of the enquiries made by the FIU if appropriate, and a description of the lessons to be learned from the reporting and investigative procedures that were adopted in the case." Additionally, new money laundering methods, as well as trends in existing techniques, are described and identified and the guidelines provide that institutions are advised of such trends and techniques.

The guidelines also consider means for providing general feedback, such as "annual reports, regular newsletters, videos, electronic information systems such as web sites, electronic databases or message systems, meetings with institutions, conferences and workshops, and working or liaison groups." The report notes that specific feedback is more difficult to provide than general feedback due to legal and practical concerns, such as potential jeopardy to ongoing law enforcement investigations and resource limitations, and secrecy laws relating to the financial intelligence or general privacy laws. Still, whenever possible, specific feedback should include acknowledgment by the FIU of receipt of the report and advice to the institution that a particular agency will investigate the report when this occurs and if the investigation would not be adversely affected. "If a case is closed or completed, whether because of a concluded prosecution, because the report was found to relate to a legitimate transaction or for other reasons," the institution should be notified of that decision or result.

FATF's External Relations and Other International Initiatives: As the third component of its mission, FATF undertakes external relations actions designed to raise awareness in non-member countries or regions on the need to prevent or combat money laundering, and offers the Forty Recommendations as a basis for doing so. In September 1997, FATF's external relations included a mission to Cyprus, resulting in Cyprus undergoing a joint Council of Europe/Offshore Group of Banking Supervisors mutual evaluation of Cyprus' money laundering system in the spring of 1998. In October 1997, FATF helped organize a conference in St. Petersburg to complement a high-level mission to Moscow in 1996. Various new and proposed countermeasures are in place and in the works in Russia.

FATF-style regional bodies are active. CFATF has grown to twenty-four states and has instituted measures to ensure the effective implementation of, and compliance with, the Forty Recommendations. The CFATF Secretariat monitors members' implementation of the Kingston Ministerial Declaration through the following activities: self-assessment of the implementation of the Recommendations; an on-going programme of mutual evaluation of members; coordination of, and participation in, training and technical assistance programmes; biannual plenary meetings for technical representatives; and annual Ministerial meetings.

The report notes that "supported by, and in collaboration with UNDCP, the CFATF Secretariat has developed a regional strategy for technical assistance and training to aid effective investigation and prosecution of money laundering and related asset forfeiture cases." In 1997-98, three mutual evaluation reports were discussed and six on-site visits occurred. A timetable was set for the remaining mutual evaluations. In July 1997, the Working Party meeting of the Asia/Pacific Group on Money Laundering made progress. It currently consists of sixteen members that "have started to exchange information and to examine the strengths and weaknesses of their systems through the mechanism of jurisdiction reports." Measures have been proposed to improve technical assistance and training, strengthen mutual legal assistance and improve cooperation with the financial sector. FATF adopted a policy for assessing the implementation of anti-money laundering measures in non-member governments. The procedure will encourage countries and territories not only to implement anti-money laundering measures, but also to improve the countermeasures already in place. In this regard, the FATF assessed the CFATF, the Council of Europe and the OGBS's mutual evaluation procedures as being in conformity with its own principles. As the latter is comprised of representatives of banking supervisory authorities, the FATF has sought formal political endorsement of the procedures and the forty Recommendations from those governments of the members of the OGBS that are not represented in either the CFATF or the FATF.

FATF cooperates with other international organizations. In this regard, the U.N. Office for Drug Control and Crime Prevention has started the Global Programme Against Money Laundering, a research and technical cooperation programme. In the context of the GPML, the UNODCCP organized several important international anti-money laundering events in 1997-1998, including awareness-raising seminars for West Africa in Ivory Coast, and for South Asian countries plus Myanmar and Thailand. On June 8-10, 1998, the U.N. General Assembly on international narcotics trafficking adopted a political declaration in which U.N. members undertake to make special efforts against the laundering of money linked to drug trafficking.

The declaration recommends that states that have not yet done so adopt by the year 2003 national anti-money laundering legislation and programmes in accordance with relevant provisions of the 1988 Vienna Convention Against the Traffic in Illicit Narcotic and Psychotropic Substances, and a package of countermeasures that were adopted at the same session. The Commonwealth Heads of Government recently has held summits calling for concerted anti-money laundering actions.

At its June 1998 London meeting, it considered four main items:

- Improving domestic coordination through national interdisciplinary coordinating structure;
- The special problems of dealing with money laundering in countries with large parallel economies;
- Strengthening regional initiatives for more effective implementation of anti-money laundering measures; and
- Self-evaluation of progress made in implementing anti-money laundering measures in the financial sector.

The Inter-American Development Bank has held meetings and is starting to become involved in anti-money laundering activities, such as training, supporting dialogue with the private sector, and funding programmes). The Organization of American States/Inter-American Drug Abuse Control

Commission have a group of experts that meets twice a year. In May 1998, it "approved a training programme for judges, prosecutors, FIU personnel and law enforcement. It also undertook to amend the model regulations to expand the predicate offence for money laundering and to provide for the establishment of national forfeiture funds." It finished a directory of contact points to effect information exchange and mutual legal assistance that would be accessible through OAS's webpage.

The expansion of the FATF network and of the scope of its countermeasures will mean that launderers will use their power and know-how to try to take advantage of globalization and new technology, and to identify and exploit jurisdictions whose systems are vulnerable. For a five-year assessment, noticeably absent in the discussion is the use of international relations and particularly international-regime theory, including the rise and fall of linkages that make regimes rise and fall, and the targeting of key elements within such regimes.

Additional limitations that exacerbate the absence of this element of its strategic planning are the temporal—its existence is limited to five years—and informal commitments—FATF is still not a formal entity. Given the threats arising from money laundering, one would think the world community would make commitments commensurate with the threats, but then progress in evolving international enforcement regimes can be slow. During 1996-97, progress was made in combating money laundering, both within and outside the FATF membership. Implementation of the Forty Recommendations by FATF has again improved and the monitoring mechanisms have been further strengthened and refined. The international anti-money laundering activities undertaken by FATF and other international organizations have increased.

On June 23-24, 1997, the Egmont Group, composed of specialists in financial investigation from thirty-six countries and seven international organizations, including Interpol and Europol, approved at its fifth meeting a declaration of principles to harmonize policies and intensify its efforts in combating money laundering. The Spanish Executive Service of the Commission to Prevent Money Laundering and Financial Offences organized the meeting at the Bank of Spain.

Among the principles agreed upon were the following: the stimulation of exchanges among various FIUs; the adoption of a programme of communication among FIUs through the Internet; the holding and development of regional workshops or seminars for their members and their units and sub-units; and the study of a formal structure to maintain the continuation and consolidation of the Egmont group and the articulation of procedures for FIUs and their counterparts.

The Egmont Group was established on June 9, 1995, at the palace of Egmont-Arenberg in Brussels as a result of an international movement directed at the promulgation in all countries of a norm pertaining to the prevention of money laundering and the establishment in each state of an organization to fulfill the obligations imposed on FIUs. The Egmont Group does not constitute an international organization or set forth hard law obligations under an international agreement, but rather provides an informal means for interested entities to meet and cooperate voluntarily.

The conclusions of the meeting indicate that Spanish norms on preventing money laundering and collaboration among credit entities, banks, and savings and loan associations, have gained momentum. Sepblac took action during 1989 on 1,530 cases on various fronts. In the matter of international business transactions, Sepblac verified the fulfillment of requirements of enterprises owned by foreign shareholders. In so doing, it discovered the manipulation in the formation of stock exchange prices. Furthermore, Sepblac observed foreign loans that hide increases of capital in Spanish affiliate enterprises abroad.

In the matter of money laundering, Seplac transmitted and finalized 412 cases in 1998, 58 of which were referred to the antidrug prosecutor, 54 to the special anti-corruption prosecutor, 10 to different judicial authorities, and 43 to police authorities. The remaining cases were shelved without further investigation or prosecution. Sepblac also investigated, among other activities, suspicious dealings in sectors such as jewelry and precious metals, the importation of vehicles, contraband tobacco, hotel businesses, the industry of information technology and products, value added tax fraud, and casinos. The work of the Egmont Group and Sepblac indicate the emergence and coalescence of a financial enforcement regime, of which money laundering is an important component. The cooperation within the Egmont Group exemplifies the role of informal cooperation and its impact on the formation and growth of national enforcement activities.

The achievement of a financial enforcement regime has occurred within the goals and activities of both formal organizations and obligations—such as the U.N. Drug Programme, the 1988 U.N. Vienna Convention Against the Traffic in Illicit Narcotic and Psychotropic Substances and the European Union, and the 1991 EU Anti-Money Laundering Directive—and informal organizations and undertakings—such as FATF and its Forty Recommendations, and the Caribbean FATF and its additional recommendations.

On December 10, 1997, at a meeting in Washington, D.C., ministers from eight industrialized governments agreed to combat cybercrime with enhanced technology and a harmonized crime legislation. The arrangements to cooperate against cybercrime result from the ongoing discussions among the G-7 nations, that is, the G-7 Economic Summit countries—plus the European Union and Russia. In particular, the governments agreed to cooperate in investigations and enforcement actions involving cyber criminals. The G-8 countries agreed on a series of principles, such as denying a safe haven to abusers of information technology. Just as important will be the establishment of a network and contacts to assist in investigating and arresting perpetrators of cybercrimes, including computer hackers, online peddlers of child pornography, drug traffickers, organized crime, and people who use computer networks to perpetrate illicit activities.

The ministers agreed on the following steps:

- Ensuring that law enforcement is properly staffed and trained to fight cybercrime;
- Developing improved means to quickly trace attacks coming through computer networks; allocating the same time and resources to the prosecution of cybercriminals who have attacked other countries as would be allocated for domestic attacks, if extradition is not possible due to nationality;
- Ensuring the preservation of electronic evidence and developing solutions for transborder searches and computer searches involving data whose location is not known to officials;
- Cooperating with the private sector to develop new solutions for preserving and collecting critical evidence;
- Accelerating the process by which traffic data from communications carriers can be obtained;
- Ensuring expeditious responses to mutual assistance requests, in appropriate cases, by voice, fax, or e-mail communications followed by written confirmation, if needed;
- Encouraging, the development of international standards for reliable and secure telecommunications and data processing technologies;
- Using compatible forensic standards to retrieve and authenticate electronic data; and
- Including cybercrime issues when negotiating mutual assistance agreements or arrangements.

A 1996 survey of the Computer Security Institute revealed that forty-two per cent of Fortune 500 companies had experienced an unauthorized use of their computer systems during the last year. While U.S. Attorney General Janet Reno has said that the action plan does not require new legislation by the United States, wiretap laws must be adjusted to accommodate the digital era. All ministers promised to review their legal systems, "to ensure that [their laws] appropriately criminalize abuses of telecommunications and computer systems and promote the investigation of high crimes." During the week of the meeting, the vulnerability of the Internet to such crimes was emphasized when hackers broke into computers at Yahoo!, one of the most popular sites on the World Wide Web, and threatened to infect users' computers with a damaging computer virus unless an alleged hacker was released from jail.

Many cyber crimes involve fraudulent pyramid schemes distributed by electronic mail. Another fraud includes tricking Internet users into relinquishing passwords that can be used to access their accounts. The G-8 agreement is an effort by national governments to enable international criminal cooperation developments to keep pace with technology and its use by transnational criminals.

On September 23, 1997, the Basle Committee on Banking Supervision, the central bank organ of the G-10 countries, agreed on a final version of supervision principles to strengthen the supervisory regime. While the new guide contains no substantive changes, the text has gained support.

For example, delegates attending the Denver Summit endorsed it. The Committee also obtained comments from many countries outside the group, including Chile, China, the Czech Republic, Hong Kong, Mexico, Russia, and Thailand. In addition, bankers and banking regulators from Argentina, Brazil, Hungary, India, Indonesia, South Korea, Malaysia, Poland, and Singapore contributed to the summit.

Major financial countries have been asked to endorse the two principles by no later than October 1998. The principles "outline the basic elements of a banking supervisory system including licensing and structure, prudential regulations and requirements, methods of ongoing banking supervision, information requirements, the formal powers of supervisors and cross-border banking." A compendium of laws accompanies the regulations that banks are requested to update on a regular basis.

The Basle Core Principles aim to provide a basic reference with which supervisory and other public authorities worldwide may supervise all of the banks within their jurisdictions. Central banks that endorse the principles will review and update their own current supervisory arrangements in accordance with the principles.

The Committee urged national legislators to ensure that required changes in the law be enacted quickly. Since the measures outlined in the principles took one and a half years to coordinate, and since they are minimum requirements, the Committee observes that many countries may want to tighten their own rules further than the principles require. The Committee pledged technical assistance and training for regulatory agencies from non-G-10 countries that want to take advantage of the principles.

The continued review and strengthening of global and domestic financial supervisory mechanisms has become more urgent in a globalized world in which transnational crime and organized groups operate. Increasingly, international organizations and groups, such as the Basle Committee, the FATF, the World Bank Group, and Interpol, are exchanging information and cooperating among themselves to complement their regulatory and enforcement frameworks.

On April 24, 1997, members of the European Parliament proposed to enact legislation against certain cybercrimes, namely pornography, paedophilia, and racist material. The measures will include establishing teams of cyberpolice to monitor the Internet, requiring industry self-regulation, and concluding international enforcement cooperation agreements. The European Union also scheduled for July 6-8, 1997 a ministerial conference on global information networks that was intended to lead to a declaration on regulatory principles.

The MEPs will try to strike a balance between protecting the public from obscenity and respecting an individual's right to free speech and privacy. The United States, Germany and France have regulated the Internet, but with limited success. The French and German authorities have focused on Internet service providers.

For instance, Karlheinz Moewes, the chief officer of the Munich police, heads the first German force to combat Internet crime. His team of five Internet police investigated 110 cases of child pornography worldwide in 1996. They patrol the Internet on a regular basis, searching for child pornography and trying to follow and penetrate groups of paedophiles.

In Belgium and the United Kingdom, similar law enforcement groups operate. For instance, in the United Kingdom the teams cooperate with the Internet Service Providers Association, which blocks access if illegal sites are discovered. The difficulty is that the persons responsible for perpetrating the crimes may be outside the European Union and in remote parts of the world where law enforcement cooperation is not effective. MEPs have called on the European Commission to propose a common framework for self-regulation and to agree on a code of good behaviour. According to EU Industrial Affairs Commissioner Martin Bangemann, the EU must introduce binding measures on service providers, with penalties. MEPs believe that service providers must be liable for illicit material on their systems.

In April 1997, German authorities charged the managing director of CompuServe in Bavaria with providing access to pornographic and racist material. The situation is seen as a test case. Service providers contend that they should be treated like telecommunications companies, who are not prosecuted when criminals use their lines. French MEP Pierre Pradier wants to make users responsible because families can use software devices to screen criminal and harmful material. One problem is the classic issue of whether the law can keep up With the technology.

Undoubtedly, the European Union and other major powers will need to update their laws constantly. Meanwhile, criminal organizations are likely to search for, identify, and utilize the states that intentionally or accidentally have the lowest law and regulatory regime. At its meeting on November 4-7, 1997 in Lima, Peru, CICAD, a branch of the OAS, made several decisions and recommen-dations of importance to international enforcement, including steps to undertake an ongoing assessment of money laundering in the hemisphere, the creation of national FIUs, and measures to strengthen the training of officials and the exchange of information and reciprocal judicial assistance.

Creation of Financial Intelligence Units

The CIAD recommended to CICAD the amendment of the Model Regulations as follows: In accordance with the law, each member state shall establish or designate a central agency responsible for receiving, requesting, analyzing and disseminating to the competent authorities, disclosures of information relating to financial transactions that are required to be reported pursuant to these Model Regulations or that concern suspected proceeds of crime. The recommendation explains that the objective is to receive and analyse information so that it can be utilized by the competent authorities.

The entities can be referred to variously as Financial Intelligence Units, Financial Investigation Units, Financial Information Units, or Financial Analysis Units. Depending on its location in the governmental structure of a country, FIUs may assume one of the following modes as identified by the Egmont Group: a police model; a judicial model; a mixed police and judicial model; or an administrative model.

Ongoing Assessment of the Plan of Action of Buenos Aires

After discussing the results of responses to a questionnaire on the status of anti-money laundering regulations in twenty-one CICAD countries, the CICAD Group of Experts determined that the top two priority areas on which to focus their efforts for the immediate future would be the training of officials, and strengthening the exchange of information and reciprocal judicial assistance. Training should focus on officials who work in FIUs or in other entities—whose purpose is to receive and analyse information, investigate on the basis thereof, or both—transactions that appear to involve money laundering.

Training also is required for investigators on the applicable investigation methods and techniques for money laundering offences and on methods of presenting evidence regarding money laundering before the courts or other competent entities. Moreover, training is required for prosecutors and judges to ensure full understanding of the offence, the importance of stringent conviction and. prosecution, evidence in money laundering cases, international cooperation among judges for mutual legal assistance purposes, the importance of seizure, confiscation pending trial, ultimate forfeiture of laundered assets and instrumentalities, and the difficulties in securing convictions.

Training also is required for officials of supervisory and regulatory agencies responsible for overseeing financial institutions. In this connection, training should be focused on the development and application of the appropriate control systems over financial institutions. It should also include training with respect to reporting systems for required cash and suspicious transaction reports, on the authority and law under which the agency operates, and on comparative approaches in other countries.

The Group of Experts will organize an informal working group for the purpose of identifying a training programme based on the priority areas identified in the Group's discussion and the replies to the questionnaire. The Group discussed the difficulties in investigating and proving money laundering, especially due to its transnational nature that complicates, in particular, investigation and issues of proof. These aspects require a high level of international cooperation, formal and informal, that must be efficient and effective. There must exist a reciprocal capability to seize and freeze assets as well as to provide for their confiscation when they are situated in a country other than where the investigation and trial are occurring.

The Group noted the importance of studies to facilitate the compilation, systematization, and diffusion of information on applicable national and international norms to identify the appropriate central authorities to give effect to the intended cooperation. For their next meeting, the Group of Experts agreed to consider the applicability of developing a manual on these matters that would set out the applicable laws and contact points in the various administrations in CICAD member states. The Executive Secretariat will develop a model outline for such a manual for the next meeting of the Group. To assist in this work, CICAD members will provide an explanatory report on these measures and identify the competent authorities. The Group of Experts agreed that a typologies exercise will become part of their ongoing agenda. For the next meeting certain countries would prepare, on a voluntary basis, a report on their experience in detecting money laundering typologies.

On May 12-14, 1998, the OAS-CICAD met and agreed to strengthen anti-money laundering enforcement efforts. This section outlines the Commission's initiatives.

- *Training:* The Group approved a training plan based on modules for the training of judges, prosecutors, FIU personnel, and law enforcement officials. Wherever possible, the training plan would be implemented on a sub-regional basis, following a needs assessment and diagnosis to determine the priorities of each country or region.

- *Amendments to the Model Regulations:* To bring the model regulations approved in May 1992 in line with the broad international policy guidelines, especially those contained in the Summit of the Americas Plan of Action of Buenos Aires of 1995, the model regulations will incorporate the concept of "serious offences," so that anti-money laundering laws and regulations are designed to counteract serious crimes rather than just drug violations. As a result, the title of the regulations was modified to read Model Regulations Concerning Laundering Offences Connected to Illicit Drug Trafficking, Related and Other Serious Offences. As defined, "serious offences" means "those defined by the legislation of each country, including, for example illegal activities that relate to organized crime, terrorism, illicit trafficking of arms, persons or body organs, corruption, fraud, extortion and kidnapping." Another change is that under new Article 7(d) CICAD members will "facilitate the sharing of the objects of the forfeiture or the proceeds from their sale, on a basis commensurate with participation, with the country or countries that assisted or participated in the investigation or legal proceedings that resulted in the objects being forfeited." In addition, new Article 7(f) obligates members to "promote and facilitate the creation of a national forfeiture fund to administer the objects of forfeiture and to authorize their use or allocation to support programmes for judicial management [and] training," as well as for counterdrug efforts and related programmes,
  The group adopted a proposal by St. Lucia to amend Article 10, [sections] 1(b) to broaden the definition of financial institutions to include businesses authorized to conduct "offshore" financial activities. The group deferred until the next meeting action on proposals of St. Lucia to add collective investment funds, such as mutual funds and unit trusts, to Article 9(2).
- *Manual on Information Exchange for Anti-Laundering and Mutual Assistance:* Consideration was given to the information page that could become a valuable tool for all countries in facilitating points of contact for information exchange and mutual legal assistance. The pages would be accessible through CICAD's webpage and would be kept current.
  The United States discussed the operation of the Egmont web site system as an example of how secure information exchanges are

occurring among the FIU Egmont members. Eventually, the CICAD system may be set up for secure information exchange.

- *Cooperation with the CICAD Working Group on the Multilateral Evaluation Mechanism:* The Group of Experts agreed that they would offer their assistance and technical capabilities to the CICAD Working Group on the Multilateral Evaluation Mechanism. The assistance would permit the experts can help with anti-money laundering evaluation, so that once the OAS members agree to undertake multilateral evaluations of the member's counter drug policies.
- *Permanent Council Working Group:* The Group of Experts reviewed the draft resolution to the OAS General Assembly of the Permanent Council Working Group—that was established to consider the desirability of an Inter-American convention against money laundering. The Experts will advise the working group of their own views on a convention from its technical perspective.

Analysis

The expansion of the anti-money laundering efforts in the Western Hemisphere to include serious crimes rather than just drug trafficking brings this group current with practice in the rest of the world. The consideration of a multilateral evaluation mechanism, the exchange of information, training, and even a convention are all efforts to strengthen compliance and indicate broader political agreement and acceptance of the purposes of anti-money laundering.

The ongoing assessment, the establishment of FIUs, and the typologies exercise are small steps towards cooperation in hemispheric anti-money laundering enforcement. Meaningful and effective cooperation, harmonization of laws and standards, and effective establishment of an anti-money laundering regime must await the establishment of a proper network. A solid legal infrastructure with funding for professionals is needed for intensive and daily work on compliance with conventions and resolutions, harmonization of laws, collaboration on common approaches to mechanisms and technology, and common approaches to operational problems. At present, the governments and international organizations in the Western Hemisphere are searching for ways to develop ad hoc solutions to individual criminal problems, such as anti-money laundering.

SUBSTANTIVE LAW OF ANTI-MONEY LAUNDERING

Since the initiation of international anti-money laundering efforts in the mid-1980s, various substantive requirements have been established: the requirement to criminalize money laundering activities; the requirement that covered persons must know-their-customer; the requirement to identify and report to authorities suspicious transactions; the requirement to freeze, trace, seize, and ultimately forfeit the proceeds and instrumentalities of money laundering crimes; the requirement of covered persons to have a compliance officer and to train employees; the requirement for covered persons to have outside audits the compliance of their organization with anti-money laundering standards; and the prohibition of secrecy as a reason for a country and covered persons to refuse to follow any of the anti-money laundering obligations.

In U.S. law, the main provisions of anti-money laundering are found in Titles 12, 18 and 31 of the U.S. Code. The Bank Secrecy Act of 1970 was a precursor to anti-money laundering. It was intended to deter laundering and the use of secret foreign bank accounts. It established an investigative "paper trail" for large currency transactions by establishing regulatory reporting standards and requirements, such as the Currency Transaction Report requirement. This requirement early distinguished the United States from other countries' approach to anti-money laundering. The BSA imposed civil and criminal penalties for non-compliance with its reporting requirements. It was designed to improved the detection and investigation of criminal, tax, and regulatory violations. A unique aspect of U.S. anti-money laundering laws that other countries are starting to emulate is the simultaneous use of anti-money laundering, tax, regulatory, and even criminal, —especially organized crime—goals.

The Money Laundering Control Act of 1986, which was part of the Anti-Drug Abuse Act of 1986, created three new criminal offences for money laundering activities by, through, or to a financial institution: knowingly helping launder money; knowingly engaging—including by being willfully blind—in a transaction of more than $10,000 that involves property from criminal activity; and structuring transactions to avoid the BSA reporting.

The Anti-Drug Abuse Act of 1988 strengthened anti-money laundering by: Significantly increasing civil, criminal and forfeiture sanctions for laundering crimes and BSA violations, including forfeiture of "any property, real or personal, involved in a transaction or attempted transaction in violation of laws" relating to the filing of Currency Transaction Reports, money laundering, or structuring transactions; requiring stronger and more precise identification and recording of cash purchases of certain monetary instruments; allowing the Treasury Department to require financial institutions to file additional, geographically targeted reports; requiring the Treasury Department to negotiate bilateral international agreements covering the recording of large U.S. currency transactions and the sharing of such information; and increasing the criminal sanction for tax evasion when money from criminal activity is involved.

In 1992, the Housing and Community Development Act of 1992 made changes in anti-money laundering laws. It strengthened penalties for financial institutions violating anti-money laundering laws, and allows regulators to close or seize institutions by appointing a conservator or receiver or terminating the institution's charges.

Regulators can suspend or remove institution-affiliated parties who have violated the BSA or been indicted for money laundering or criminal activity under the BSA. It forbids any individual convicted of money laundering from unauthorized participation in any federally insured institutions. Under the Annunzio-Wylie Act, the Treasury must issue regulations requiring national banks and other depository institutions to identify which of their account holders—other than other depository institutions or regulated broker dealers—are non-bank financial institutions, such as money transmitters or check cashing services.

Treasury, along with the Federal Reserve, must promulgate regulations requiring financial institutions and other entities that cash checks, transmit money, or perform similar services to maintain records of domestic and international wire transfers that are useful in law enforcement investigations. Under the Act, the U.S. Government has established a BSA Advisory Group that includes representatives from the Departments of Treasury as well as Justice, and the Office of National Drug Control Policy and other interested persons and financial institutions.

The group was created for the purpose of developing a harmonious private-public cooperation on anti-money laundering.

Under the Annunzio-Wylie Act, Treasury can require financial institutions to adopt anti-money laundering programmes that include: internal policies, procedures, and controls; designation of a compliance officer; and continuation of an ongoing employee training programme; and an independent audit function to test the adequacy of the programme. Treasury can require any financial institution, or any financial institution employee, to report suspicious transactions relevant to possible violation of law or regulation under the protection from civil suit arising from such reports by virtue of a "safe harbour." The American Bankers' Association and the banking industry had long sought such a safe harbour.

Under the Act, a financial institution or employee may be prosecuted for "tipping off"—that is, if they disclose, to the subject of a referral or a grand jury subpoena, that a criminal referral has been filed or a grand jury investigation has been started concerning a possible crime of money laundering and BSA laws. Officers who improperly disclose information concerning a grand jury subpoena for bank records are subject to prosecution.

The 1998 U.S. Money Laundering Act: Fostering Partnerships and Better Targeting

Before adjourning in 1998, Congress considered and almost enacted the Money Laundering Deterrence Act of 1998. On October 5, 1998, it passed in the House, but died in the Senate. Because it has the support of the Administration and many other people, the bill is worth considering. It would amend title 31 of the U.S. Code to improve methods for preventing financial crimes, and for other purposes. It amends Title 31 of the U.S. Code to improve methods for preventing financial crimes.

Section 1 notes that organized crime groups are continually devising new methods to launder money, "including the use of financial service providers that are not depository institutions, such as money transmitters and check cashing services, the purchase and resale of durable goods," and the exchange of black market foreign currency. The involvement of international criminal enterprises engaged in money laundering is complex, diverse, and fragmented. Many foreign gangs and groups have financial management and organizational infrastructures that are highly sophisticated and difficult to track because of the globalization of the financial service industry.

Section 2 lists as the purposes of the Act to provide the law enforcement community with the necessary legal authority to combat money laundering, to broaden the law enforcement community's access to transactional information already being collected" in a non-financial trade or business, and " to expedite the issuance by the Secretary of the Treasury of regulations designed to deter money laundering activities at certain types of financial institutions."

Section 3 amends the suspicious activity reporting requirements in the Bank Secrecy Act to facilitate the flow of financial regulatory agencies.

Subsection broadens the "safe harbour" provisions of 31 U.S.C. [sections] 5318 to independent public accountants who file Suspicious Activity Reports. It is hoped that accountants conducting audits and routine examinations of a financial institution's books and records will report wrongdoing. Subsection limits the circumstances under which the filing of a SAR may be disclosed. Subsection "provides financial institutions with immunity from liability when making employment references that include suspicion of a prospective employee's possible involvement in a violation of law or regulation," unless the financial institution knows such suspicion "to be false or if the institution acts with malice or reckless disregard for the truth in making such a reference." Subsection makes SARs available to self-regulatory organizations as defined by the Securities and Exchange Act of 1934.

Section 4 expands the scope of the summons authority under 31 U.S.C. [sections] 5318(b)(1) from merely "investigations for the purpose of civil enforcement" of the Bank Secrecy Act to "examinations to determine compliance with the Bank Secrecy Act, as well as investigations relating to reports filed pursuant to the Act." The expanded summons authority will help in the case of non-depository institutions whose activities are not subject to regulatory oversight.

Section 5 "clarifies existing statutory language making it illegal to violate reporting requirements mandated by a geographic targeting order issued by the Secretary of the Treasury or the funds transfer record-keeping rules."

Section 6 eliminates Treasury Secretary's obligation "to report to Congress on the status of states' adoption of uniform laws regulating money transmitters." The Treasury Department's recently promulgated regulations for Money Services Businesses, which include money transmitters, has rendered this directive unnecessary.

Section 7 "exempts Bank Secrecy Act reporting requirements, including those imposed by geographic targeting orders, from consideration under the Paperwork Reduction Act."

Section 8 "transfers from the Internal Revenue Code to the Bank Secrecy Act the requirement that any person engaged in a trade or business file a report with the Federal government on cash transactions in excess of $10,000." Reports made pursuant to this requirement "provide law enforcement authorities with a paper trail that can help identify a lifestyle that is not commensurate with an individual's known sources of legitimate income."

Under prior law, non-financial institutions had to report cash transactions exceeding $10,000 to the Internal Revenue Service on IRS Form 8300. Because such reports must be filed pursuant to the Internal Revenue Code, Form 8300 information is considered tax return information. As such, it may not be disclosed to any persons or used in any manner not authorized by the Internal Revenue Code. Authorized disclosures of Form 8300 information are subject to the procedural and recordkeeping requirements of Section 6103 of the Internal Revenue Code. For example, Section 6103(p)(4)(E) requires agencies seeking Form 8300 information to file a report with the Secretary of the Treasury that describes the procedures established and utilized by the agency for ensuring the confidentiality of the information.

The IRS requires that agencies requesting Form 8300 information file a "Safeguard Procedures Report," which must be approved by the IRS before such information can be released. While the IRS uses Form 8300 to identify individuals who may be engaged in tax evasion, the information collected on the form can also be useful to other law enforcement agencies investigating other financial crimes, including money laundering. Form 8300 information can be instrumental in helping law enforcement authorities trace cash payments by drug traffickers and other criminals for luxury cars, jewelry, and other expensive merchandise. However, Form 8300s are not accessible to law enforcement authorities and, as a result of the above-mentioned restrictions under Section 6103, they cannot be retrieved electronically from a database maintained by the Treasury Department. The change will make the reports much more accessible.

Section 9 requires that within 120 days of enactment the Treasury must promulgate know-your-customer regulations for financial institutions. The regulations have been under discussion and study among Federal banking and financial regulatory agencies, including the Treasury Department, the Federal Reserve Board of Governors, the Office of the Comptroller of the Currency, and the Federal Deposit Insurance Corporation. The regulations "are intended to assist financial institutions in verifying that their customers' funds are derived from legitimate sources."

Section 10 extends the statute of limitations period from one to two years in forfeitable fungible property in bank accounts under 18 U.S.C. [sections] 984. It provides that all bank deposits are fungible and authorizes the forfeiture of money held to prove that the money in the account on one day is the "same money" as was in the account on a prior occasion.

Section 11 requires the Treasury Secretary, in consultation with "federal banking agencies" and within one year of enactment of [the law], to prepare a report on the nature and extent of private banking activities in the U.S.; regulatory efforts to monitor private banking activities and ensure that they are conducted in compliance with the Bank Secrecy Act; and policies and procedures of depository institutions that are designed to ensure that private banking activities are conducted in compliance with the Bank Secrecy Act.

Section 12 requires the Treasury Secretary, to prescribe regulations requiring financial institutions to maintain all accounts in such a way as to ensure that the name of an account holder and the number of the account are associated with all account activity of the account holder, and to ensure that all such information is available for purposes of account supervision and law enforcement.

Section 13 "expresses the sense of the Congress that the Secretary of the Treasury should make available to all Federal, State and local law enforcement agencies and financial regulatory agencies the full contents of the electronic database of reports required to be filed under the Bank Secrecy Act."

Section 14 "directs the Secretary of the Treasury, in consultation with appropriate Federal law enforcement authorities, to develop criteria... to identify areas outside the [United States] in which money laundering activities are concentrated, and to designate any areas so identified as foreign high intensity money laundering areas." Section 15 "authorizes the doubling of criminal penalties for Bank Secrecy Act violations committed with respect to a transaction involving a person in, a relationship maintained in, or transport of a monetary instrument involving a foreign country known to have been designated as a foreign high intensity money laundering area" pursuant to Section 14, which refers to the portions of the Department of State's annual International Narcotics Strategy Control Report that identifies foreign countries that serve as safe havens for money laundering.

Erosion of Secrecy

For professionals involved in the international transfer of wealth techniques, financial privacy is an important principle. Fiduciaries have obligations under law—both common law and statutory law in some countries—contract, and ethics to uphold confidentiality. Increasingly, in the era of globalization and since the start of the anti-money laundering regime in the mid-1980s, secrecy is sometimes overridden by obligations of banks, financial institutions, solicitors, and other covered persons to "know their customer" and identify and report suspicious transactions.

Two developments indicate the fragility and nature of exceptions to bank secrecy: the initiatives to rectify the Nazi gold losses and the intensive efforts by liquidators of a Cayman bank to recover computer bank records turned over by its former chairman and managing director to the U.S. Government.

Swiss Foreign Minister Reassures Swiss Bankers on Secrecy: One of the exceptions to bank and business secrecy has been the effort to ascertain the extent of wrongdoing and pay compensation to the victims of the Holocaust. The effort is sometimes referred to as the Nazi gold debacle. The various investigations, agreements, and lawsuits all have succeeded in overcoming bank secrecy in Switzerland and other countries, and demonstrate yet another exception to such secrecy.

In this context, the Swiss Government has tried to assure its investors about its efforts to maintain legitimate secrecy. On September 5, 1997, Flavio Cotti, Switzerland's foreign minister, assured Swiss bankers that the Swiss Government would not buckle to international demands to dilute Switzerland's bank secrecy laws, one of the main factors for Switzerland's dominance in the private banking business.

His remarks were made during the annual meeting of the Swiss Bankers Association in Berne and were designed to reassure Swiss bankers that Swiss authorities are aware of the financial risks facing the banks in the aftermath of growing criticism of the banks' wartime role in dealing with the accounts of Holocaust victims and looted Nazi gold. According to Cotti, the Swiss

Government would ensure that the Swiss banking industry remains a "central pillar of the Swiss economy." The banking sector generates ten per cent of gross domestic product, employs 108,000 people, and contributes eleven per cent of tax revenues.

Cotti complimented Swiss bankers for helping improve Switzerland's international image and for the "extraordinary speed" with which they had prepared a "package of measures comparable to no other." In addition, Cotti noted that the issue of "unfair tax competition" had assumed greater significance and that "Swiss banking secrecy and other laws supporting the Swiss financial centre had become frequent targets of criticism at OECD meeting." Cotti also discussed the role of the Swiss banking community in accepting assets of "dubious origin from heads of state." In this connection, the Swiss Government had responded in an "active and efficient manner" in 1997 to block the Swiss bank accounts of ex-President Mobutu. The lessons from this and other cases is that "[t]he efficiency of Switzerland's financial centre attracts assets of criminal or dubious origin and it was in the deepest interests of the financial centre to keep such monies at a distance."

Ultimately, the lifting of bank secrecy helped facilitate the agreement announced on August 12, 1998, whereby representatives of Swiss commercial banks and Holocaust survivors reached a settlement, in which the banks agreed to "pay $1.25 billion in reparations to victims of the Nazi era, in exchange for the dismissal of three class action suits... and recommendations by the victims groups that the state and local authorities cancel plans to impose sanctions." Cotti's remarks and the lifting of bank secrecy to resolve the controversy over the claims of Holocaust victims indicate the transition that the Swiss government and private sector are undergoing with respect to bank secrecy, vetting to exclude illegitimate money, the new anti-money laundering regime concerning "know-your-customer", "identifying and reporting suspicious transactions", "criminalizing money laundering", and freezing and forfeiting illegal proceeds and the instrumentalities of the same.

The transition becomes more complex when governments, international organizations, non-governmental organizations, and public opinion assess and impose moral judgements about the private sector and the government's role during World War II nearly forty years later.

A case involving an effort by the Cayman Government to reclaim computer bank records obtained from a former managing director and target of a U.S. law enforcement proceeding provides a perspective of the practical limitations of bank secrecy in an increasingly shrinking world. On May 7, 1997, the U.S. District Court for the District of New Jersey issued an order denying a petition by liquidators of a Cayman bank seeking the return of its computer bank records that its former chairman and managing director had turned over to the U.S. Government. The managing director was a target of a law enforcement proceeding when he "voluntarily" turned over the documents. The liquidator then filed a petition for the return of property pursuant to Federal Rule of Criminal Procedure 41(e). On January 18, 1995, the Cayman Government appointed an interim controller to take control of the affairs of the offshore bank. At the time, the offshore bank had approximately 1,000 clients, including corporations, trusts and individuals, some of which were U.S. residents.

On January 24, 1994, the Cayman Government revoked the offshore bank's "category `B' Bank and Trust company licenses" and closed the bank. The Cayman Government also filed a petition for an order to wind-up the affairs of the offshore bank due to "serious irregularities" identified in the conduct of the offshore bank's business.

On February 10, 1995, the Grand Court of the Cayman Islands ordered the offshore bank "wound up". On June 21, 1996, a federal grand jury in Newark, New Jersey returned a multi-count indictment charging the individual defendant and others with conspiracy and money laundering. FBI agents subsequently arrested the individual defendant.

In June 1996, the individual defendant gave the FBI a tape containing "copies of certain computer back-up tapes containing detailed financial and operating records of the [Offshore] Bank." The individual defendant voluntarily gave the tape to the Federal Bureau of Investigation "without the issuance of a warrant, subpoena or other compulsory process." It remains in the possession of the U.S. Government. The FBI contacted the Royal Cayman Islands Police and sought assistance in its efforts to gain access to the information stored on the tape. On August 6, 1996, Christopher Johnson, the liquidator, "filed a formal, written complaint of the `theft' of the tape to the Cayman Police." The petition focused on the inevitability of the eventual transferal of the tape to the IRS "for the purpose of investigating and, where appropriate, prosecuting any bank clients subject to U.S. taxation."

The Advisory Committee's Report for Rule 41(e) of the Federal Rules Criminal Procedure provides "that an aggrieved person may seek return of property that has been unlawfully seized, and a person whose property has been lawfully seized may seek return of property when aggrieved by the Government's continued possession of it." Moreover, Rule 41(e) allows a court to "order either the originals or copies of seized documents be returned to their owner and permit the Government access and/or use of the information." Using four factors in entertaining a Rule 41(e) motion, the court denied the order. The first factor is "whether the Government displayed a callous disregard for the constitutional rights of the petitioner." The Cayman liquidator and government did not meet the test. The Johnson court noted that the U.S. Government had no role in the procurement of the tape. Instead, the individual defendant voluntarily provided the tape to the U.S. Government. Since there was no U.S. Government involvement in the procurement of the tape, no constitutional rights were at issue in the instant case.

Thus, the Johnson court held that the rights afforded by the Fourth Amendment are "wholly inapplicable to a `search or seizure, even an unreasonable one, effected by a private individual not acting as an agent of the Government or with the participation or knowledge of any government official.'" Because the documents were voluntarily given to the U.S. Government, the latter's "use of the tape in its investigation of the suspected tax evasion scheme and other suspected financial crimes connected to the offshore bank and in future prosecutions will not violate the constitutional rights of the offshore bank or any of its clients." The second factor the Johnson court considered was whether the petitioner had an individual interest in and need for the property he wanted returned. The court found against the petitioner, stating that the petitioner already possessed the information contained on the tape and, hence, its return did not appear necessary for petitioner to carry on the offshore bank's business.

That the offshore bank was in liquidation and apparently would be defunct shortly invalidated the claim that petitioners did not need the tape to undertake their duties. The Johnson court found unpersuasive the speculative argument that the use of the tape may expose the offshore bank to "numerous complaints and claims" because U.S. nationals are in any event "required to reveal the existence of foreign bank accounts and report certain foreign transactions." The reporting requirement meant that the U.S. nationals lacked a reasonable expectation of privacy in the offshore bank records.

Upon consideration of the third factor, the Johnson court found that the offshore bank would not suffer "irreparable harm" if the tape was not returned, since the offshore bank's licenses have been revoked and the bank was in liquidation. The court also considered and rejected the fourth factor, whether the petitioners had an adequate remedy at law. Even if the petitioner was able to establish that the bank would suffer irreparable harm, the court found that the exercise of equitable jurisdiction to forbid the Government the use of the tape was not justified. Generally, even when the U.S. Government improperly has possession of evidence, and when the aggrieved party's Rule 41(d) motion is successful, courts have permitted the Government to retain copies of the evidence.

The Johnson court rejected the petitioners' argument that the doctrine of international comity requires the suppression of the tapes. While comity is "the spirit of cooperation in which a domestic tribunal approaches the resolution of cases touching the laws and interests of other sovereign states," it must yield to domestic policy. In particular, the Johnson court stated that no country will suffer the law of another to interfere with its own to the injury of its citizens.

Here, the court noted that the U.S. Government declared that the information on the tape constitute "significant evidence" of a "widespread tax evasion scheme" and has "initiated multiple investigations concerning suspected criminal activities by customers of the Offshore bank." The Johnson court rejected the arguments that disclosure of the information contained on the tape to U.S. Government agencies, such as the IRS, may expose the offshore bank to numerous complaints and claims.

The court noted that, notwithstanding the Cayman Government's claim that its Mutual Legal Assistance in Criminal Matters Treaty enabled the United States to obtain the information on the tapes from it on request, the U.S. Government is not able to obtain information on pure tax matters under the Cayman-U.S. MLAT. In rejecting the arguments of the petitioner under international comity, the Johnson court found the speculative arguments regarding harm that may result to the offshore bank and the banking industry of the Cayman Government insufficient to overcome the interest of the United States in its ongoing criminal investigation.

The case represents a setback to Cayman secrecy and indicates the practical limitations of secrecy. Any person who relies on secrecy of one country now must factor into the equation the limitations that may eventually eliminate the confidentiality on which it seeks to rely.

Due Diligence

Since the mid-1980s, a major component of international anti-money laundering efforts has been due diligence requirements. These requirements include: the duty to know-your-client, the duty to identify and report to authorities suspicious transactions, the requirement to appoint a compliance officer with access to the top executives of an organization, the duty to train employees on anti-money laundering, and the duty to ensure that anti-money laundering obligations are properly audited so that any violations will be detected and remedied. Increasingly, those bodies covered by due diligence include non-bank financial institutions, such as money transmitters. In addition, the requirements for bank and financial supervisors to monitor and audit continue to multiply. On November 19, 1998, the release by the British Government of its report on financial services in the Channel Islands initiated a number of changes in due diligence to prevent and combat money laundering.

In its November 1998 report on problems in international financial services in the Channel Islands, the British Government called for reforms, many of which presage similar reforms it will demand from other offshore territories. The so-called Edwards report—named for its author, a former top official at the British Treasury—reviews financial supervision in the Channel Islands and calls on them to strengthen restrictions on offshore companies and start cooperating with foreign financial investigations. Lord Williams, a British Home Office minister, subsequently agreed to chair a series of meetings with the three territories starting in January 1999, to follow up on the list of proposed reforms in the Edwards report.

The Edwards Report applauds the efforts of the islands, which are self-governing dependencies of the British crown, to strengthen standards in their 350 million [pounds sterling] financial industry. The report notes that one-third of investments come from U.K. residents. However, the report contains detailed recommendations for major reforms focusing especially on the rules for establishing offshore companies and trusts used to shelter assets from tax or from outside scrutiny.

While all three islands have accepted the recommendations generally, they resist a number of specific recommendations—such as requiring companies to file audited accounts, and, in the case of the Isle of Man, vetting companies established on the island—in the hope that new measures to control company agents will solve the problem. The report calls on all of the islands to improve the regulation of companies and company directors. The islands' low tax rates and relatively flexible regulatory controls have attracted large numbers of international companies.

Approximately 100,0000 companies are incorporated in the islands, especially in the Isle of Man. Many more are administered from, but not incorporated in, the islands. According to former Minister Edwards, company regulation requires tightening in all three islands. The priority for the authorities in all three islands is to cooperate fully with other countries in the pursuit of financial crime and money laundering.

In recent years, several high profile financial court cases have called attention to the Channel Islands' regulatory procedures. For example, in 1998 Bank Cantrade was forced to pay fines of $3 million because one of its traders had misled investors by showing profits of $15 million on foreign currency transactions when he had actually lost $11 million. In 1995, when the Barings merchant bank failed, "the bank's Guernsey subsidiary had lent deposits well in excess of its capital base and was technically insolvent.

However, the unit was not declared insolvent while the authorities tried to find a buyer." According to the Edwards Report, these and other cases indicate the need for more on-site inspections of financial institutions as well as the need some kind for of reform, moratorium, or administration procedures as in the United Kingdom to assist them in dealing with insolvency. The report also calls for a financial ombudsman to deal with customer complaints.

The Edwards Report recommends that the Isle of Man strengthen its regulation of companies. Thousands of companies are incorporated in the Isle of Man and thousands more are administered from Guernsey and Jersey, if not actually incorporated there. Most of the companies are private and formed by non-residents or trusts to hold assets or interests outside the islands. The Isle of Man has no system to vet new companies that want to register or for persons to obtain disclosure about the companies already registered. For Guernsey, the Edwards report calls for dealing with the problem of nominee directors—the so called "Sark lark." This phenomenon involves residents of Sark, a small island under Guernsey's jurisdictions, who sit as directors on many different company boards. While the population of Sark is only 575, the total directorships held amount to approximately 15,000. Three residents hold between 1,600 and 3,000 directorships each.

Guernsey has started to crack down on "false domiciles," whereby islanders were responding to phone calls for companies located elsewhere. However, the island has resisted divesting residents of their directorships. In general, the islands reacted positively to the Edwards report. However, bankers complained that the report's recommendations would erode client confidentiality. The financial industry is likely to oppose and resist many of the detailed changes, including comprehensive customer compensation schemes in Jersey and Guernsey, and some changes in trust law.

The Edwards report recommends the establishment of a confidential hotline for whistle blowers, such as the person who reported improprieties in Cantrade, but was ignored by his superiors. Jersey authorities are considering providing statutory protection for such informers. The Jersey Bankers Associations has indicated that it favours the release of information to other authorities where the latter are investigating crimes. However, they worry about "areas which potentially affect the fine dividing line between protecting [their] clients' confidentiality and the disclosure of information about customer affairs to authorities outside the jurisdiction of Jersey."

The preparation and release of the Edwards report takes place in the context of the OECD Report on Harmful Tax Competition and the EU initiative towards tax harmonization and imposing minimum withholding tax, reporting requirements for the payment of interest to residents of other EU countries earned on bank deposits in the other host country, or both. In fact, the United Kingdom's membership in the European Union has been a contributing element in its own initiatives to strengthen international financial supervision in its dependent and overseas territories. The Edwards report takes a balanced approach of acknowledging and applauding the comparatively favourable financial supervisory standards in the three islands, considering the dependence of each of the islands on international financial business. The recommendations recognize the need to help the international financial services sector evolve rather than trying to destroy them.

The pragmatic approach to improving financial supervisory standards is prudent, especially given the positive attitude of the three jurisdictions to cooperate in the implementation of the recommendations. Regulators and professionals in jurisdictions in which international financial services are an important part of the economy will recognize that many recommendations of the Edwards report will be adopted by international organizations active in the relevant subject matter areas.

The Proposed U.S. Know-Your-Customer Rule Will Formalize Internal Control Procedures:

- *The Proposed Regulations*: The proposed know-your-customer regulation contained in the Board of Governors of the Federal Reserve System's memorandum dated September 28, 1998, requires banks to develop for the first time their know-your-customer programme, and continues to generate discussion. The proposed rule will also apply eventually to non-bank financial institutions and will have broad implications for private banking, offshore accounts, and the imposition of responsibility on covered persons to design, implement, and regularly update and adjust their know-your-customer internal control systems.

The proposed regulation will require institutions supervised by the Federal Reserve Board to develop and implement a know-your-customer programme. According to the proposal, the establishment of a know-your-customer programme is designed to protect the reputation of the bank; facilitate the bank's compliance with all applicable statutes and regulations and with safe and sound banking practices; and protect the bank from becoming a vehicle for or a victim of illegal activities perpetrated by its customers.

Because the Board recognized that banks vary considerably in the way in which they conduct their business, the proposal permits each bank to develop its own know-your-customer programme as a system designed to meet the goals of the proposal.

The proposed Federal Register notice will require banks to develop a know-your-customer programme that at least will provide a system for handling the following tasks:

- Determining the true identities of the bank's customers;
- Determining the customer's sources of funds for transactions

involving the bank, including the types of instruments used and the sources from which the funds were derived or generated;

- Determining the specific customer's normal and expected transactions involving the bank;
- Monitoring customer transactions to ascertain if such transactions are consistent with normal and expected transactions for that particular customer or for customers in the same or similar categories or classes, as established by the bank;
- Identifying customer transactions that do not appear to be consistent with "normal and expected transactions for that specific customer or for customers in the same or similar categories or classes, as established by the bank"; and
- Ascertaining if a transaction is unusual or suspicious, in accordance with the Board's suspicious activity reporting regulations, and reporting it accordingly.

The proposal permits each bank to decide how best, consistent with its own business practices, it can identify its customers, understand the normal and expected transactions of its customers, and then monitor on an ongoing basis the transactions of its customers. Under the proposal, a bank must decide the know-your-customer programme suited to its specific needs, delineate the programme in writing, and demonstrate that it is complying with the programme.

The proposal will require banks to understand to whom they are providing their services at the start of the relationship, to develop an understanding of the transactions the customers will be conducting, and then to monitor the transactions of those customers.

Some banks, especially those offering private banking services, have raised concerns about identifying their clients, especially since a main tenet of such services is the confidentiality offered and demanded by these customers through the use of intermediary entities, such as private investment companies, trusts, private mutual funds, or investment advisory accounts, and since these entities are often based at offshore locations. The Federal Reserve is convinced that the beneficial owner's identity is usually well known to bank personnel or that banks can obtain waivers from their customers for any perceived restriction of the release of beneficial owner information.

In this regard, the Federal Deposit Insurance Corporation seeks comments on whether any actual or perceived invasion of personal privacy interest is outweighed by the compliance benefit.

While the proposal's requirement of identifying the true beneficial owner of each account of the bank is not intended to force a bank to disclose information in violation of foreign law, allowing any bank to avoid identification of beneficial ownership of any account would defeat the main purpose of the proposed rule—to ensure that each bank knows to whom it is offering its service. In this connection, the proposed rule responds to the criticism of a recent General Accounting Office report that U.S. banks lacked sufficient documentation regarding the beneficial owners of offshore entities that maintained accounts in the United States.

In response to concerns raised by several banks as to the severe hardship and cost of the new monitoring requirements, the Board of Governors has emphasized that the regulation will offer flexibility and require banks to develop and implement effective monitoring systems, commensurate with the risks presented by the types of accounts maintained at the bank and the types of transactions conducted through those accounts. The effectiveness of the monitoring system of a bank's know-your-customer programme will be based on that particular bank's ability to monitor transactions consistent with the volume and types of transactions conducted at the bank. The FDIC is seeking comment on whether the benefits of implementing the know-your-customer requirements outweigh the costs involved and whether there should be a minimum account size threshold below which the requirements should be waived.

The design of a monitoring system should correspond to the risk associated with the types of accounts maintained and types of transactions conducted through those accounts. Hence, the design of such a system could involve the classification of accounts into various categories based on such factors as the type of account, the types of transactions conducted in the various types of accounts, the size of the account, the number and size of transactions conducted through the account, and the risk of illicit activity associated with the type of account and the transactions conducted through the account. For certain categories of accounts, it may be sufficient for an effective monitoring system to establish parameters for which the transactions within these accounts will normally occur. Instead of monitoring each transaction, an effective monitoring system may involve monitoring only for those transactions that exceed the established parameters for that particular category of accounts. The proposed know-your-customer rule asks for the public to provide input on specific questions. The Federal Reserve wants comments to focus on the proposed definition of "customer" to ensure, at a minimum, that the definition is not overly broad and adequately covers "beneficial" ownership-related issues. Respondents are asked whether the proposal creates an uneven playing field for non-bank financial institutions, such as money transmitters and broker-dealers.

The proposed rule arises out of the Congressional hearings that have produced the enactment of the Money Laundering Deterrence Act of 1998, which requires that the Secretary of the Treasury implement know-your-customer regulations within 120 days of passage of the legislation. Congressman Leach's staff informed the Federal Reserve that the primary reasons for the provision in the draft legislation is to ensure that legal enforceable regulations exist to require that financial institutions adopt know-your-customer procedures and that similar regulations are developed for the non-bank financial sector, including broker-dealers and money transmitters.

The Federal Reserve will continue to work with FinCEN and will start to coordinate with the staff of the SEC in helping programme such rules for non-bank financial institutions. The Federal Reserve is awaiting feedback from other regulatory agencies, especially the Office of the Comptroller of the Currency and the Office of the Thrift Supervision, before submitting the proposal to the Federal Register. It is also awaiting input from the Board of Directors of the FDIC on whether know-your-customer standards should be issued as regulations or guidelines.

The Federal Reserve believes that the proposed know-your-customer rule will enable financial institutions to obtain information from their customers regarding the identity, the types of transactions to be conducted, and the source of funds, among other things. Obtaining and reviewing such information will assist financial institutions in making a risk-based determination on various matters—including the extent of identifying necessary information and the amount of monitoring required—by permitting institutions to categorize their customers into different groups based on the types of services being requested and the magnitude and extent of the transactions being conducted.

Effective know-your-customer programmes will require that banking organizations develop "customer profiles" to understand their customers' intended relationships with the institution and, thereafter, to determine realistically when customers conduct suspicious or potentially illegal transactions.

Legally, the Federal Reserve's proposal will revise 12 C.F.R. pts. 208, 211, and 225 by requiring state member banks, certain bank holding companies and their non-bank subsidiaries, U.S. branches and agencies and other offices of foreign banks, and Edge and Agreement corporations to develop and implement a know-your-customer programme within their institutions. The proposed rules define "customer" as "the person or entity who has an account involving the receipt or disbursal of funds at a bank and any other person or entity on behalf of whom such an account is maintained." The term encompasses direct and indirect beneficiaries of the account when the activity in the account involves the receipt or disbursal of funds. "It also includes a person or entity who owns or is represented by the customer."

Hence, a customer would include an account holder, a beneficial owner of an account, or a borrower. A customer could also include "the beneficiary of a trust, an investment fund, a pension fund or company whose assets are managed by an asset manager, a controlling shareholder of a closely held corporation or the grantor of a trust established in an offshore jurisdiction." The proposed rule underscores the need to target private banking operations, since these customers utilize such account vehicles as personal investment companies, trusts, personal mutual investment funds, or are clients of financial advisors.

Such accounts help protect the legitimate confidentiality and financial privacy of the customers that use such accounts. However, the need to identify properly the beneficial owners of such accounts, through an effective know-your-customer programme, is required to continue safe and sound operation of the bank. Hence, know-your-customer procedures for identifying the beneficial owners of private bank accounts should be no different than the procedures for identifying other customers of the bank. By developing special protections to limit access to information that would generally reveal the beneficial owners of these accounts, a private bank can address any needed confidentiality.

Once the proposed rule is published in the Federal Register, the public will have sixty days from that date to comment on the rule. The final rule may take effect at the start of the year 2000. Once the rule becomes final, the Federal Reserve will allow covered financial institutions a six-month grace period to fully implement know-your-customer programmes, after which time bank examiners may bring disciplinary action against institutions that violate the rules.

During the annual American Bankers Association/American Bar Association conference on money laundering, Susan Tucillo, Vice-President and Senior Compliance Officer of Citibank, N.A., noted that the know-your-customer rules will generate a substantial amount of new employment because of the complexity of issues raised, thereby requiring "a fundamental retooling of the branch operation process." The proposed rules cover virtually every product line and will particularly cause problems for attorney trust accounts, escrow accounts, other high-turnover attorney accounts, letters of credit, and other banking and lending transactions.

The know-your-customer rule would require that banks ensure that all documentation on accounts domiciled in the United States. be made available to Federal Reserve examiners within forty-eight hours of a request. U.S. banks are concerned that these rules will limit their ability to do business in offshore jurisdictions where they compete with foreign banks from jurisdictions with less restrictive know-your-customer rules. An important issue raised is the definition of customer. The preamble explains that "customer" includes "direct and indirect beneficiaries" of the account, as well as "a person or entity who owns or is represented by the customer." The proposed regulation specifically the beneficial owners of PICs, trusts and "personal mutual investment funds," clients of financial advisors, and "borrowers." The Federal Reserve and FDIC maintain a customer also could include the beneficiary of an investment fund, a pension fund, a company whose assets are managed by an asset manager, or a controlling shareholder of a closely-held corporation.

The regulations and preambles are conspicuously silent on what a customer does not include, for example, shareholders of publicly-traded corporations or of widely-held non-publicly traded businesses. Further, the regulators state that in some cases persons with the know-your-customer obligation might need to obtain information about the controlling owners of a business or other legal entity.

Hence, the definition of customer may have significant impact on many fiduciaries. In this connection, the Federal Reserve and FDIC are seeking comments on whether the proposed definition of "customer" is adequate to include all persons who "benefit from the transactions conducted at the bank, such as persons who establish off-shore shell companies... or otherwise conduct business through intermediaries." In addition, they seek comments on whether the proposed definition of customer is too wide and will unnecessarily include persons that pose minimal know-your-customer risk, that is, whether additional regulatory exceptions are appropriate.

At present, the proposed regulations do not have exceptions for foreign banks, foreign broker-dealers, or foreign investment advisors that are regulated in their home countries or in certain home countries that have sufficient anti-money laundering countries. Similarly, no exceptions exist for foreign open-ended collective investment funds such as mutual funds, which may have thousands of investors.

However, the regulators would expect banks to identify the shareholders of a mutual fund established in an offshore jurisdiction that has a limited number of shareholders. In the case of accounts opened by mail or Internet, banks and other covered persons must give special attention to verifying addresses and telephone numbers, and to use commercially available data sources to verify the customer's date of birth and social security number. The regulations require the bank to identify the beneficial owners of account holders that are offshore private investment companies, trusts, "private mutual funds," or investment advisors—in other words, high-risk customers—and to maintain data about the beneficial owner to the same extent as for U.S. persons. In the event that banks maintain the documentation about the identity of foreign beneficial owners, such as customers of a foreign investment advisor or the principal of a personal investment company outside the United States in a foreign branch or holding company, regulators would require that the bank furnish the documentation to a bank examiner in the United States within forty-eight hours of the examiner's request. No exceptions exist if bank secrecy or other law, such as the EU privacy directive, would preclude providing the documentation in the United States, especially with respect to existing customers.

Opposition from Private Sector and Congress: On February 3, 1999, a dozen members of Congress introduced four pieces of legislation:

- *H.R. 220*: Freedom and Privacy Restoration Act of 1999 to prohibit the federal government from creating a national ID and medical ID by repealing sections of the laws passed in 1996 and would prohibit the use of social security numbers as an identifier.
- *H.R. 516*: Know-Your-Customer Sunset Act of 1999 would bar agencies from following through on proposed Know-Your-Customer regulations.
- *H.R. 518*: Bank Secrecy Sunset Act would repeal the law that gives federal bank regulators monitoring authority and devolves the power to the states unless Congress passes a better version of the law.
- *HR 517*: FinCEN Public Accountability Act of 1999 would let bank customers check their own files and challenge information they believe to be false or inaccurate.

On March 4, 1999, Comptroller of the Currency John D. Hawke, Jr. testified that federal banking regulators' proposed know-your-customer rules should be withdrawn at the end of the public comment period. Hawke said any marginal advantages for law enforcement would be strongly outweighed by its potential for inflicting lasting damage on the banking system.

Christie Sciacca, associate director of FDIC's division of supervisor, also testified that his agency believes the "proposal cannot become final in its current form, if at all." Sciacca explained that most comments from the banking industry involved concerns about "the cost of compliance, customer privacy, and the competitive disadvantage if all financial institutions are not subject to the same requirements." At present, the status of the know-your-customer regulations are uncertain and controversial.

International Standards for Accounting in Anti-Money Laundering Campaigns

An important development is the establishment of international standards for accounting in anti-money laundering and financial crimes. The goals of accounting, as defined by the American Accounting Association, are to make decisions on the use of limited resources, including crucial decision areas, determine goals and objectives, direct and control effectively an organization's human and material resources, maintain and report on the custodianship of resources, and facilitate social functions and controls. Auditing encompasses the following three major categories: financial statement audit; operational audit; and compliance audit. In particular, a compliance audit has as its principal goal determining whether the entity under audit is following procedures or rules established by a higher authority.

Both accounting and auditing include within themselves certain fundamental notions on conformity with, and obedience to, applicable legal authority. These basic concepts involve the intersection of accounting and money laundering. In every jurisdiction, accountancy contains long-standing and deeply rooted requirements of impartiality, objectivity, and accuracy, using uniform standards and principles, and a code of mandatory professional ethics to support those obligations. These obligations entrust accountants with the responsibility for determining whether financial statements are free from material misstatements, and for auditing internal controls and procedures relevant to the production of those internal controls. The "core competence" of accountancy in the area of internal controls and the accountant's obligations for impartiality, objectivity, and accuracy have led many countries to rely on accountancy in detecting and preventing money laundering and financial crimes such as fraud.

Training provides accountants with the requisite professional tools and expertise to enable them to compare different entities within a single industry and thereby detect certain anomalies. Accountancy emphasizes operational knowledge of industries audited and appropriate internal controls, applied to a particular industry. A growing requirement in accounting jurisdictions to combat financial crimes requires accountants to report discoveries of serious abnormalities to higher authorities in appropriate circumstances.

Worldwide accounting organizations have begun to give guidance to their accounting professionals concerning money laundering issues. However, little or no international coordination has occurred, despite accountancy's overall global harmonization and increasing emphasis on international accounting standards. The Basle Committee on Banking Supervision of the Bank for International Settlements has issued its Core Principles for Effective Banking Supervision. In particular, Principle 15 states that "banking supervisors must determine that banks have adequate policies, practices and procedures in place, including strict `know-your-customer' rules, that promote high ethical and professional standards in the financial sector and prevent the bank being used, intentionally or unintentionally, by criminal elements." In addition, Principle 14 provides that bank supervisors must ensure that banks employ "appropriate independent internal or external audit and compliance functions to test adherence to" policies, procedures, practices and legal requirements, which include know-your-customer and anti-money laundering rules.

In the United States, the Bank Secrecy Act Advisory Group has established a sub-group, in coordination with appropriate accounting organizations and headed by an industry expert, to explore appropriate guidelines within the United States concerning money laundering. The group will explore issues and develop guidelines or suggestions on how to effectively provide useful guidance to the U.S. accounting profession on money laundering. Accounting bodies and researchers working on money laundering problems have concentrated on six important issues: legal issues; auditing issues; internal controls; reporting obligations; effect on financial statement presentation; and enforcement activity. With respect to legal issues, all jurisdictions whose accounting bodies have worked on accounting guidance concerning money laundering have provided an explanation in layman's terms of appropriate legal issues that an accounting professional is likely to encounter.

For auditing issues, many accounting jurisdictions have issued a checklist of significant indicators accounting professionals can apply to potential money laundering concerns. Such guidance assists accountants in effectively performing their duties. Clear, specific guidance on standards within an audit of potential money laundering are critical to the accounting profession. While the technical specifics of accounting standards may differ throughout the world, the indicators of potential money laundering often do not. Use of harmonized checklists and indicators are important since money laundering is often transnational; prevention and investigation thus may require cooperation between accounting professionals in various jurisdictions.

Comprehensive internal risk control assessment is critical to application of auditing standards. The Swiss and U.S. professionals have provided effective models for internal risk assessment with respect to money laundering. Various jurisdictions have provided guidance as to the obligations of an accounting profession when potential money laundering is discovered. The guidance is divided between legal requirements and ethical obligations to report. While accounting professionals have ethical obligations of confidentiality towards clients, exceptions apply with respect to reporting crimes, such as money laundering.

With respect to the effect on financial statement presentation, several jurisdictions have discussed such effect after discovery of potential money laundering. The questions concern whether, and to what extent, an accounting professional must report to the audited entity the discovery of potential money laundering in the financial statements. Conflicts may exist between ethical and legal obligations of accounting professionals to disclose fully and impartially all relevant or material information in a financial statement on the one hand, and legal restrictions on the notification to unauthorized personnel of potential money laundering on the other.

Enforcement of accounting standards in money laundering is largely self-regulatory and authorizes a self-regulatory body to impose sanctions. One accounting jurisdiction has already imposed sanctions on a member based on money laundering and in the absence of any legal sanctions against that member. The accounting professional can play a critical role in preventing money laundering, especially in the development and application of internal controls and the assessment of risks. International cooperation is critical to effectively combating money laundering.

Case Law and Developments

In many countries around the world, major litigation is raging over the implementation of national anti-money laundering laws, often continuing for five years or more. For instance, the anti-money laundering litigation in the early 1990s in Luxembourg over assets of the Cali cartel in Luxembourg generated simultaneous litigation in Panama and New York, and subsequently resulted in criminal proceedings against one of the U.S.-based attorneys for the Cali cartel over his conduct in handling the case.

The broad nature of money laundering laws means that it can, and often is, added by U.S. prosecutors as a charge whenever a crime has been committed involving the transfer of money, property or both. Moreover, the technical distinctions in money laundering statutes sometimes can be important internationally.

Antigua Government Announces the Failure of a Russian- Owned Bank

During the first week of August 1997, the Government of Antigua and Barbuda announced the failure of the European Union Bank —a fraud warning— and appointed Coopers and Lybrand as the receiver of a Russian-owned bank. The Antiguan Government further announced that it was pursuing Serbeveo Ushakov of Texas and Vitali Papsouev of Ontario, Canada, two Russian nationals who founded EUB and are believed to have fled. According to a media report, Evan Hermiston, resident manager in Antigua of Coopers and Lybrand's Caribbean branch, said the Antiguan Government had asked his firm to start investigating the bank during mid-July. Hermiston delivered a report during the first week of August. The webpage established by EUB on the World Wide Web invited depositors to take advantage of "excellent interest rates, offered in a stable, tax-free environment, with utmost privacy, confidentiality and security." In October 1996, both the Bank of England and the U.S. Comptroller of the Currency issued warnings on EUB's operations.

Two Russians, Aleksandr P. Konanikhin and Mikhail B. Khodorovsky, founded EUB in June 1994. They described themselves as "brokers of oil, metals, and construction supplies and officers of the Menatep Bank of Moscow." U.S. and British officials allege the bank is linked to Russian organized crime. According to U.S. officials, Konanikhin was arrested in the United States on visa violation charges and is accused of embezzling more than $8 million from a Moscow bank.

Both Konanikhin and Khodorovsky have since severed their formal connections with the EUB. Two other Russians, Ushakov and Papsouev, who have disappeared, were listed as the bank's directors when it collapsed. As part of EUB's marketing on its now dormant Internet webpage, the bank stressed the benefits of the lax regulatory climate. The webpage announced that "since there are no government withholding or reporting requirements on accounts, the burdensome and expensive accounting requirements are reduced for you." EUB's Internet webpage allowed clients anywhere in the world to open accounts, transfer money, write checks by computer, and obtain credit cards twenty-four hours a day.

Although the Antiguan Government is claiming confidentiality laws and has declined to provide information regarding the number of depositors at EUB or the amount of money it had reported in accounts, bank records show the bank violated the rules almost from the start. Indeed, in October 1995, an official letter from the Ministry of Finance noted that the bank had failed to file an audited financial statement for 1994. In May 1997, the Idaho Department of Finance "declared the bank to be operating illegally" and ordered it to "stop soliciting deposits from Idaho residents over the Internet." As a result of international pressure—that is, the warnings issued by the Bank of England, the OCC, and the U.S. State Department—the Antiguan Government closed another five Russian banks established in Antigua and issued new anti-money laundering regulations. The combination of the U.K. and U.S. warnings and the latest problems experienced by EUB clearly hurts the reputation of Antigua and Barbuda as stable and secure environment. Indeed, over reliance on secrecy and insufficient regulatory frameworks and supervision can undermine stability. Ironically, secrecy and lack of regulation also focus the attention of foreign regulators and international financial organizations on financial institutions in such jurisdictions.

Nevertheless, since the British Government has closed many of the offshore banks and financial institutions in the Caribbean Dependent Territories, and since more traditional jurisdictions such as Panama and the Bahamas have tightened their own vetting and regulatory processes, unsavory characters and organized crime have targeted countries whose frameworks and vetting processes are comparatively liberal. John E. St. Luce, the Antiguan Finance Minister, has claimed that his government has passed strong legislation on anti-money laundering and has a committee reviewing these developments.

Earlier statements from the Antiguan Government stating that it had remedied the problems of offshore banks, however, have proven to be mere rhetoric and little substance. On May 6, 1998, the U.S. Attorney filed an indictment in the U.S. District Court for the Northern District of Florida charging "the Caribbean American Bank of Antigua and eight individuals with a loan scam that allegedly bilked more than $60 million from hundreds of people in ten countries and with related money laundering." The indictment seeks as one remedy the forfeiture of all the bank's funds and assets.

Canadian Supreme Court Orders Extradition for U.S. Money Laundering Sting

On July 26, 1997, the Canadian Supreme Court reversed the Ontario provincial appeals court and held that a Canadian citizen should be extradited to the United States. On a dual criminality issue, the Court concluded that the failed sting constituted the offences of attempt and conspiracy in Canada. Arye Dynar, a Canadian citizen, was the subject of a U.S. money laundering investigation during the 1980s. In 1990, the FBI in Nevada began recording telephone conversations between Dynar in Canada and a cooperating informant in the United States known as "Anthony." According to the Court, "Mr. Dynar agreed with alacrity to launder money for Anthony." Moreover, these conversations indicated that the money to be laundered was drug money. However, as it was a government sting, no real drug money existed. Dynar refused to travel to the United States. Instead, it was determined that Dynar's associate, another Canadian citizen named Maurice Cohen, would meet with Anthony's associate in Buffalo, New York, collect the money, and return it to Dynar in Toronto where it would be laundered. Cohen would return the laundered money less, of course, Dynar's commission. Cohen entered the United States and met with undercover U.S. law enforcement agents. No money was transferred, and the FBI aborted the operation by pretending to arrest one of the undercover officers.

Subsequently, the United States sought the extradition of Dynar on a two-count indictment returned in Las Vegas, Nevada. The indictment charged Dynar and Cohen with violations of U.S. money laundering laws of under the sting provisions of the U.S. Code. The first count of the indictment accused "both Dynar and Cohen of attempting to conduct a financial transaction involving property represented by a law enforcement officer to be the proceeds of drug dealing and the second count accused the two of conspiring to do so." The United States requested the extradition of Dynar from Canada in 1992. Following an extradition hearing, Dynar was ordered committed for extradition. Dynar appealed to the Ontario Court of Appeal.

The Ontario Court of Appeal reversed and set aside the extradition on the basis that there was a lack of dual criminality under Canadian law. According to the provincial appeals court, Dynar did not commit a crime under Canadian law because at the time of the activity no sting provision existed. As such, the money must in fact be derived from the commission of a crime. The Crown appealed to the Supreme Court of Canada.

The Supreme Court framed the issue before it in this way: The issue in this appeal is whether the respondent's conduct in the United States would constitute a crime if carried out in this country, thereby meeting the requirement of "double criminality" which is the precondition for the surrender of a Canadian fugitive for trial in a foreign jurisdiction. This issue requires the Court to consider the scope of the liability for attempted offences and conspiracy under Canadian criminal law, specifically, whether impossibility constitutes a defence to a charge of attempt or conspiracy in Canada.

A majority of the Court ruled that "Dynar's conduct would have amounted to a criminal attempt and a criminal conspiracy under Canadian law." Even though Dynar's plan, if successful, would not have constituted a violation of the substantive criminal law in Canada at that time, the Court found that "the steps that Mr. Dynar took towards the realization of his plan to launder money would have amounted to a criminal attempt and a criminal conspiracy under Canadian law." As a consequence, the Court ruled that the trial court was correct in holding Dynar extraditable on both the charge of attempt to launder money and conspiracy to launder. The extradition order was reinstated.

United States and Mexico Duel over Money Laundering Case

A case that illustrates the tension over international money laundering and corruption between the United States and Mexico is a case resulting from a sting operation conducted by U.S. authorities primarily against Mexican banks. On May 18, 1998, a federal grand jury in Los Angeles charged three Mexican banks and twenty-six Mexican bankers with laundering millions of dollars in drug profits. According to an announcement by Treasury Secretary Robert Rubin and Attorney General Janet Reno, the charges represent the first time that

Mexican banks and bank officials were directly linked to laundering U.S. drug proceeds for the Cali cartel of Colombia and the Juarez cartel of Mexico. The indictment was the culmination of "Operation Casablanca," a three-year undercover sting operation led by the U.S. Customs Service that resulted in the arrests of twenty-two bankers from twelve of Mexico's nineteen largest banking institutions.

The indictment indicated gaping loopholes in U.S. and Mexican laws that permit traffickers to move their proceeds relatively easily in spite of various anti-money laundering and reporting laws and regulations in both countries. The loopholes have been widely reported by law enforcement authorities. This section outlines some of the highlights of the investigation, the indictment, responses by the Mexican Government, and its consequences for U.S.-Mexican law enforcement cooperation.

Indictment

The three Mexican banks charged were Bancomer and Banca Serfin—Mexico's second- and third-largest banks, respectively—as well as Banca Confia, a smaller institution recently bought by Citibank. On May 18, 1998, the Federal Reserve Board announced it was filing civil actions against five banks with branches in the United States. Shortly after the indictment, Banca Serfin announced it would plead not guilty and asked William Isaac, former Chairman of the FDIC, to conduct an independent investigation of the accusations.

In a statement announcing the indictment, Secretary Rubin said that "by infiltrating the highest levels of the international drug trafficking financial infrastructure, [U.S. Customers officials were] able to crack the elaborate financial schemes the drug traffickers developed to launder the tremendous volumes of cash acquired as proceeds from their deadly trade."

Attorney General Reno said that "the arrests and seizures disrupted a major money laundering operation that had served as an engine of the international drug trafficking trade." Since its start in November 1995, the undercover sting was kept secret from the Mexican Government. On May 18, 1998, Mexican officials first learned of the investigation when Reno notified Mexican Attorney General Jorge Madrazo Cuellar by phone. Secretary Rubin also alerted his counterpart, Jose Angel Gurria Trevino, Secretary of Finance and Public Credit in Mexico.

U.S. authorities said that they discovered nearly 100 bank accounts in the United States had been used by drug traffickers to deposit laundered funds. On May 18, 1998, investigators seized those accounts that they estimated to hold approximately $122 million. The investigation began after the U.S. Customs Office in Los Angeles discovered that drug cartel members had laundered proceeds from U.S. drug sales in branches of Mexican banks near the border. The investigation grew to include the financial infrastructure of the Ciudad Juarez cartel. During the investigation, Customs Service undercover agents established a front company, the Emerald Empire Corp., with offices in the Los Angeles suburb of Santa Fe Springs, and posed as middlemen between the cartel financial directors and the Mexican bankers, who agreed, for a fee of four or five per cent, to launder funds.

The bankers had established phony accounts and used bank drafts to evade money laundering regulations. The indictment indicated gaping loopholes in U.S. and Mexican laws that permit traffickers to move their proceeds relatively easily in spite of various anti-money laundering and reporting laws and regulations in both countries. The loopholes have been widely reported by law enforcement authorities.

According to the indictment, between February 1997 and May 1998, Confia branch lawyer Miguel Barba Martin and employee Jorge Milton Diaz managed to direct $11 million in drug money deposits into false accounts and transfer the funds into easily cashed bank drafts and other instruments. At one time, Reyes Ortega warned Victor Manuel Alcala, alias Dr. Navarro, an alleged capo for the Juarez cocaine cartel, that the new Mexican banking rules would make it more difficult to launder money in Mexico. Hence, in late 1996, $650,000 from one deposit turned up belatedly in a phony business account established in the Cayman Islands as part of the scheme. "New accounts in false names were regularly opened and closed in various offshore locales to avoid detection." For instance, Alcala is alleged to have established "a textile company as a front in Tepatitlan, which opened accounts at Banoro, where the branch manager also proved helpful."

On May 18, 1998, the Federal Reserve issued "`cease and desist' orders against five foreign banks, including two of those under indictment, for failing to address serious deficiencies in their anti-money laundering programmes." The banks are Banca Serfin, Bancomer, Banamex and Bital of Mexico and Banco Santander of Spain, each of which operates offices in the United States. The Federal Reserve order requires the banks to implement new anti-money laundering procedures.

Mexico will Prosecute U.S. Agents Who Operated Sting

Attorney General Madrazo Cuellar accused the United States of deceiving Mexico by making officials there believe that the entire three-year undercover operation had been conducted inside the United States. President Ernesto Zedillo ordered his diplomats to deliver the protest after he determined that conducting a hidden operation on Mexican soil violated the terms of several agreements between the two countries as well as the spirit of the close bilateral relationship. On May 21, 1998, the Mexican Permanent Commission, which represents Mexico's Congress when it is not in session, voted unanimously to demand an investigation into "Operation Casablanca" and criticized possible intervention by U.S. agents.

On June 3, 1998, the Mexican Government advised the United States that it would prosecute U.S. Customs agents and informers who executed an undercover money laundering operation in Mexican territory and would seek the agents' extradition in connection with the charges. At a meeting on June 1, 1998 in Caracas, Venezuela, Foreign Secretary Rosario Green of Mexico handed to U.S. Secretary of State Madeleine K. Albright a list of Mexican laws that the Customs agents violated according to preliminary results of Mexican investigations. In news interviews, Secretary Green reported that "Mexico is preparing to accuse the agents of entrapment, engaging in money-laundering, and usurping the authority of Mexican law enforcement." Meanwhile, Secretary Albright acknowledged that ties with Mexico had been damaged at a meeting of the Organization of American States in Caracas.

In the aftermath of the indictments against Mexican banks and bankers resulting from "Operation Casablanca," Secretary Green has stated that Mexico now has evidence that U.S. agents broke Mexican laws during their investigations. The inducement of illegal acts, apparently conducted during the three-year money laundering sting when U.S. agents posing as drug traffickers persuaded Mexican bankers to launder alleged drug profits, violates Mexican law. As a result of the U.S. handling of the investigation, the whole structure of U.S.-Mexican antidrug cooperation will be reassessed in future meetings with U.S. officials. Mexican officials are angry that indictments were issued only against Mexican banks and bankers, while U.S. banks named in the investigation went unindicted. The indictments "also reinforced perceptions of corruption in Mexican law-enforcement institutions and undermined efforts by the Zedillo government" to strengthen Mexican agencies responsible for monitoring and combating money laundering.

U.S. Response on its Lack of Notification to Mexico

In January 1996, U.S. officials informed Rafael Estrada Samano about the operation and asked for his help. Separately, however, U.S. officials gave a less detailed presentation to a deputy finance minister, Ismael Gomez Gordillo. Although U.S. officials asked Estrada to conduct a joint investigation, he did not respond and the United States abandoned the idea. Attorney General Madrazo Cuellar has said that the United States was vague about the operation and asked Gordillo only for information on some Mexican bank accounts, which he provided. Yet, U.S. customs officials grew suspicious about the lack of response they received from Mexican officials. Julie Shemitz, an Assistant U.S. Attorney in Los Angeles, stated that U.S. officials did not share any information about the operation with Mexico while it was under way out of fear for the safety of the undercover agents. Shemitz said "[i]t's not that we don't trust Mexicans. We just didn't tell anyone. This kind of operation is so dangerous, and you can't play games with the lives of the officers." As a result of the indictment, hopes of obtaining diplomatic protection for U.S. law enforcement agents have been discarded. Similarly, thoughts of following up on the investigation are fading.

Tax Developments

Professionals involved in international wealth transfer techniques must be aware of developments in international tax enforcement. Moreover, practitioners working in international tax enforcement must be aware of several important trends. Recently concluded and ratified tax treaties indicate the trend towards more active enforcement and cooperation within such treaties and increased merging of provisions from treaties of mutual assistance in criminal matters with traditional tax treaty provisions. The United States has concluded several treaties with key countries used in international tax and estate planning, such as Switzerland, Austria, Luxembourg, and Ireland. These treaties contain active enforcement cooperation provisions.

The trend towards increased unilateral assistance in tax enforcement affects clients and practitioners in sometimes unexpected ways. While U.S. tax authorities have been in the forefront, many other countries, sometimes under pressure from multilateral development banks in the context of structural readjustment programmes, are conditioning loans on better tax administration and more active enforcement.

Multilateral development banks are also making effective tax administration part of their good governance programmes. In recent years, the unilateral extraterritorial tax enforcement has manifested itself in draconian reporting requirements for foreign persons, foreign trusts, and persons who expatriate, such as surrendering their citizenship. A growth area in international tax enforcement concerns pre- and post-judgement attachment, seizure, and freezing of assets.

Increasingly, tax officials recognize that in an interconnected world at the end of a controversial tax dispute the ability to move funds instantly may make for a hollow victory unless tax authorities have the means to seize the funds in dispute or obtain sufficient security in lieu of the funds. Increasingly, the tax and non-tax enforcement areas are interacting. In this regard, tax enforcement officials and law enforcement officials are cooperating in an effort to combat the threats from transnational crime, especially transnational organized crime. An engine of increased international tax enforcement is multilateral tax cooperation. International organizations, such as the OECD, economic integration groups, and ad hoc groups are developing novel enforcement cooperation approaches and a more institutionalized approach. In particular, the OECD Harmful Tax Competition report has significant implications for fiduciaries operating internationally.

Asset Forfeiture

From the beginning, one goal in anti-money laundering and other anti-crime initiatives has been to immobilize criminals and their assets by identifying, freezing, tracing, seizing, confiscating, and forfeiting the instrumentalities and proceeds of the crimes.

Some countries, such as the United States, have active criminal, administrative, and civil asset forfeiture programmes. Some prosecutors prioritize asset forfeiture over criminal prosecution of defendants, especially in cases in which prosecution of defendants may not be possible. Two Swiss cases discussed below indicate the increasing cooperation by the Swiss Government in assisting foreign governments prosecute corruption cases against former high level officials. The discussion below of the Mexican Government's seizure of accounts illustrates how many governments that traditionally have not had active anti-money laundering programmes are now implementing new programmes.

Swiss Freeze $13 Million of Bhutto Accounts

On October 15, 1997, the Swiss police announced that it identified SFr20 million in frozen bank accounts belonging to the family of former Pakistani Prime Minister Benazir Bhutto, in connection with corruption enquiries. During the weekend of October 10-11, 1997, Bhutto denied for the first time that the Swiss accounts belonged either to her or to her relatives. Bhutto had been fired as Prime Minister in November 1996 on charges of corruption and misrule. As a result of the freeze order that followed the provisional blocking of the assets—a preventive measure taken the month preceding the freeze—the assets will remain frozen until the end of the investigation. The Swiss authorities responded to a formal request for judicial assistance from the Pakistani Government. Pakistani investigators claim that the Bhuttos have deposited between $50-80 million in Swiss bank accounts. According to Falco Galli, Swiss federal police spokesman, the Swiss police "have not excluded the possibility of freezing more accounts."

According to Galli, the Swiss police froze seven accounts in seven different Geneva-based banks in three stages—on September 8, September 17, and October 8, 1997. The owners of the frozen accounts are Bhutto, her husband, Asif Ali Zardari, and her mother, Nusrat Bhutto. Senator Saifur Rehman, who heads a Pakistani government corruption commission investigating the affair, said that he would visit Switzerland to give evidence to Swiss authorities and request the freezing of more accounts. The freeze orders and provisional blocking of funds, along with the Swiss actions in the Mobutu case and the overriding of bank secrecy in dealing with the accounts related to the Holocaust, indicate a new environment of Swiss cooperation with respect to foreign asset forfeiture cases. Nevertheless, the Swiss will act only in response to an actual criminal investigation and a request for judicial assistance, mutual assistance, or both, in connection therewith.

The Swiss action indicates the increased cooperation by governments when they are requested to provide assistance in corruption cases. Until the mid-1990s, governments and courts were reluctant to act in corruption cases, especially when they concerned former high level officials or political leaders.

Swiss Supreme Court Forfeits Portion of Marcos Money

On December 10, 1997, the Swiss Supreme Court, in a landmark decision after eleven years of litigation, ruled that $100 million of assets belonging to the late dictator Ferdinand Marcos must be returned to the Philippines Government, provided certain conditions are met. The decision applies to $100 million of the $500 million frozen in Swiss bank accounts since Marcos' abdication in 1986.

According to Peter Cosandey, the Zurich District Attorney, a decision on the disposition of the remaining funds would be forthcoming. The court ordered that the money be placed in an escrow account at the Philippine National Bank, which is partly owned by thc Philippine Government. Provided certain conditions are met, the court has ordered that the funds held by Swiss Bank Corporation must be transferred to the Philippine courts, which will decide how to distribute them. The same decision will apply as well to the funds held by Credit Suisse, which are subject to the jurisdiction of another Swiss canton.

The order reverses prior rulings that the disputed assets could not be released until Imelda Marcos, who also claims the money, was convicted by a Philippine court. While she has been convicted and sentenced to a total of forty-two years for corruption, Marcos has not served time in prison. Instead, she is an active member of Congress. To ensure the transfer of the money, the Philippine Government must demonstrate and guarantee that the money "will be distributed by a court complying with the United Nations standards of legal process." The order also requests information "about deliberations on the award of the money and measures being taken to compensate victims of human fights abuses under the Marcos regime." The ruling represented a setback for approximately 9,500 victims of international human right violations during the Marcos regime who have already obtained a judgement but are trying to levy against many of the same assets that the Philippine Government is seeking. Approximately one week before the order, a U.S. federal appeals court dismissed a lawsuit by Philippine human rights victims who had also made claims upon the money in the Swiss banks. The court ruled that the Swiss decision to block the Marcos accounts forestalled any action on the matter by U.S. courts.

In 1994, a U.S. federal jury in Hawaii found the Marcos Administration guilty of murder, torture, and violations of the provisions of international human rights conventions. It awarded the plaintiffs $1.2 billion in damages. But the pendency of the court actions by the Philippine Government left Swiss courts and banks in a quandary. While they feared having to pay twice, they wanted to demonstrate that they would not protect a corrupt government that had stolen so much money over a long period of time. Activity is underway in Manila to resolve the dispute between the Philippine Government and the Marcos family. The initiative is led by Magtanggol Guunigundo, chairman of the Philippines Presidential Commission on Good Government, which was established by former President Corazon Achino in 1986 to recover assets fraudulently amassed under Marcos and the Marcos family. Now, both the government and the Marcos family have said they want a final settlement. However, differences regarding the amount of Marcos assets still outstanding complicate such a settlement.

The decision represents a victory for those wanting to pursue civil prosecution against corrupt politicians, even when the assets are moved to foreign jurisdictions in which strong secrecy laws predominate. The effort to forfeit the Swiss assets of Marcos was especially difficult because the environment to penetrate and forfeit assets of government corruption was much less developed in the late 1980s than today.

The case is also a precursor to future efforts to pursue the assets of corrupt leaders. C. Mexican Seizure of Gaxiola Bank Account Signals New Cooperation and Tension in Anti-Money Laundering Enforcement Cooperation. Testimony by U.S. Deputy Treasury Secretary Lawrence H. Summers before the Senate Foreign Relations Committee on March 12, 1997, as well as other reports, indicate that the Mexican and U.S. Governments are actively cooperating in freezing and seizing assets, and on prosecuting money laundering, although tension exists over the effectiveness of the cooperation. On January 8, 1997, the United States requested that the Mexican Government freeze assets belonging to a drug-trafficking suspect, Rigoberto Gaxiola Medina. The United States believes that substantial amounts of money may have flowed out of the account after the freeze request was made, perhaps because of corruption and a tip-off. Rather than seizing $183 million, only $16.7 million was frozen and seized.

According to a media report, two confidential chronologies of the case produced by U.S. officials show that agents of Mexico's National Institute for Combating Drugs did not act on the January 8, 1997 order until January 20. Another problem was that the Mexican official in charge of executing the order was Colonel Jose Felix Name, the Institute's chief of investigations. Name has been under suspicion since he was arrested and charged with allowing Humberto Garcia Abrego, a man accused of being one of Mexico's most important money launderers, to escape from custody. When Mexican authorities reported to the U.S. Customs Service on the Gaxiola case, they reported that the accounts in question were depleted and only about $16.7 million remained. Mexican officials argued that the $183 million requested seizure did not take account of the frequent withdrawals Gaxiola had made over a thirty month period.

According to media reports, on March 11, 1997, at a meeting of law enforcement officials of the two countries in Mexico City, Assistant U.S. Attorney General Mary Lee Warren protested the apparent disappearance of the money.

However, a senior Mexican Justice official who was present said "in no way" did the United States complain about the matter. Mexican officials have stated that Gaxiola's accounts contained only $393,000 on December 31, 1996. On January 10, 1997, just before the Mexican Government moved to seize the accounts, the accounts contained $1.47 million. After the money was frozen on January 23, 1997, the combined balance was up to $16.7 million. These new deposits seem to rebut allegations of a tip-off. The case indicates that, despite thc tension between the two governments, progress is occurring in establishing legal and law enforcement framework to freeze assets in Mexico. The next push will come in the effort to enforce Mexico's anti-money laundering laws.

The Fourth Amendment Right Against Unlawful Search and Seizure

"All searches and seizures in the U.S. must fulfill the requirements of the Fourth Amendment." Hence, a search warrant issued pursuant to a treaty request must fulfill U.S. constitutional requirements regarding probable cause, specification of the place to be searched, and specification of the things to be seized.

The majority of U.S. mutual legal assistance treaties in criminal matters specifically provide authority to U.S. courts to issue search warrants in execution of requests for assistance under such treaties. While some of treaties do not expressly confer such authority on U.S. courts, they still require the United States to conduct searches and seizures at the request of its treaty partners if the request contains information justifying such action under U.S. laws.

"The absence in some cases of specific statutory authorization raises the issue as to whether those treaties sufficiently authorize the courts to issue such warrants." In a decision that has potentially important implications for international criminal cooperation, the U.S. District Court for the Central District of California held that a freeze of a target's bank account of a U.S. securities enforcement investigation is unconstitutional as violative of the Fifth Amendment right to due process and the Fourth Amendment right to be protected from unreasonable seizures.

The case began as a derivative action of an Securities and Exchange Commission enforcement action. The SEC sued one of the plaintiffs, Michael Colello, for his role in a pyramid scheme. Colello asserted his Fifth Amendment right against self-incrimination during the investigative stage and has continued to maintain his silence. The day before the Commission filed the enforcement action against Colello and the other defendants, the SEC sought the freeze Colello's Swiss bank accounts.

The U.S. Department of Justice transmitted a request under the U.S.-Swiss Mutual Legal Assistance in Criminal Matters Treaty and Swiss authorities complied. Simultaneously with the SEC enforcement action, the court issued a temporary restraining order in the enforcement action, freezing all the defendants' assets located in the United States, including Colello's. The court, in a decision by U.S. District Judge Richard A. Paez, refused to grant the SEC's motion for a preliminary injunction against Colello, and the domestic asset freeze dissolved along with the temporary restraining order.

Colello and plaintiff Robert Romano—who was not a defendant in the enforcement action—filed a separate case on September 2, 1994 to challenge the constitutionality of the Swiss asset freeze, Colello and Romano named as defendants, among others, the SEC, its lawyers, and the Director of the Department of Justice Criminal Division's Office of International Affairs. The SEC had commenced its investigation in October 1993 against Cross Financial Services, Inc., after discovering through a newspaper article that CFS promised very high rates of return to investors in a "government receivables" investment programme.

On December 3, 1993, the SEC issued a formal order of investigation. In April 1994, the SEC subpoenaed records and testimony from Michael Colello in connection with the investigation of CFS. During his testimony, when SEC lawyers questioned Colello about Carroll Siemens, letters of credit, European and American banks, and his bank accounts, he asserted his Fifth Amendment right against self-incrimination and refused to answer. On June 13, 1994, the Department of Justice sent a request under the U.S.-Swiss treaty for assistance from the Swiss Government, "seeking documents and testimony from banks in Switzerland to establish whether CFS made false statements about its investment scheme to induce people to invest and, thereafter, misappropriated investors' funds in violation of U.S. federal securities laws." In addition, the SEC requested that any funds "traceable to the subject matter of the request be frozen so that the funds later may be returned to the U.S. to compensate the victims of the fraud."

On June 15, 1995, the Swiss Federal Supreme Court rejected plaintiffs' contention that the asset freeze was improper. It explained, "In matters of judicial assistance, the Federal Supreme Court examines an administrative court complaint only to determine whether the preconditions for the provisions of judicial assistance have been fulfilled." If the judicial assistance is requested by the United States, the request cannot be denied merely on the basis of deficiencies in the U.S. proceedings, because the treaty does not contain any corresponding provision.

Meanwhile, in ruling that the freeze was an unconstitutional seizure in violation of the Fourth Amendment to the Constitution, the Colello court rejected the government's contention that plaintiffs "assumed the risk" of depositing their money in a foreign country. The court stated that U.S. citizens are protected by the Bill of Rights from incursions by the U.S. Government on them or their property, regardless of its location. Similarly, the court found no authority for the government's notion that it "can circumscribe or limit the entitlement of citizens to constitutional rights via a treaty."

The court was troubled that freezing is permitted under the treaty based on "reasonable suspicion," whereas the Fourth Amendment requires showing "probable cause." The court appeared troubled by the failure to implement legislation and regulations, although legislation was initially contemplated. The court also noted that, while the Department of Justice manual governs the conduct of the SEC and the Department of Justice, it does not require them to notify "the subject of a Treaty request or to provide a hearing before or after making the request."

Additionally, the court noted that the manual contains no standards and includes a disclaimer stating that the manual provides only internal Department of Justice guidance and "is not intended to, does not, and may not be relied on to create any rights, substantive or procedural, enforceable by law by any party in any matter civil or criminal." Finally, the manual states that no limitations are placed "on otherwise lawful prerogatives of the Department of Justice."

The absence of U.S. statutory and regulatory provisions contrasts with Switzerland's approach. Switzerland has enacted law and guidelines under the treaty. The Federal Law on the Treaty with the U.S. on Mutual Legal Assistance in Criminal Matters of October 3, 1975 provides for certain "precautionary measures" to guarantee due process through requiring notice to the affected parties. In addition, the Federal Office for Police Matters has also issued guidelines to inform interested authorities and citizens on what is meant and encompassed by international mutual assistance in criminal matters.

The decision may presage trouble on other criminal mutual assistance agreements when the U.S. Government tries to enforce them in courts. Indeed, although the American Bar Association and other interested bar groups testified previously against excluding from such treaties due process protections for defendants and third parties, the U.S. Government vehemently opposed such arguments.

The decision seems to indicate that at least the court believes that a better balance is constitutionally required. A similar difficulty may arise in the tax information exchange and cooperation area. There, in order to secure support for ratification of the Council of Europe and OECD Treaty on Mutual Administrative Assistance in Tax Matters, the U.S. Department of Treasury promised to issue regulations and stated that it would consider extending such regulations across the board to all tax information exchange agreements. Indeed, such due process seems compelled.

However, many months after the Convention has taken effect, Treasury officials claim that their workload does not permit time for such a project. It appears that the role of courts can be important in developing incentives for officials to prioritize due process rights. The absence of adequate rights within enforcement cooperation treaties, together with aggressive enforcement actions and the inevitable cases where rights of individuals have been abused, may jeopardize the potential for success in enforcement actions. International anti-money laundering efforts will increase as transnational crime and especially transnational organized crime continue to spread.

The efforts of the United Nations and the G-7 Economic Summit Group to develop a convention and other mechanisms to tackle transnational crime illustrate the political consensus behind the new efforts. Some of the prospects for international anti-money laundering efforts can be viewed in the March 1997 release of the International Narcotics Control Strategy Report, which contains a large section on anti-money laundering. It is worthwhile to summarize some of the discussions in order to identify trends, as well as develop and improve due diligence. Finally, a common forum for major international bankers and government policy makers was organized. In 1997, FATF's high-impact initiative external relations programme that began in 1992 and 1993 succeeded in establishing agreements with the Council of Europe, the Offshore Group of Banking Supervisors, and the CFATF. These agreements are intended to secure evaluation by outside experts to determine whether the majority of financial centre countries were properly implementing the minimal global standards on anti-money laundering.

During 1996, increased cooperation with foreign governments on major money laundering cases occurred. Asset sharing cooperation increased, as did the amount of U.S. mutual assistance treaties in criminal matters, all with important anti-money laundering and asset forfeiture-sharing provisions. Adverse developments identified by the INCSR include the further penetration of financial systems by organized crime groups. Transnational crime groups increasingly have used "new drug transit routes across ever more remote countries, most of which have no or few anti-money laundering laws." The result is the ability to move crime proceeds to the countries and systems whose financial standards are vulnerable and easily manipulated. Transnational crime groups can more easily identify and exploit "the differential between the levels of compliance with international anti-money standards," especially in Asia and Latin America.

Mutual Cooperation Mechanisms

Increasingly, practitioners must be aware of an ever-growing web of bilateral and multilateral treaties, executive agreements, and memoranda of understanding that enable governments and law enforcement officials to obtain information on various crimes. Sometimes tax crimes are covered. For instance, all the modern U.S. mutual assistance in criminal matters treaties cover tax. On October 21, 1998, the U.S. Senate voted to approve for ratification thirty-nine treaties providing for international criminal cooperation, including nineteen mutual assistance in criminal matters treaties, eighteen extradition treaties, and one prisoner transfer treaty.

The evidence law enforcement officials need to prosecute tax crimes is often the same evidence that is required to show wrongdoing with respect to securities or commodities futures trading, drug trafficking, or transnational bribery. For instance, the OECD Convention on Combating Bribery of Foreign Public Officials in International Business Transactions, which took effect on February 15, 1999, obligates signatory countries to provide evidence in connection with alleged bribes of foreign public officials and eventually will require all signatories to eliminate tax deductions for payments that are bribes. Similarly, in the investigation and prosecution of transnational organized crime, many law enforcement officials can obtain evidence on a variety of economic matters. Many governments, such as the United States, target alleged transnational organized crime members for tax crimes, as the United States did successfully with Al Capone. Proactive policing vis-a-vis transnational organized crime has produced transformations in international criminal cooperation law in the United States and throughout the world, especially in the development of a financial enforcement regime.

Antimoney laundering and immobilization of the assets and profits of criminals play an important role in these efforts. Globalization ensures that the number of transnational criminal investigations and prosecutions involving the United States will increase. Undoubtedly, an increasing number of cases will bring into play the potential applicability of the various rights guaranteed by the U.S. Bill of Rights or applicable provisions of international human rights conventions, such as the International Civil and Political Covenant. "The tension between the need for the United States to cooperate more with national governments and international tribunals and the concern for the fulfillment of constitutional and international human rights standards is likely to continue to grow."

Counsel representing investors, business entities, and fiduciaries can increasingly resort to international human rights provisions—in national judicial fora, international tribunals, or both—to adjudicate conflicts between new intrusive law enforcement techniques and substantive laws and international human rights and constitutional rights. These conflicts often result in intrusive search and seizure cases, enforcement of new due diligence requirements for businesses and individuals, asset forfeiture cases, restraint of individuals at borders, and so forth. The discussion of the restrictive provisions in U.S. mutual legal assistance treaties and the efforts to conduct intrusive search and seizure and evidence gathering without proper safeguards illustrate the types of defences that persons implicated by these provisions can raise.

U.S. MLATs Restrict Their Use to Governments

Recent U.S. MLATs in criminal matters that grant the government compulsory process rights, as delimited by the respective treaties, expressly state that the treaties do not create the right for a private person to obtain evidence.

The purpose is to prevent the use of its MLATs for suppressing or excluding evidence or for impeding its investigations. Hence, if an adversely affected person wants to prevent the execution of a request that he believes was made in violation of the treaty, his only recourse under the treaty is to the executive authority of the requested country, not to its courts. Similarly, if he wants to contest that the requested country violated the terms of the treaty in executing a request, he may do so only to the executive authorities of the respective countries. The treaty provisions do not prevent a person adversely affected by a request or its execution from asserting whatever rights he has under the laws of the appropriate country in its courts. For instance, a person whose home or place of business was searched and whose property was seized under a search warrant issued pursuant to a treaty request may assert whatever rights he has under the laws of the requested country to prevent that property from being turned over to the requesting country.

Similarly, a person whose records have been subpoenaed pursuant to a treaty request may assert whatever rights he has under the laws of the requested country, to prevent the production of those records, their transmittal to the requesting country, or both. An affected person would also presumably be able to seek to enjoin the requested country from taking an action not authorized by the treaty or its laws. In at least one case in which a defendant sought to use a U.S. MLAT to obtain evidence from a treaty partner pursuant to a treaty that was silent with respect to a defendant's right to seek evidence under it, "the trial court directed the Department of Justice to make a treaty request on behalf of the defendant."

The U.S. Government has agreed to provisions in its MLATs that accommodate concerns of its treaty partners about safeguarding provisions on international human rights. For instance, in the MLAT between the United States and Australia signed on April 30, 1997, the term "essential interests" that may be invoked to deny assistance to a requesting state includes a discretionary limitation on providing assistance in death penalty cases.

Potential remedies for rectifying apparent violations of binding provisions of international human rights include the following: to urge governments and international organizations to condition applicable MLATs, extradition treaties, and other international criminal cooperation agreements to comply with such provisions; to urge judicial tribunals through amicae briefs to condition criminal cooperation agreements on international human rights obligations; and, where appropriate, to help aggrieved persons initiate and prosecute actions in international human rights fora in order to reflect equitably their respective contributions.

Bibliography

A Satish Babu: *Tourism Development in India : A Case Study*, APH Publication, Delhi, 2008.

A.K. Bhatia: *Tourism Development : Principles and Practices*, Sterling Publication, Delhi, 2001.

Ashok Sharma: *Tourism Development*, RBSA Publication, Delhi, 2008.

Atul Shrivastava: *Tourism Planning and Management*, Centrum Press, Delhi, 2010.

B S Badan and Harish Bhatt: *Tourism Planning and Development*, Commonwealth Publication, Delhi, 2007.

B S Badan and Harish Bhatt: *Travel Agencies and Tourism Development*, Commonwealth Publication, Delhi, 2007.

Banwari Lal Raheja: *Tourism Development Strategies*, Arise Publication, Delhi, 2006.

Devesh Nigam: *Tourism Planning and Tour Operation*, Shree Publication, Delhi, 2008.

E K Murthy: *Tourism Planning : Concepts, Approaches and Techniques*, ABD Publication, Delhi, 2008.

Jagpradeep: *Tourism Development*, Murari Lal and Sons, Delhi, 2008.

K P Lakshman: *Tourism Development : Problems and Prospects*, ABD Publication, Delhi, 2008.

Kailash Hariharan Iyer: *Tourism Development in India*, Vista International Publication, Delhi, 2006.

M.G. Chitkara: *Tourism Development*, APH Publication, Delhi, 2012.

Manish Ratti: *Tourism Planning and Development*, Rajat Publication, Delhi, 2007.

Manjula Chaudhary, K.K. Kamra, S.S. Boora, Ravi Bhushan Kumar, Mohinder Chand and R.H Taxak: *Tourism Development : Impacts and Strategies*, Anmol Publication, Delhi, 2007.

Meenakshi Thakur: *Tourism Development : Problems and Prospects*, Omega Publication, Delhi, 2008.

Nikunj Tarun: *Tourism Planning in 21 Century*, Alfa Publication, Delhi, 2006.

O.P. Kandari and Ashish Chandra: *Tourism Development Principles and Practices*, Shree Publication, Delhi, 2004.

Palash Handique, Hemanta Saikia and Ratul Kumar Lahon: *Tourism Development and Planning in India*, SSDN Publishers, Delhi, 2014.

R K Gupta: *Sustainable Tourism Planning*, Sumit Enterprises, Delhi, 2007.

R.K. Arora: *Tourism Planning and Human Resource Development*, Mohit Publication, Delhi, 2007.

Ranjit Taneja: *Tourism Planning*, Alfa Publication, Delhi, 2006.

S Sutheeshna Babu; Sitikantha Mishra and Bivraj Bhusan Parida: *Tourism Development Revisited : Concepts, Issues and Paradigms*, Response Books, Delhi, 2008.

S.C. Bagri: *Sustainable Tourism Planning and Development : All India Tourism Teacher's Association National Seminar Proceedings*, Bishen Singh Mahendra Pal Singh, Delhi, 2006.

S.P. Bansal: *Tourism Development and Its Impact*, Shri Sai Printographers, Delhi, 2001.

T.K. Sathyadev and P. Manjunath: *Tourism Development*, Pacific Books International, Delhi, 2012.

T.K. Sathyadev and P. Manjunath: *Tourism Planning*, Pacific Books International, Delhi, 2012.

V P Sati: *Tourism Development in India*, Pointer Publication, Delhi, 2001.

Vijay Sinha: *Tourism Planning and Management*, Random Publications, Delhi, 2012.

Vikas Choudhary: *Tourism Planning and Management*, Centrum Press, Delhi, 2010.

Virender Kaul and Sarika Bajpai: *Tourism Planning : An Introduction*, Shri Sai Printographers, Delhi, 2007.

Yashodhara Jain: *Tourism Development : Problems and Prospects*, APH Publication, Delhi, 2013.

Index